Among Muslims

EVERYDAY LIFE ON THE FRONTIERS
OF PAKISTAN

Kathleen Jamie

SEAL PRESS

FOR MY MOTHER, ISABEL

AMONG MUSLIMS: *Everyday Life on the Frontiers of Pakistan*

Copyright © 2002 by Kathleen Jamie

Published by
Seal Press
An Imprint of Avalon Publishing Group Incorporated
161 William St., 16th Floor
New York, NY 10038

Previously published by Sort Of Books, London, 2002. An earlier edition of this book was originally published as *The Golden Peak* by Virago, London, 1992.

Library of Congress Cataloging-in-Publication Data is available.

ISBN 1-58005-086-7

9 8 7 6 5 4 3 2 1

Designed by Henry Iles

PICTURE CREDITS: Phil Butler (Prologue; Gilgit Going; Karimabad Side; Askole by Night), Jamie Marshall (Shia Girls; In Baltistan; Epilogue).
Printed in the United States of America

CONTENTS

Prologue: In Fife

Ours is a small, rural Scottish town. There are shops, parks, a school, and a Victorian museum which displays, amongst other things, a two-headed weasel and a Zulu shield. Stolid stone houses, some painted a grudging cream or pale blue, line a long main street. There are no front gardens. It's the kind of place where you acknowledge the people you pass. There is too much traffic, always going elsewhere.

Because it was Guy Fawkes night, we were going to buy fireworks. The kids ran ahead, while I walked past six or seven houses, all with lace curtains, all with closed doors. When the doors are closed, the town can take on a dour, forbidding look. From The Tay View came a sudden male roar. Rangers must have been winning the football.

The kids were excited about their fireworks. They were going to have friends over, and eat sausages. We'd left their dad building a bonfire at the top of our long garden. They danced on ahead toward the Post Office cum toyshop.

Beyond the Co-Op the pavement widens out to accommodate a flowerbed and a couple of benches. And there, in a circle, cross-legged on the pavement, were a dozen Pakistani men.

The impression was all of textile, of fabric. They were sitting on a brightly patterned cloth, they wore white turbans, green bandannas and beards, and baggy shalwar-kameez, with anoraks and leather blouson jackets against the Scottish cold. One had a fine brown blanket draped over his head and shoulders. Another, a little bright green mirror-work hat. The youngest was a doe-eyed lad of about twenty with a few wisps of beard, the eldest would be about fifty, a doughty, confident personage we came to know as Mahmood. I say cross-legged, but one of the men was kneeling, with his back to the road, swaying back and forth as he read aloud from the Qu'ran.

Duncan came running back to me.

"Mummy! Come on! Let's get our fireworks!"

"In a minute . . ."

"No, Mummy, come on!"

We bought the fireworks, and a paper, and some milk. The paper had a front-page picture of an Afghan woman in a pale blue burqa. These men could easily have been taken for Afghanis, maybe that's why no one seemed quite sure what to do with them. No one seemed to have approached them, though a couple of women in tweed coats stood at the bus stop, talking in low voices.

With a child in either hand, I made a move, and two of the men clambered to their feet.

A-salaam aleikum, I said.

Aleikum a-salaam!

•••

Since the war in Afghanistan I'd been thinking a great deal about Pakistan. The TV news carried nightly reports from Islamabad and Peshawar and Quetta. There were refugees and anti-US riots, and once, the BBC even suggested that the road into the Northern Areas, the Karakoram Highway, was in the hands of the Taliban, but I didn't believe it.

It was ten years since I'd last been there, and although we'd lost touch, I'd written a letter of concern to the women who had befriended me in the northern town of Gilgit, but they keep purdah, and it was all a long time ago, and I didn't really expect a reply.

All the men in the circle were looking at us. They smiled and nodded.

"You're from Pakistan! I'm pleased to meet you," I said, and held out my hand, but the man with the green bandanna backed off from it, smiling and bowing.

The two tweedy women had ceased talking to watch.

And that's how come we went out for fireworks and came home with three Punjabi men in full fig. I was wearing my frump-at-home dark blue skirt, which reaches almost to my ankles, and, for once, was glad of it. I'd mustered my few words of Urdu: tea, house, husband; and three accepted. We made a jolly party, striding up the pavement, exchanging names, and fussing over the children. They made an enormous fuss over the children. The wind tugged their turbans and shirt-tails.

We led the men through the green gate which leads into our yard, and I sent Duncan up through the garden to find his dad, while the rest of the party followed.

The gardens are our town's best kept secret. Behind the closed doors and the dour privacy of the street are plum orchards and apple orchards, sunlit lawns, bee-hives and vegetable plots, and views of the wide, blue Firth of Tay and the Carse of Gowrie to the north.

Walls and fences are little more than a gesture, everyone just knows whose is whose, so the impression you have is of sunlit openness. The three Pakistani men stood under the plum trees and exclaimed. They turned, exclaiming about the sudden view of the river. I wanted to tell them that it was the same, that when I myself had been admitted through the austere green street-gates of Gilgit, I had found gardens and vegetable plots, family compounds, children, and an insistent hospitality.

Phil came striding down. In his younger, mountaineering days, he too had spent time in Pakistan, but that was before we met. We often spoke about the place, and promised ourselves that one day, when the kids were much older, we'd go back.

The men shook hands and exchanged names. The biggest, with the black beard, he was Mahmood. He was, he said, a miner, but that was disingenuous. His card, which he flourished from an inner pocket, named him as chief executive of five mineral-extraction businesses in the Punjab. The man called Nazir was thinner, he wore a parka over his shalwar-kameez.

"He is the mayor of our town!" said Mahmood.

"Scotland must seem cold, after the Punjab," I said, but as if to concede that Scotland was cold would be to insult it, Nazir turned his head and smiled.

"Not cold. Scotland is very fine. Scottish people very kind."

The third was an older man, who spoke little. He had a kindly, thin face and wore a fine woollen blanket like a shawl over his head and shoulders. I never learned his name.

We ushered our three guests indoors. As they demurred and we fussed, I saw my house through new eyes. What did we have that they would recognise? A decent front room for visitors? No. They were shown into our cramped kitchen. An elegant matching tea set? Fat chance. The cooker hadn't been cleaned for a week. There was much courtesy over chairs, but eventually the three men were seated and I began to make tea, which I knew they'd find insipid and bitter. Sugar. We needed sugar. We needed clean cups. Spoons, why are there never any spoons? I flapped the cat out of the kitchen.

"You alright with cats?" I asked Mahmood.

"Cats, yes. Dogs," he tilted his head. "Dogs, no."

They sat at the table. Phil and I stood. The children stared. We named the places in Pakistan we'd known, Phil and I. Rawalpindi, Islamabad, and especially, the mountainous Northern Areas . . . It was before the kids were born. The men fussed over the children, toyed politely with their tea, and with courtly gestures refused the shortbread we offered. Everyone was merry. But, we asked, why on earth they were *here*?

They told us they were on a "Peace Walk." They had started in Aberdeen, back in August, and were walking through all the small towns of Scotland, until, at length, they reached Glasgow. It would take, they said, four months. *Four months?* I glanced down at their shoes. I'd been chided in Gilgit for the unladylike state of my own, but theirs were not fit for four months' walking in a Scottish winter.

"Yes. It is at our own expense. Our purpose is to be here and say to Scottish peoples, we can be understanding. In every town we are making some talk, some communication. Muslim and Western, we are all the Children of Adam, you understand? In every town we arrive, and sit . . . as you saw."

And then?

Mahmood gestured toward our ill-painted kitchen ceiling, and said something about Allah.

"In every town the people have been most kind. We are in need of accommodation. Very simple place. Church hall, community hall . . ."

I glanced at Phil.

"Give us that again. You need somewhere to stay. What, ten, twelve of you?"

"If you can help with this thing . . . otherwise it is no problem. We have a van . . . we can sleep on the . . ."

"Not another word. We'll see to it. Wait here, please. You are our guests."

Go to Pakistan, and those are the words you will hear. "You are our guest." That's what people said to me, ten years ago when I did as these men had done, that is, I turned up in a small northern town and threw myself on people's kindness. "You are our guest" and "where is your husband?"

In those days I had no husband. But now I did, and I conferred with him in the hall. We had to find them someplace. We had to find these men a place for the night; these peace-walkers with their strange garb and beards, their curious habit of sitting on the pavement, these men without women. I fell into a complete passion about it. What if people got the wrong end of the stick? What if they thought these men were Afghanis, and all Afghanis were Muslims were terrorists? All we got on the news was anthrax and bombs and bin Laden. People might take them for a Taliban invasion force. God knows what people might think, if all they knew of Muslims were TV pictures of men with beards and turbans and Kalashnikovs.

"We'll see to it," I said. "Please, wait here."

"You are very kind."

Nazir was fiddling with his teaspoon, as though unsure where to put it. We possess but one saucer, and the cat drinks from that.

As man of the house Phil would stay here and hold the fort. Being a woman, and possessed of the female arcane lore of who lives where and is related to whom, and who goes to what church if any, I went running down the street.

As I did so, I understood for the first time some things I'd remembered fondly, even written a book about, but had never acutely understood. Things about honour, and danger. I under-stood at last what my host in Gilgit, Major Shah, had actually meant when he thumped his desk that distant, hot afternoon and roared, "I will find accommodation for you. IT IS MY HONOUR!"

Well, it was my honour now. I went running down the street. We needed a church hall. We could rely on Christians, couldn't we? Peace walk, stranger at the gate and all that.

The woman who looks after the Ecumenical church hall was out. Geraniums crowded her windows. Next, I stopped in at the bakers, because the woman who works there belongs to one of the town's old extended families. She'd have an idea what to do, but it was her day off. Her deputy wiped floury hands on a cloth and said: "Oh, I saw them! My daughter was scared! She thought they were going to bomb us or give us anthrax . . ."

"Do you know who looks after the Kirk hall?"

"No, but you'll see all the churchy-folk in the morning. A' wi' their hats on."

The board of the Baptist church displayed a poster with a fluffy duckling and a notice about a Salvation choir. Of course it was shut. It was Saturday afternoon, after all. The community centre has doors like a castle, and they were firmly closed. I ran on, smiling and waving as I passed the remaining Pakistanis still sitting in their circle on the pavement. I knew the pharmacist, a likeable woman my own age, went to the Church of Scotland, maybe she could help. She stood in her white coat among the vitamins and lip salve, as I gab-bled something about Pakistanis, and she said,

"Oh, that's who they are! We saw them. Oh, how interesting. I would like to have spoken to them, but I didn't know how . . ."

"One of them is a pharmacist, apparently . . ."

"Oh, how interesting!"

She gave me the name I needed, and an address, just round the corner. I ran on.

The door was surrounded by a cotoneaster, the garden was flawless. A man I didn't recognise glanced out of the window at my knock, then came to the door, and looked down on me as I stood on the step, and said my piece.

He said, "We know. The Post Office called at lunch time. There's nothing we can do. It's not suitable. There's communion tomorrow. Really, you'd think they'd have something organised."

I didn't argue, merely closed the little black garden gate behind me. I didn't argue that the whole point of the men's mission was to have nothing "organised." The point was to walk into a town, sit on the ground and see what panned out. To force a situation where we had to talk to each other, the "Children of Adam," instead of blowing each other to bits.

So much for the church halls. Who else? Who could accommodate twelve? Not for the first time I wished we had a huge house. A huge huge house. I went home by a back way, because I felt embarrassed to be seen yet again running up the main street, past the group waiting on the pavement, and their few bemused spectators. This was a fine pickle. What kind of impression would they have, these men, if they found the town was shut up and barred?

I swung back into the kitchen. Only Phil was there. He sat alone at the table, reading the paper. The men were all gone. We had failed.

"Gone? Naw, they're not gone," said Phil, laughing. "They're up in your garret, praying."

A pharmacist, a draper, a glass-merchant, the town's provost, a businessman involved with minerals, a teacher of Arabic, a student of economics. "We are spending only our own money." We sat in a circle on the floor of a large room. The room belonged to a man called John. John was an artist, a man in his fifties. When the USA and UK began bombing Afghanistan, it was John who circulated e-mails and petitions of protest. He was new to town, and the ground floor of his house was a disused shop. He'd phoned us, just as I was explaining to our guests that we were experiencing some difficulty, and said,

"I hear you've got a problem . . ."

He offered the empty shop to the peace-walkers. There was no electricity, but there was water, plenty of floor space and an old lawnmower. The men were gracious, and they drove up their support van, a blue Transit stuffed with all their accoutrements. Then, to the frank astonishment of passers by, they filed back and forth into the empty shop with tin cook pots, kerosene stoves, bright mats, and sleeping bags. Their clothes billowed in the November wind.

"This is kind of you, John," I said.

He said, "I was just worried about them being out when the pubs were closing, you know? Just in case . . ."

If I'd understood about honour, I also now understood about danger.

No wonder my hosts in Gilgit had used the word. If we were worried about twelve men who could probably handle a couple of drunks, little wonder my Gilgiti hosts were so beside themselves with concern about me, a lone Western girl with a taste for being out after nightfall.

We had our fireworks, in the dark garden. The wind had swung to a bitter north, and the bonfire crackled. There were eight adults, and as many kids. John came, but none of the Pakistanis, though we'd invited them. I don't suppose they fancied sausages and wine. The word was out, though. John told us that, as he had walked up the street to our house, two wee boys had accosted him.

"Mister," said one, "are you an Afghani?"

"Does he look like an Afghani?" said his pal.

We had a good time with our friends and all the children, and of course we talked about the group of Pakistani men, who were sitting in the dark with their candles and kerosene stoves in a strange, foreign town, while, outside, rockets shrieked and banged.

The following day, Sunday, we woke to the sound of the green gate opening, a shuffling in the yard and a nervous clatter of the letterbox. It was seven o'clock; the sun was not yet risen.

"Please," said Mahmood with a bow. "We have come to pray."

"You better go up in the study again."

"First, wash."

"Of course. I'll fetch towels."

"Hot water!" They grinned.

There was some urgency. The sun was rising, time was short. Mahmood washed in the bathroom, Nazir in the kitchen sink and the third man in the brown shawl filled a milk bottle with hot water and went to hunker in the yard. The spot he chose overlooked our neighbour's door. Please God, I thought, Please Allah, don't let the neighbour open his door at this moment. Because if he does, his three large dogs will come bounding out and leap up against the wall, just where this Muslim man is making his ablutions.

They left their shoes in the hall and filed up the narrow attic stair to my study. I shut the door.

"What way is Mecca, anyhow?"

Phil yawned.

"We discussed that yesterday. You know how the Cupar road curves south, out of town, past the petrol station? If it maintained that curve for a few thousand miles, you'd be there, apparently."

They wanted to leave by eleven, for the next leg of their walk, so we went to John's house to see them off. But first, we wanted to talk. In John's living-room, we sat in a circle on the floor. We spoke, for a short while, about the bombing of Afghanistan, about bin Laden, about the men's extraordinary project. We'd assumed, of course, they'd been prompted by September 11th, but they had in fact been here since August, and the trip had been planned for a long time before that. I would like to have known more about their thinking and planning—why Scotland, why now?—but I didn't want them to feel they were bring interrogated. The only time they seemed impatient was at the mention of Bin Laden. We asked them what they thought of him, and realised they'd been asked five hundred times before.

"This is political games. Games for the control of Afghan-istan. They have all tried and failed, British, Russia, Taliban, now USA. These Afghanis are proud people. We are not interested in polit-ical games . . . we are Peace Walk."

I thought I felt an undertow to the answer: "We are not Afghanis." Any more than we Scots were French. We commended the men on their bravery, especially after September 11th, because, said John, of the images we get on the media . . .

"Media!" spat Nazir, and they all shook their turbanned heads.

When it was time to go, we stood on the pavement as all their bags and gear were ferried from the shop back into the Transit. Duncan sat grinning on the passenger-seat beside two cloth-wrapped copies of the Qur'an and a bottle of Irn-Bru. The pleasant, shy man, the one who wore a brown shawl over his head, and who had washed in our yard, hunkered before our daughter and spoke in Urdu, but Freya hid her face in my skirt.

"He is saying she is same! He has one daughter, who is also three and she is same!"

"I think he's missing her."

"Yes."

Then it really was time to go, if they wanted to reach Cupar before dark. But first, the gifts. To Duncan's high delight, he was presented with a small ceramic vase, decorated with Scottish this-tles. John received an astonishing Chinese-made thermos flask in bronze plastic, in the shape of Aladdin's lamp. His eyes widened.

"Now that," I said, sotto voce, "is a truly Pakistani object," but I was overheard.

"No, please, it is belonging to one womans, here. She gave us some food, but, please, could you find this woman . . ."

" . . . and see that she gets it back?"

"Please. She is most kind."

I gave them a copy of the book I wrote, an account of my adven-tures in Northern Pakistan, and that went down well, and was passed from hand to hand.

"Is this book available? Here?" asked Nazir.

"No," I said. "It's out of print. There are very few copies left. But I'd like you to have one."

"You see! It is because you came to Pakistan, that is why you helped us. Now if you come back to Pakistan we will help you. There will be understanding, communication. This is Peace Walk!"

They ruffled Duncan's hair, admired Freya, shook the hands of Phil and John and offered effusive thanks to us all. The van set off. The walkers took to the road.

A walk. A bottle of hot water. A few words of another language. A garish thermos flask. The sound of a green gate, opening. A paper-back book. Such are the arts of peace. They're pretty banal. They're also quite funny. John ushered us back into his house and, behind the closed door, we all began to laugh.

"Have you had breakfast?" said John. "I have. I had curry and rice pud. And what do I do with this flask?"

We spoke for a while about our strange weekend. And over the next few days, when people heard about the Pakistanis, what they said was much what Susan the pharmacist had said: "Oh, I'd liked to have talked to them, but I didn't know how . . ."

When we came back to our own house the telephone was ringing. This is the truth: the telephone was ringing and the call was for me. It was a publisher.

"Your book about Pakistan," she said. "It's out of print, isn't it? That's a pity, because we think it says something necessary. Because of all the awful dehumanising images of Muslims we're getting these days. We know your book is about Pakistan, of course, not Afghanistan, but we think it counteracts some of the negative images we have about Islam. We wondered if you'd consider re-publishing it. We wondered if you'd consider—and this is absolutely your choice—we wondered if you'd consider going back?"

This book is called *Among Muslims*. It concerns a small part of the Muslim world, the Northern Areas of Pakistan. This has frontiers with China, India and Afghanistan. Its major river is the Indus, and its mountains are among the highest in the world. My story begins in the early 1990s, when I crossed the Khunjerab Pass from China.

November 2001, Fife, Scotland.

Pakistan, everything possible!

1 Gilgit Going

From the roadside, a nomad herdsman watched our charabanc rumble by, then turned his horse and was gone. To the east the distant ridges of Mustagh Ata rose purplish from the plain; west, the mountains of the Hindu Kush. For the thousandth time I shifted, trying to get comfortable. For the thousandth time I leaned my head against the window, but still it shook too much. How I longed to be that herdsman, laughing as he rode.

The air was growing thin and chill, with a hint of snow. We were getting higher and no one spoke much now, except the Pakistani lad who still stood swaying at the front of the bus, trying to rouse us in a merry chorus. "He is jolly boy," said the young man next to me, wearily, as he laid his aching head in his arms. Jolly boy sang and lurched and twirled his luxuriant moustaches. He put on a tape of shrieking Hindi film music, so at odds with the wide lands through which we passed, but the Chinese driver vetoed it.

At the Chinese customs post, a row of lily-shaped streetlamps rose from the desolation. There were no lilies here; in a few months the snow would come again, and the Khunjerab Pass close for the long winter. We were ordered off the bus, and spent four hours huddled against a wall, wrapped in shawls, with strewn glass and gravel to sit on as the Chinese officials grimly processed our passports, and then refused to let our bus through. One can understand their intransigence; no Roman foot soldier on the bleak cold moors of Hadrian's Wall would have had much to smile about. But the Pakistani lads had exhausted the delights of Kashgar and wanted to go home. They invaded the wretched customs house and waved and swore at the Chinese officials behind the desk, who merely stared them down. There is no love lost between the peoples who together built the "Friendship Highway." Then it was decided that to be rid of us was the better option, and with infinite slowness the bus made its way out of Pirali and up towards the watershed. The Pakistani lads—and they were all lads—banged on the windows and jeered.

Higher and higher the bus climbed. It had been a two-day ride from Kashgar, because in China drivers stop at night, and so incur the derision of the Pakistanis, whose drivers just light another joint and keep on going: twenty, thirty hours. Already we had broken four fan belts, and spent the night in a dosshouse in Tashkurgan—forty people, only three of them female, in twenty-eight single beds. A miners' trip to Blackpool was nothing like this.

Pockets of snow lingered on the dark side of rocks. The pass is wide, and very beautiful. At the concrete post which marks the border, the bus stopped and the lads poured out. They come from the sweltering plains of the Punjab, and snow was something new. They were as children; moustachioed businessmen danced about in their sandals and threw snowballs down each other's necks. They piled back aboard and the bus tipped for the descent into Pakistan. The border was crossed, they cheered loud and long. Only then came the moment we had really been waiting for. Jolly boy stopped mid-cheer, turned deathly pale and keeled over like a tree. As he fell sprawling on the boxed-up tea sets and thermos flasks stacked in the aisle, there rose another cheer. Alcohol and altitude had got to him at last.

In Kashgar there are beer and brandy, massage parlours, women unveiled and business to be done. Behind our bus there followed a wagon, laden with more tea sets, pencils, shoes and silks. Trade was their excuse and they were sticking to it. Like the yak-caravans of yore we laboured on. I looked off into the distance, because the wide grassland would be our last sight of space until we crossed the Karakoram and emerged in the Punjab, hundreds of miles below. From now on we would be among mountains. An ibex bolted from view. We tipped downhill, and followed the river into a gorge. Gradually the wide sky closed to a mere strip of blue above our heads. China was finished.

The curled-up fellow lifted his head. "You are Gilgit going?"

"Yes. You?"

"Inshallah." God willing.

Many hours later we reached another huddle of buildings: Sost. A painted sign read "Pakistan Customs and Anti-Smuggling Post." I stared at that sign. I could read it. It spoke to me. In China, I could read nothing. I could not tell a bank from a laundry, a tea-house from a barber-shop. Green flags fluttered in the slight breeze, and a soldier emerged from a tent to raise the barrier: a wooden pole lashed down and counterweighted by a basket of river-stones. The customs officer lounged on his verandah, and seemed little interested in the passports stacked before him. There was no hurry; the Chinese bus would go no further, and no transport to Gilgit would appear before morning. The Pakistani lads queued to clear their huge baggages of tea sets. Their luggage was searched for drink.

I was allowed to enter Pakistan on condition that I sent the Immigration Officer a postcard from Scotland. He thumped the rubber stamp down upon the page and said, "This China, no good. Welcome to Pakistan. Pakistan, everything possible. Here, we are *free*."

I'd been in Gilgit a couple of times before and had stayed at the hotel called the Golden Peak. Its entrance is a decrepit green gate which stands between a gun dealer's and a disused mosque. The mosque is domed and orange, like an exotic fruit. A shouting madman lives there now. Within the gate lies a secluded lawn, shaded by three of Gilgit's magnificent walnut trees. The shade of the trees is a favourite spot for the burghers of Gilgit to take tea and talk politics. There's a collection of mismatching garden furniture. The manager has an office with a telephone and a small TV which stands on the ledge of the open window, facing out so it can be watched from the garden in the cool evenings, amongst the bugs.

Mohammed was not in his kitchen. He had washed and stacked the chipped plates and turned off the kerosene stoves. His water supply, a hose poked through a knothole in the wooden wall, dribbled on to the earth floor. Pinned to the wall, among the tea and spices, plates and cups, were two pictures torn from a magazine. One showed Benazir Bhutto, with her dupatta over her hair and her lips parted in speech. The other showed the raven's stare of the Ayatollah Khomeini.

Mohammed had been off down the bazaar. Already his summer had been too long, the guests too demanding, his boss too hard, his money too little. He came in to find me looking at the pictures, and gave a teenage grin.

"Ahh, I like." And, with a curious intimacy, "They are speaking to me! Benazir, she tell me I am good boy. Ayatollah tell me I am *strong*!"

It seemed a balanced enough parentage for a boy so long away from his village. The Golden Peak is named after the mountain, also called Spantik, which cannot be seen from Gilgit but forms the backdrop to the village of Nagar. This hotel is a Nagari stronghold. Mohammed is Nagari, as is his boss, Mr Latif. The owner of the hotel is the Mir of Nagar himself. The valley is on the east side of the Hunza, and the Nagaris have a fierce reputation. Neither Mohammed nor Mr Latif evinces this at all. Mohammed is all talk and Mr Latif is small and neat, and too concerned with his health to endanger it by fighting. He's often in the company of his friend Dr Noor.

"This doctor. You look his face!" hissed Mohammed as he brought us tea. He flew back into his kitchen and inspected his chin on a shard of broken mirror. The poor doctor had a bad complexion. I sat with him and Mr Latif and the conversation turned, as it often did, to Benazir Bhutto. Benazir was everyone's darling, her government a tender flower anxiously protected by some from the trampling feet of others. As we spoke, the call to prayer reached over the rooftops from the Shia mosque nearby.

"Mullahs!" said the doctor.

"Do you think they're dangerous? Have they influence?"

"No, but they can make a fuss. They say it is sin. She is woman. When they want, they make fuss. Do you know this item in the newspaper?" He tapped the *Daily Jang* on his lap. "From Lahore? There is an argument between landlord and tenant. The court decides that the tenant should win. What does this landlord do? Why, he goes to the tenant's house, and takes the wife and daughter, drags them into the bazaar, strips them, rapes them! And what do the mullahs do about *these* women? Nothing!"

Mr Latif, like most men, wears large rings of jasper or turquoise.

Around his thin neck there hangs a tablet of jade, in case someone poisons him. He told me how to take the stone and grind some in a little water to form a milk. Drink it, it is an antidote to everything. With the jade there hung the little sewn parcels more commonly seen on children, called *taviz*, little talismans containing a text from the Qur'an to banish ailments and night-fears. It was good to be back in Gilgit. The pace of things was slow.

The Golden Peak is by no means the best hotel—far from it. It is neither the most expensive nor the cheapest. It was built a century ago as a winter palace for the Mir, but one could scarcely even call it beautiful. It's built of stone, and squats like a toad at the end of its lawn, eyes closed in the hot sunshine. A verandah runs round each of its two storeys, with cane blinds to keep out the heat. There is a stone portico, with benches, where Mohammed often sleeps. Crowning that, a magnificent set of horns from some poor ibex. A dreadful wooden staircase reaches from the lawn to the upper floor.

The building sags and sighs. On hot afternoons it seems visibly to dissolve, like a lump of sugar in a glass of tea. Colonies of wild bees have secreted their hives under the verandah. There are mice, and bedbugs. (Mohammed slaps his backside: "*This they like!*") There are only four rooms and a couple of washing-rooms with a collection of butts and buckets. Each room has several camp beds and a lugubrious fan. The rooms are bow-fronted and cool, with woodwork painted bottle-green. There are frequent power cuts, but even when the electricity is on, the low glow of the bulb does little to cheer the rooms, even on the sunniest day.

One of these rooms is graced with wallpaper as old as the building itself. I'm fascinated by this wallpaper, and have often lain wondering about its history. It is of trellises of vines, with haughty birds who repeat themselves all over the walls, from the deep skirting boards, around the old wooden fireplace, to the cobwebby corners of the ceiling.

In the days when the Mir of Nagar built the palace, there was no road. If he chose to indulge a rich man's whim for wallpaper it would have been carried on the back of man or beast from Srinagar, and before that, who knows? Calcutta perhaps. Maybe it was ordered through a catalogue from Harrods. I can picture the rolls of birds and trellises, strapped on the back of a wizened porter and borne for days, weeks, through twisting Himalayan gorges and precipitous hillsides, to Gilgit, where it still hangs in the gloom which has done much to preserve it.

I like the Golden Peak because of the dark fireplaces and this extraordinary wallpaper, the bow windows and the incongruous camp beds. It makes me think of a Scottish drawing-room, billeted in wartime.

I was lying in the cool room thinking these thoughts when the screen door slammed and young Mohammed entered unbidden. He plonked himself on the foot of the bed, scowled, then rose again, very solemnly. "Now," he said, "I dance."

He began to turn about, lifting his feet. He closed his eyes as if entranced and hummed a long high note. It was a melancholy dance, this way and that, like the casement of an old clock. When the dance was done, he opened his eyes, sat again and tilted his teenage chin for my inspection. His encounter with Dr Noor had alarmed him.

"*Why* these things are they coming?" he said, pointing to a spot.

"It's just your age."

"M'med! M'med Hussain!" cried a gruff voice from the garden. A brace of doughty Gilgit councillors had come to take tea beneath the walnut trees. Mohammed made a foul face. "It is *too much work.*" He left to tend to the councillors, pausing as he crossed the lawn to throw an outraged stone at cats mating on the wall.

The idea of staying in Gilgit for a while was beginning to grow on me. The summer stretched ahead; I had a little money, an iron stomach and no good reason to go home. After China, Gilgit felt like normality itself. And—it had a library. To get there, I did what I did every day: walked through the bazaar.

There are no women in the bazaar in Gilgit, save one: a beggar in full black burqa who huddles at the post office every day, like a shot crow. Had I the language I would have asked her story, but I hadn't. She frightened me a little, in that black garb, just a brown hand held out for alms.

It is a long town, and the main road which reaches from the airstrip to the half-built mosque is a throng of commerce. There's little you cannot buy in the shacks of Gilgit: mounds of dried apricots and bales of Chinese silk; rat traps, microwaves, condoms and veils. New shops are being built, and although they're of concrete they retain the principle of the old wooden box, open to the road. Within the shade of the shop the vendor lies across his sacks, conversing with his friends, flicking flies.

On the main road, Japanese jeeps weave between heavy handcarts. Great trucks and military wagons occasionally roll through town, but they don't disturb the fat-bottomed goats that sit in the gutter, chewing the cud. There is a human noise of shouting and selling above the sound of machines. To look the length of the straight street is to see an astonishing uniformity of sex and dress. Men and boys, be they in shops, on wobbling bicycles, on buses, foot or jeeps, drinking in tea-houses or pulling carts, wear browns and fawn and cream. Dress in Pakistan for men and women both is the shalwar-kameez, the long shirt and baggy trousers. For every purpose: travelling, working, gardening, even sleeping. Although there are nuances of cut and fabric, finish and decoration, the shalwar-kameez is the great leveller.

Beside the half-built mosque is one narrow and fetid little alley given over to butchery. Goats' testicles hang damply from awnings, their kidneys are arranged on plates. There is always a wicker cage of chickens, and a bloodied stone over the sewer where their throats are cut in the halal manner. I don't eat meat, but would sooner walk through an honest alley of feathers and gore than a supermarket of polystyrene trays any day. There are open drains to negotiate, and the smell of fresh-baked roti, spices and blood.

I walked through the bazaar every day, because every day there was some new sensation, some gossip or new arrival. It is a rumour mill, an exchange of more than goods and money. Today two Afghan carpet-sellers had arrived, with their wares draped over their arms, and an itinerant perfumier sat among his jars of jasmine, sandalwood and rose.

Suzukis serve as public transport. They are waspish little wagons that fart from one end of the bazaar to the other. Sometimes, in the backs of these, I saw women, wrapped in chadors. Sometimes a woman, holding her black burqa at her throat, would dart across the street like a guilty thing. If I, a lone woman, took a Suzuki, I would sit next to the driver in the seclusion of his cab while the men piled into the back.

The bazaar can be stressful. Although I too wore the shalwar-kameez I sometimes got jostled on the narrow pavement, my breasts nudged. For the most part the men are mannered to the point of condescension, ridiculously courtly, and hope more to sell a tea set than to have a swift *affaire*. "Madam! What do you want? Yes! Come on!"

But outwith the bazaar it is peaceful. There are no roads, only little lanes, so no vehicles penetrate the labyrinth of homesteads. The back alleys are lined by high walls, and children play on the corners. "Angrez!" they call on seeing a Westerner. "Angrez! Angrez!"

There are a few last vestiges of British occupation here: some tired old bungalows, a cemetery behind a locked gate, and a top-heavy civil service. The Gilgit Agency was Britain's farthest out-post in India. I was looking forward to seeing the library—I'd heard it was an old building, the residence of the British Agent himself. I followed directions given by water-channel, not street, and walked upstream. The channel flowed fast down from its source in the barren mountains which surround the town. There was a dusty path beside the stream and branches of apple trees and flowering shrubs hung over the walls. There was an officers' mess, for Gilgit is full of soldiers, and little planks laid across the stream served as bridges to the gates of private houses. I could hear the voices of women inside the walls, but could see none, because the gates were invariably closed.

To eyes deprived of print and ears used to the honed-down essentials of communication, the library was a dream. It stood in its own garden, a low, white building, like a croft. The reading room was silent but for the rustling of newspapers: *The Muslim, The Daily Jang*. Men sprawled along the window seats where the afternoon breeze found its way between the fronds of bushes outside. On the straight side of the semicircular room the scholarly librarian sat at a desk. He granted me permission to look at the books. Above his head a little painted sign read "Silence is requested."

An eccentric collection it was, on tilting shelves, Books Britishers didn't want to take home had been donated wholesale, and so formed a literary timewarp: Maurice Walsh, J.J. Bell, *The Log of a Woman Wanderer*. Fifty Himalayan summers had faded the spines. There were the Brontës, and more recent acquisitions: Lawrence Durrell and Sartre's *Essays on Aesthetics* next to *The World's 100 Best Jokes*. There were volumes on computing, where there was little electricity, never mind computers. There was a room for books in Urdu, and a further archive, full of yellowing newspapers. Above the bookshelves photographs gazed severely from the washed walls; agents and governors faded away like Cheshire cats, leaving not a smile but a moustache. Polo teams stared strongly from some hot pre-Partition afternoon, and above the fireplace behind the desk was a painting of K2.

I took Seamus Heaney's *North* from the shelf—the first time, according to the label, it had been disturbed in fifteen years. I laid it on a table and a cloud of mountain dust rose from its pages.

A gentleman reading *The Muslim*, an English-language paper, obligingly moved over so that I might sit.

"You are English?" he said, from behind the paper.

"Scots."

"Switzerland?" He lowered the paper and showed himself: a broad, bearded man in his fifties, handsome and dark. He looked puzzled.

There was a 'thirties book: views of Scotland. I took it and showed him a grainy photograph of Edinburgh Castle, and then of Highland blackhouses, so like the village homes he would recognise.

He replaced the newspaper on the table in front of him. "You will come to my house!" he said, in a thunderous whisper. "Take tea! Mr Iqbal . . ."

A voice from behind the *Pakistan Times* said, "Major Sahib?"

"We are taking tea at my house with this lady. You will come?"

Mr Iqbal lowered his newspaper and revealed himself. He looked like David Niven. He eschewed the shalwar-kameez in favour of a Wodehouse garb—silk cravat and polished brogues. Skulking behind a third newspaper was Dr Noor. We all left the library and the Major led the way.

"So you are from Britain! British! We have British. This library is British!"

The Major sat and slapped his thighs.

"Wonderful bridges!" said Mr Iqbal, who crossed his legs and displayed beige socks.

"You, Sir, are too keen on these British!"

"They did good things for us, Major Sahib."

"Pah!" said the Major. "They were out for their own ends!" He cast me a laughing look. "Still are! All governments are out for their own good. Is this not true, Miss Kathleen?"

"But this road! What great benefits to our remote area!"

"SO WHAT FOR THIS ROAD, MR IQBAL! Now, Miss, you have seen this great road, this Friendship Highway, what is this? It is a means by which the Pakistan and Chinese governments can shake hands in case of emergency! Was it built for my betterment? No."

The door opened and a small boy entered, stared, and was gone.

"Doctor," said the Major, "tell this lady about the health problems of our little area."

"The people suffer chiefly from deficiency and bad sanitation."

"Do the aid programmes help?"

"AID?" the Major cried. "My opinion, Miss, about aid programmes from the West is that they should STOP, yes, STOP! And you are asking me why? It is because it is not for our betterment. It is for yours! Yes. Where is our science, where is our technology? Kept down by you!"

By now he was smiling.

"You're preaching to the converted," I said.

"The West is not giving to us, it is holding us, just here, exactly here. We will not starve, but we will not rise. Your aid promotes a state of Arrested Development. It is a state of Dependence. Enough, little, little is given, so these simple peoples think you care. So they are not angry. But not enough to make us rise. What is this Israel?"

"Israel?"

"It is a cancer in our side! It is made by the West and put here to stop the unification of Muslim peoples. And now we will take tea."

I was to grow to enjoy conversations with the Major. They were rollicking affairs. For the moment I was trying to remain polite. We sat on two sofas, facing each other like passengers in a train. The room had two doors—one opening directly from outside, which we had used, and another connecting it to the remainder of the house. This latter opened and the Major strode towards it. It opened just enough to admit a tray of tea things. I saw a woman's hand, which vanished, and the door was firmly closed.

"I served . . ." began Mr Iqbal, and I distinctly saw the Major roll his eyes.

." . . in the Bangladeshi war."

"You were a soldier?"

"Oh yes."

"I also served," growled the Major, and laughed to me. The doctor began to stroke his troubled chin. Mr Iqbal told an old soldier's tale, with the Major as chorus. It droned on like the fan which stirred the air above our heads.

"He lay upon the field of battle . . ."

"Wounded," said the Major.

"Badly wounded. With my own clothing . . ."

"You stopped the blood."

"I stopped the blood. I took him in my arms . . ."

"You embraced."

"Embraced."

In a corner of the room there stood an ibex, stuffed, with twisted horns and glassy eyes.

Mohammed ran across the lawn with eyes the size of saucers. "It is telephone! For you! This major, you know this major? Oh, he is big man, important man. But very nice! He say, you go to his office eleven o'clock."

The pounding of the Major's typewriter could be heard on the street outside. He was retired from the army, and concentrated on other things. The office was in a modern concrete block which, by dint of dust or architecture, seemed quite in keeping with the wooden shacks around it. I knew it by the sign outside—Northern Areas Trading Co.—and went in.

Northern Areas. It seems hardly the most imaginative of names for an area redolent with romantic-sounding kingdoms: Baltistan, Dardistan, Kashmir. At first I avoided using the term, because I imagined it to be as offensive to the people here as is the term "North British" to the Scots: a denial of their cultural identity and difference. I was right in one thing—it is politically loaded, but not in the way I'd supposed.

The Major shook my hand and slapped my back and dusted down a cane chair. His desk was awash with papers. A shelf of mineral samples stood against one wall.

"Again I am writing this newspaper!" he cried, and pulled the paper from the typewriter. Another furious letter to the editor. I quickly came to realise that the Major's primary concern and first amusement was loud political argument. The letter addressed Benazir Bhutto's visit to the Siachen Glacier, where the Kashmir war splutters on between India and Pakistan.

"Read!"

"The Constitutional Status question has set back our people, our culture and our economy. As we all know, India wants . . ." the letter broke off.

"What does India want?"

"To strangle this Pakistan! You will take tea, cold drink?" He crossed to the window in one stride and bawled down the street. In a few moments a scruffy lad appeared with a tray and a blue enamel teapot. To him the Major spoke in Shinas, to me in perfect English; and on the telephone, which rang loud and often, a mixture of both, plus Urdu as well.

As he spoke on the phone I stood to look at the stones. Some were very strange, like plants from under the sea. As I examined first one, then the next, he cupped his hands over the mouthpiece and hissed: "This tourmaline! This jade! Don't touch that, it's uranium!"

Equally unstable is the Constitutional Question, the Kashmir Question. As he explained to me, the Major paced about his office. He picked things up and put them down. Sometimes he fired a question at me: What do you think of this man? What is your opinion of that? But to my great relief he expected no answer.

The people of the Northern Areas have no representation in the Pakistani Parliament which administers them. They can't vote, because the question of to whom, India or Pakistan, their area should belong has yet to be resolved. The Northern Areas [of Pakistan] is that portion of Kashmir which a dismayed Jinnah seized. At Partition, the Maharajah of Kashmir opted for secular India. The Major told me that the outraged Muslim majority revolted and went for Pakistan. Indian history books, just as partisan, say the Kashmiri people themselves were happy enough with India— it was Jinnah who sent in raiders, then troops. They nearly reached Srinagar, but the raiders got drunk on the way, and were pushed back. Now the land of Kashmir is divided by a cease-fire line which severs its natural and ancient lines of communication; through Srinagar and Leh. Pakistan holds the mountainous lands from west of Gilgit through to east of Skardu: as far as the Siachen Glacier. It is a strange and forgotten little pocket.

"For forty years this has been our problem. Now we have Benazir. She has promised to help. We want to be Pakistan fifth side. My own brother was killed in this struggle. What good is this sacrifice if we cannot become Pakistan's fifth side? We overthrew this Dogra regime, and for what?"

He sat, pushed the typewriter to the side of the desk and laced his hands under his bearded chin. "And now, Miss. You are looking for accommodations in Gilgit. I have been thinking and I have the answer. It is one of my own family! An engineer."

"Have you a large family?"

"More than two thousand. He has spare rooms. You will be safe, and comfortable."

"I really don't want to live with a family . . ."

"You will have private entrance, bathroom."

"But I really don't know."

"He has agreed to this thing, because I have asked him."

"But really, if he is at all unhappy . . ."

"I have asked him. And we will go there now. You know, this thing is simple for you, because you are female. Accommodations are simple. For mens, not possible! Because you know, we are Shia."

It was a hot day in mid-July when I took my things round to the house of the Major's cousin. One of the mysterious green gates was opened to me, and I stepped into the garden within. I saw whitewashed walls, and tall orange flowers. I would, the Major insisted—nay, ordered—be safe and comfortable in the home of Murtaza, Salma, and what they called their limited family: two vivacious little children called Hina and Ali.

The couple stood before me like a Dutch painting: the Arnolfini Wedding. Salma was pregnant with a third child, and considerably younger than her husband. She took my hand in a soft, uncertain grip. She was plump of face, where he was thin and drawn. Where he was intense and anxious, she was slow and easy-going. I realised that Salma was the first Gilgiti woman whose face I had seen. She spoke no English, but Murtaza was fluent. With grave charm and manners, which I sensed covered a certain unease, he showed me around.

I was to have the suite of rooms reserved for male visitors. The seclusion of women is complete, and if the men of the house wish to entertain their friends, a space must be provided where they can go without disturbing the women. If a strange man is present, the women will not enter the room. Hence the two doors in the Major's room. I had a sitting-room, like the pristine front rooms I remembered from childhood days, which were kept dusted and spotless and where the best china was displayed, but which were never used except in the event of visitors. Here, there was a table, a sofa, a thick durrie on the floor. There was a damp little bathroom, with a shower-head and a wooden palette to stand on, a toilet and water-jug. The room was decorated with some plastic flowers in a vase, a toy aeroplane and a papier-mâché camel. On a window-ledge stood photographs of polo teams. A bedroom adjoined, with two single beds covered with rich blue brocade. French windows looked on to a small chicken yard. The back windows admitted the morning sun and, five times a day, the muezzin's sobbing call to prayer. The front room gave out on to a verandah, within a fly screen, and the verandah on to a small but crowded garden.

The Major didn't come in. "You will be comfortable!" he said, "And if there is any problem, ANY PROBLEM, you will come to me. And you will remember what I told you about male visitors. It is not our custom, and the people will be offended. Because, as you know, we are Shia."

That night, as I sat at the heavy table, the sense of foreignness closed in. I felt myself to be in a strange place, far from anywhere. A wave of panic passed through me: what friends I had in Gilgit were gone now. To calm myself, I wrote sardonic notes in my diary about how the anticipation of an event is sometimes preferable to the reality. To stay in Gilgit seemed like a good idea at the time. Gilgit interested me. These Shia people interested me. We were told to fear Shias as madmen, in the days of the Ayatollah, but that was propaganda and these people were in some way familiar. I wondered then if I wouldn't find in Shi'ite people the Calvinists of Islam. So I was an "Angrez" installed in Gilgit.

There were cockroaches scratching in the bathroom. At every little sound, I flinched. When I'd mentioned the possibility of staying to a Dutch woman I'd met in passing, she had shaken her head and said, "It is very dangerous, I think, for a woman, alone." But I sensed little danger. I felt weird, displaced, but not endangered. If anything, I was aware of being co-opted, that responsibility was being taken for me whether or not I required it. But of course I required it, I was a woman and a guest, and it was the men's God-given role to accept that terrible weight of responsibility. Responsibility was a word Murtaza often used, and the lines of it deeply marked his face.

I sat at the table, read, and wrote a letter. The shadow of the fan flicked across the page. I missed everyone I knew, and felt very much alone.

In the dark, long after the evening prayers had been called, a rhythmic chanting continued to be broadcast from the mosque's megaphone on the warm night air. It was a sound of men's voices and women's, perhaps children's too. The very darkness seemed full of this chanting, chanting. I had seen streams of people heading towards the mosque: men, and groups of women completely wrapped in shawls that crossed the nose and trailed down their backs to their heels. I was asleep before that eerie chanting ceased, well into the night.

The first time I met Rashida Shah she was standing at my table, giving me a long hard look. She startled me, like a ghost. Not that she had any ephemeral quality: on the contrary. She had dark hair and eyes, and a slightly craggy look, like a bird. Her clothes were full and modest, her hair tidily drawn back in a plait beneath a black dupatta. For a moment I forgot I was in Pakistan and thought "Victorian." If she was a Victorian, then I was the ghost; the brash ghost of the future which she was puzzled to find in the drawing-room. I stood, and gravely we shook hands. We were of similar age. She said, "What is your opinion of Pakistan girls?"

I said I had met few, but I knew that if I were a Pakistani girl, I couldn't do the things I was doing, which would be a great loss to me.

She considered and said, "Yes, Islam is very strict religion." She put one hand over the bridge of her nose. "We are purdah-observing. We work in burqa. My sister is teacher. I too did apply for the position of teacher, but was not selected. I am BA."

I was to learn two things which astonished me: one, that this rather formal speech was given in Rashida's seventh language; and two, that I was the first and only native speaker of that language she had ever met. Her eyes left my face, which they had given close examination, and began to travel down my frame.

"You do not wear dupatta?" she said, around my shoulders, and at my feet she heaved a sorrowful sigh: "This is not beautiful shoes."

Rashida is one of Salma's younger sisters. She lives with her parents and remaining unmarried siblings in a large pink house, but a step away through a connecting gate. She led me there. She showed me the spartan rooms of her house. In her brothers' bedroom there hung but one picture: a huge poster of the Ayatollah Khomeini.

The gravity which I would come to associate with Shi'ite people does not extend to dress. Once requirements of modesty are satisfied by the shape of the shalwar-kameez, anything goes. Rashida's elder sister, Jamila, appeared in an astonishing outfit of turquoise rayon, splashed with leopard-prints. In her arms she carried another polyester creation and, worse, she was giving it to me. At first, when all the unfamiliar names confused me, I thought of Jamila as "the leopard woman," because of her outfit, her fast, leaner way of moving, and the dark mischief in her eyes.

Good manners demanded I put the shalwar-kameez on, and fold away the old blue cotton which had served me well, with its masculine accoutrements, like pockets. The whole thing was worse than I feared. Unfolded, the full horror of the leg-of-mutton sleeves was revealed to me. And the design was of leaves in hateful shades of mustard and fawn, like a crazed autumn wood. It trailed far over the offending footwear. I rolled the vast waist over and over upon itself and pulled the tie round hard. The roll showed through. I heard my grandmother's voice: "Hen, ye've got a bumfle!" Abjectly I stood as Jamila laughed. Rashida gravely pronounced me beautiful. The sandals couldn't be helped at the moment, but we could at least go and see Mother.

They led me through a back gate and out into a secret world of tiny connecting passages. Dark shadows clung to the walls, like dogs. So narrow were the lanes a man had to stand back into a gateway to let us through. He passed the time of day with us, but the two girls averted their faces as they replied. We stepped across a conduit which was running cobalt blue and arrived at a wooden door that opened not to a house, but to a walled garden.

There was every fruit tree, and almonds, bushes of okra, spinach, onions and radishes, and flowers too. High walls cast shadow over scrubby lawn where a milk-cow grazed. It was a far cry indeed from the bazaar.

"It is our mother," said Jamila. At first I thought she meant the garden itself, for I could see no one. Mrs. Shah was so impossibly tiny. A little, tanned, merry lady with a figure like an eighteen-year-old. She emerged from the flowers like a pixie, wearing an outfit I immediately coveted; it was young and fresh in purples and pinks. For myself, I felt like a poodle in a tutu, but Mrs. Shah took both my hands in hers and looked up at me, talking fast.

"She says you are welcome, you are very welcome. You are her daughter." I felt quite overcome. We all went back for tea.

Three daughters remain unmarried and at home, and to them falls the housework. Mrs Shah led me into the family's sitting-room—not, this time, the men's parlour. We kicked off our sandals and ducked through the curtain which served as door. There was none of the stuffed furniture and plastic flowers. A fridge stood beside the door and on top of the fridge, on a doily, a TV set. A set of newly built cupboards lined one wall. And what, I wondered, when the carpenter comes? Do the women all hide in the kitchen? There was no sofa, no furniture at all, but a much more comfortable arrangement of carpets and cushions on the floor against the wall. Two embroideries decorate the walls, because the littlest sister, affectionately known as Moon, is a student of needlework. Again I thought "Victorian." The whole family gathered for lunch. Father, a heavy-jowled, French-looking man. An elder brother, newly back from China where, Rashida said, he was looking for shoes. A younger brother, a fine young man of fourteen who attended a high school on the other side of town. His school uniform was English style, grey trousers and a blue shirt and jacket. A cloth was spread on the floor and a meal of chapati and garden vegetables arrived, prepared by Jamila.

I would often accept their invitations to lunch, and spend an hour or two in the living-room with the girls. They were not bored, they said, but I thought the days needed only the heavy ticking of a clock to turn them into a Scottish Sunday. It was summer, so Jamila was on holiday from school. She hunkered on the floor, sewing a new shalwar on a hand-turned sewing machine. Moon was teaching her small nephew his letters. Rashida and I sat on the low cushions around the wall. The arrangement of cushions was a good one. You could hold sisterly conversations with your neighbour, or cross-family debates.

Rashida said she would like to continue her education. "I am BA in Islamic Studies: Persian, Arabic. It is my ambition to attain MA; but is not possible."

"Why not?"

"We are purdah-observing! The MA is available only at college. This BA I did attain at home. For examinations only I did leave the house."

I don't know which surprised me more: that she had learned all she had at home, or that college was debarred to her.

"My father will not permit."

"Where did you learn your English?"

"School. Film, and TV; newspapers. Also my father is speaking, you have heard! You know I have a good friend, she is from very near. She is in Abbotabad, student of medicine. Very modern family. She did travel alone to Bangkok! One other is taking a BSc in Lahore. But they admire me, because I am purdah-observing. And now I will show you the photographs of my engagement party."

No visit to a Pakistani household is complete without the photographs. They're usually stacked up in a corner. Look upon the albums, ye mighty, and despair. The snaps showed an affair of women and hennaed hands, of make-up and voluptuous fabrics. There were no men at the engagement party.

"At our parties there is much dancing, men and women both, drinking too."

"It is very strange to us."

There were more photographs—of the elder brother, a hostile, bearded man of thirty. He had been to Japan on a trade delegation, and showed the pictures.

"This Canadian." He pointed to a girl in red. "This Japan, this France."

Rashida began: "If God gave me the golden opportunity to see your country . . ." but he shook his head. He drew in the photographs.

"What if your brother came, or your father?"

"It is not possible," said the brother, wagging his beard.

"We have not permission," said Rashida.

"Whose, for heaven's sake?"

"To travel to another country, we need permission of father or husband."

"Well, where may you go?"

"To our place of education or work. In burqa. Look . . ." She held out her hands. "Hands may show. Feet may show." She scraped her hair from her brow. "Hair may not show."

She fetched her burqa to show me.

"Like a moving tent!" roared father from the garden.

"Do you think it is a good thing that your daughters look like tents?"

"They have peace, and no worries."

Rashida nodded. "We are satisfied," she said.

There was a pounding of mortar fire all the afternoon, when the mountains were hazy in the heat. A convoy of military trucks had rolled into the bazaar, and soldiers in uniform, a grey-belted shalwar-kameez, ran along the gutters like rain. They carried rifles—some automatics, two with mortars. Somewhere a rock-face was being blasted, and the sound rolled and rebounded off the mountains. The strange chanting came again that night, like a shanty, led by a boy and echoed by a thousand men. Murtaza looked in later. He said they had been at the mosque, but the kids were fractious and Salma tired, being so pregnant, so they'd come home early. He seemed inclined to talk, and sat at the table in his slippers and a light white shalwar-kameez. He looked very drawn. He told me he had undergone eighteen months" treatment for TB, which may have accounted for his pallor. He told me about his early days, when he was manager of a pre-casting plant in Karachi.

"But," he said, "I resigned my post, because Karachi knew no peace. And now Gilgit also. Where can one go for peace?"

"Why are there so many soldiers in Gilgit?" I asked.

He laid his head in his hands, and straightened up. "It is because of this massacre, last year. You know?"

I had heard. A stupid brawl in the bazaar blew up into a short internecine war. Passengers heading into Gilgit found themselves jumped at the roadsides as their buses and jeeps were overrun by Sunnis, who ran amok.

"Fifteen villages," he said. "Fifteen. They burned . . . the people, the animals, even the pigeons. Such was their cruelty, they even killed the pigeons. In my own village, there are three thousand people. Twelve thousand invaders came . . ."

"Your people . . .?"

"My brother was there. His house was burned, his animals were slaughtered."

"And your parents?"

"My parents, thank God, were in Gilgit. And when all this happened, where were the authorities? Sitting in Gilgit, doing nothing."

"Why?"

"Because they were part of it. This Zia was part of it. We lived under his army, his law."

"Now he's gone."

"This bastard Zia!"

"He was Sunni?"

"You know about Sunni and Shia? The difference is only the personality of the Prophet."

Murtaza went off to bed. I could hear the murmur of his praying through the wall.

The weekend consists of one day, Friday, which is Saturday and Sunday rolled into one. It is an endless round of social calls. The lanes are full of gangs of veiled women, in lines, like geese, going to visit each other.

"Always they are coming!" growled Jamila. "Make tea, make sweets, sit one minute only, make tea, make sweets." The aunts, the sister-cousins, the in-laws, their babes in arms, they come. Some have lived through many Fridays and eaten many sweets.

"This my cousin," whispered Rashida, and the curtain was flicked aside and a file of women entered. "This also my cousin, she is fat!"

Their babies are plentiful, plump and ghastly with kohl smudged round their staring eyes. The aunties dandled the babies. How I remembered it all—the Sunday visiting, the aunts, the fancy teacups. The "My! aren't you getting tall, and how's the school?"

Some aunts and cousins are dark and craggy, like closed umbrellas; some are great and doughty, breasting the alleyways like galleons, with their veils billowing around them. When they enter the low gates of the garden they tug down the veils from their faces, to dangle beneath the chin like false beards at a party. They deflate themselves on to the floor and await the tea and sweets. It was Moon's turn, which she took with the best teenage ill-grace. Had there been doors she would have slammed them hard.

When the guests had gone, Mrs. Shah lay back on the cushions. She looked like nothing so much as Chagall's *Poet, Reclining*. She asked for a cigarette and puffed on it gleefully.

"Your mother smokes?" I said to Rashida, who scowled.

"Also her sister is smoking."

Mrs. Shah pointed the cigarette towards Rashida and sang, "Hussain Ali! Hussain Ali!" Rashida went very red.

"It is her fiancé," said Jamila, and poked her sister.

"Do you see him?"

"No, not until we are married."

I wondered what to say. "Is he a good man?"

"Oh, yes!"

"Well, how do you know?"

"Because he is my cousin."

"But aren't you frightened?"

She looked downright surprised.

"And will you go on honeymoon?"

This time she looked coy, and hooked her black dupatta back over her ear. "Yes, maybe. *Then* we can meet and talk."

"You know, this is the thing we find most strange. To marry someone you do not know. To obey your parents and marry someone you don't know."

"Yes. But you are much divorce. Our marriage is success. No divorce."

There are worse things, I thought, than divorce, but it wasn't the first time I held my tongue. "You'll be having babies soon, then."

Both girls screwed up their faces as if they'd trodden in dog-shit. Jamila positively grued. "Creation of babies is . . . difficult."

Though Mrs. Shah understood not a word of our conversation, she followed it all, giggling. Rashida cupped her hand to my ear and whispered, "But I see!"

"How?" I asked, imagining clandestine meetings and all sorts of romance.

"Because he lives next door! Why you are laughing? His house is next door, and he stands on the roof, and I see from my brother's bedroom window. Stop laughing! Come, I show you."

We scampered up the stairs into the small bedroom the three girls shared. There was room enough only for three small beds, a wardrobe. Rashida hauled a suitcase out from beneath the bed and rummaged in it until she found a small photograph. It showed a lanky, bespectacled man of about thirty, wearing a checked jacket. The picture was taken in front of the Kashgar mosque. She looked at it for a moment, then stuffed it away. "He is jobless," she said, fondly.

"I thought you said he was a lawyer? Who ever heard of a jobless lawyer?"

Jamila stood with arms folded. "When he finds a job, we will give to him the hand of Rashida."

"Come on!" They led me up another stair and across a spartan bedroom. At the window, they lifted the blind a chink. "Look!"

Sure enough, I could look down upon the little clay chimneys of next-door's flat roof. I could imagine Ali stood there beside the firewood, like Romeo, looking up at nothing but an enigmatic flutter of the curtain. *We are purdah-observing.*

Jamila grinned handsomely. "Our marriage is success, no divorce!"

My not-beautiful shoes still caused comment. Beneath the burqa, my friends wear sexy high heels in flashing colours. I understood the fuss Victorian men made about ankles.

"And your feet are not soft," said Jamila, in her best school-marm voice. She gave me a pitying look. I decided that a change of outfit was imperative. Rashida had offered to make me a new suit, and I announced one day that I was going to the bazaar to buy not only fabric, but beautiful shoes as well. They were mortified. Always running round the bazaar in this unseemly manner. I said that in my country shopping was very much a women's activity, and men were often to be seen parked at shop doorways on a Saturday morning, with their hands in their pockets and a very bored look on their faces.

"But, you take from here!" said Jamila. "Our mother's shop, cloth, shoes . . ."

"Beautiful shoes?"

She punched my arm. "Very beautiful!"

And here was a new surprise. Women don't go to the bazaar, but keep their own shops within their homes. Mrs. Shah had a room given over to bales of cloth and sandals. When I asked Murtaza, he obligingly opened their shop-room and showed me baby clothes and ornaments. It made sense of a sign I'd seen on another lane: "Lady Shop." I chose some cotton, and paid for it, and then some sandals which showed to high advantage life's marks: my bunion and corns. I was a disaster.

Mrs. Shah made me a gift of some of the fabric I'd so much

admired on the first day. She pressed her finger to her lips: Don't tell Him.

Mr. Shah was at once scary and avuncular. He parked himself on his garden chair, and as Rashida cleverly cut out my new shalwar—I'd begged for the simplest style, no puffed sleeves, straight hem—he called loud questions through the door. He was retired from a senior post in education; he did much what old men do everywhere: sat about on benches and watched the world.

"AND YOUR FATHER DOES NOT TRAVEL?" he roared.

"No, he prefers to sit at home and watch TV."

"My father also," said Rashida.

"WHAT IS THE LAND AREA OF YOUR COUNTRY?"

Rashida began to giggle.

"I really don't know, there is water, water everywhere . . ."

"AND NOT A DROP TO DRINK! MILTON?"

"Coleridge," I replied, in some surprise.

"THE NAME OF THIS POEM?"

"The Ancient Mariner?"

"YES!" he cried, "I READ THIS POEM IN 1952, BUT NOW I AM RETIRED, AND FREE. WHAT IS YOUR OPINION OF MY WIFE?"

Ignoring Jamila's laughter, I gave an honest reply. I thought she was a lovely lady, mischievous and fun.

"MY WIFE IS BEAUTIFUL!" he roared, "WHAT IS YOUR QUALIFICATION?" With that he reeled off the academic success of his thirteen children. "AND THAT IS WHY MY WIFE IS LOVELY, SHE HAS GIVEN BIRTH TO THIRTEEN CHILDREN!"

She was tiny, quite tiny. Touching five foot, and thin and lithe as a girl.

"And you are very proud?"

His voice softened. "No, I am humble man. Great Allah has given this to us." He gestured wide to include his wife, his children, their home, the garden in the evening light, the green trees and the towering mountains: a great and lovely world in which he, in his garden chair, was the enviable centre.

"Great God has given this to us."

When I met Salma on a backstreet I knew her only by little Hina dancing on her arm, for she was swathed in black, to make the short walk to see the newborn baby of a friend. I looked up that passage in the *Alexandria Quartet*, where Balthazar knows Justine only by her scarab ring. Salma kept to the back lanes. I walked down the bazaar, where a wandering salesman displayed a dubious cure-all and muscle-building lotion made of tourmaline. In the pharmacies you can buy everything: Mogadon, strong antibiotics, preparations of testosterone called Stallion, and some frightening substance: "virgin-tight."

To go with the cloth merchants there are alleys of cross-legged tailors; since the advent of the Japanese ghetto-blaster, there have evolved repairers of same. Of necessity, everything can be repaired and recycled in a way which we are only just rediscovering. Old tyres are reused to mend shoes, and as a container for the huge lumps of ice which are dragged through the streets. The dust jackets of Australian chemistry textbooks have found their way to Gilgit bazaar, there to be turned into covers for school-jotters. Once the jotters are used, the pages of careful sums are gummed to make bags for samosa-fryers and sweet-sellers.

There were two chained prisoners today, being tugged through the street, stopping now and again to exchange a few words with shopkeepers, but the news was of Benazir, who was visiting the Northern Areas. Her helicopter had chugged over our heads. She had gone to the Shandor Pass, and given a sermon on the mount to an assembly of polo fans, who poured back into town on jeeps to fill the tea-shops with their news. An old bright-eyed man declared, "She is sweetly speaking! She is lifted by God, but . . ." he tapped his temple. "She is clever,

clever, she is watching. Her eye is here, here, when she is sweetly speaking."

As if at a vision of the Virgin, he lifted his face. "She say, I am with you always, I am with you always!"

There used to be posters of General Zia, moustachioed and baggy-eyed. Only a few remain. They were switched with almost mercenary haste after his death in a plane crash. Who killed him? A councillor in the garden of the Golden Peak draped his arm over the back of his chair and summed it up: "Who knows? It is of no concern. I think the CIA. But he is gone! This bastard Zia is gone."

Gone too are many of the soldiers from the streets, the unhappy atmosphere. In place of the old posters are pictures of the sweetly smiling Benazir, with the dupatta draped over her hair. They show her with her father's spirit hovering at her shoulder, or Benazir and her mother forming into a dynasty. "She is clever, clever." Hers is a lonely position. She fulfils every role model at once.

Though leaders come and go, the idea of Pakistan is still fresh and new. A fierce pride in Pakistan—or rather, a universal loathing of India—fills the people. It is refreshing to be in a country which believes the future will be better than the past. Corruption is rife, governments are unstable and nepotistic, wealth is greedily held in private hands, but Pakistan is still an idea. Some say it is a bad idea, a theocracy, an idea doomed to failure; but when I come home I feel the West, in comparison, to be a place of slow but certain decline.

The holy month of Muharram was passing. Each evening the silent throng gathered at the mosque to chant into the night. At the Golden Peak young Mohammed arched his back and screwed his face in a mock rictus of pain. "*This* I do! This! This!" He turned and grinned. "You like? Is good?" He shrugged. "For me, is good."

Rashida had said merrily, "You will see much blood!"

Mohammed fetched a parcel of newspaper. He unwrapped it

almost reverently and showed me a grim little object: a number of leaf-shaped metal blades attached by short chains to a wooden handle. "The peoples say: Stop! Stop! Is too much! More I do, more. You will see."

It was with a certain dread that I waited for the occasion of the Muharram procession. On its eve the Shia quarter was already quiet, and the bazaar closed early. The sky turned grey, as if it too were in mourning. Rashida touched my arm and said, "*Please understand, it is a very sad time for us.*"

When morning came, the sky was still clouded and the air cool. No one saw me when I went out. The aura of grief so tangible within the family's compound pervaded the whole quarter. The shops were shuttered and closed. No traffic moved. I had never seen the bazaar so desolate. Closed, but not empty, because under every tree, in the entrance to every alley, in shop doors and hunkered in the gutters, were soldiers armed with sticks and rifles. One had a tear-gas gun. At the Sunni end of town business went on, a touch more quietly than usual. Between the two quarters, police and soldiers manned a buffer zone of a hundred yards.

I knew this was the quiet before the storm. A macabre curiosity held me, though I wondered if, as a woman and a Westerner, it wouldn't be politic to clear off.

From the direction of the mosque came the first rumblings of movement. A thin line of spectators was forming, closely watched by the police. I took a place at the *chowk*, where beside the road there is a sorry attempt at a garden, surrounded by a low wall. A few older men were standing on the wall. At the bottom of the garden was an unsuitably colourful canvas screen. I peeked through a gap, and saw it was shielding a row of beds and buckets of water. My heart, already low, sank altogether.

It was a strange excitement I felt on the street, not gay or childish. Not sexual, but not dissimilar. Perhaps the grim excitement of battle is a little like this. From the mosque came a noise:

a flutter of a rhythm, then nothing. Again, like an engine reluctant to fire, a rhythm, which died. And then it began, a low beat as of drums, and male voices, chanting.

Far from being shooed away, I was ushered forward, and friendly hands lifted me to a vantage point on the low wall. None of the lolling soldiers challenged me. I could feel the low exciting throb set off adrenalin, despite myself. The air filled with the chant. Slowly the men were coming this way, filling the bazaar with their press of bodies. My heart thumped. A long banner was walked before the demonstration, and behind the banner boys of eight or nine, proud and bewildered. The procession swelled; by the time they reached the chowk the chanting and drumming had worked its anaesthetic, and you could smell the blood.

Two boys broke from the crowd and ran to a roadside stone, ostensibly to sharpen their blades, but they took a long time over it, like schoolboys excused to go to the toilet. They had their shirts on, and a little blood was seeping through. They looked proud, horrified and scared. The press of their chanting sweat-soaked elders encouraged them from behind.

The crowd pressed on a few yards and the chant was now clear: *Ali! Hussain! Ali! Hussain!* At every beat of the names the men raised a fist to the sky and pulled it hard down upon their chests. Like the awesome machinery of some Victorian steam engine, the arms were raised and pulled down on to the naked chests. The skin was beginning to split. *Ali! Hussain! Ali! Hussain!* There were groups, lodges, each led by its own black-swathed Suzuki wagon, where a man with a megaphone led the chanting. I could smell their sweat as they pressed by. A few lurching steps, then they would stop, arranged in eights like dancers in a macabre eightsome reel, and the cycle of pounding and chanting would begin again. When the chanting ceased the men stood swaying and lurching, but only for a moment, for then there came a sound I will never forget: a merry tinny rattling, strangely reminiscent of Christmas. There was a whirling of arms and metal flashed, and the men in their prime, stripped to the waist, were flaying their backs raw with the blades.

I felt a terrible nervous urge to laugh. The sun was breaking through and the smell rose of sweat and blood and press of male bodies. Little dramas began to break out. I watched one young man being dragged out, his chest and back bloody. His friends pulled him, shouted at him, implored him to come to his senses; the relief station was waiting with water and beds. But he pulled back, he wasn't through yet, his protest and sacrifice were not yet enough. I watched and all at once thought, "He's hamming."

Stood on my wall I could watch them all, the chins back, the raw chests beaten, the young and strong and the old more meekly by their side. And they were watching me. The young men, strong and stripped in an un-Muslim manner, pounding their arms down on their broad chests. I caught the eye of one and he held my look too long, and began to lash himself with even greater fervour than before. It was true—if they saw me watching they beat themselves the more. This was a strange sort of sexuality indeed. I jumped down from the wall and left.

I walked up the quiet back lanes until the chant was far away. In his weariness Murtaza had said such a radical thing: "*You know about Sunni and Shia? The difference is only the personality of the Prophet.*" Few would agree with him. I felt I had seen into the psyche of my new friends and ought to be frightened, disturbed and disapproving, but I wasn't. I was shaken, and tried to calm myself with analogies and comparisons. I thought about the Orange walks I'd been taken to as a very young child near Glasgow. I remember being dangled out of tenement windows to hear that tremendous tribal drumbeat, and see the order, the snapped-shut faces of the Orangemen. But this felt different. The Orange walks were aggressive, they feared and loathed the Other. What I had seen on the faces of the Shia men was not aggression but anguish. Passion. I thought of the Passion of Christ, the blood and nails. The Passion without the Resurrection. Down on the bazaar I had felt from the men real anger and grief and rage; also dramatics, and young men's fervour. I thought about the underdog. This was no victory parade, like those of the Romans or Orangemen. This was the rage of the oppressed.

I turned on to the back road home, but an officer barred my way with his rifle. "This danger-day!" he said.

If you ask for a reason, you will be told of the murky power struggles and schisms at the dawn of Islam. Shias were those who had backed the wrong horse. A grievous injustice had been done on this day many hundreds of years ago, and the old wound was literally opened every year. It's the story of Ali and Hussain. When the Prophet died, he nominated as his successor on earth his son-in-law Ali. Shi'ite means party; the Shias were the party of Ali. Those who would become Sunni insisted on a succession devoid of family or tribal connotations.

Ali was passed over three times until he was granted the Caliphate, but murdered after only five years. Neither of his two sons succeeded him. The first was poisoned, and the other died a noble death on the battlefield when he and his followers were set upon in the desert. This is the death honoured on the streets. "Live like Ali, die like Hussain!" is what they say, and the family has taken on a mystical quality; the Shia pantheon.

Still it puzzled me. It didn't seem enough of a reason. But, I told myself, these are the Middle Ages, and didn't medieval Europe see some strange scenes?

A man called to me. He was keeping one of the few open shops. I must have looked worn, because he made me sit down and pushed before me a tin plate. "Have some halva! It's traditional at this Muharram time. We make it for the children."

The halva was good, thick and full of plump raisins, but I didn't feel like eating. From over the rooftops came the throbbing and chanting. "I can't get back, the soldier won't let me pass."

"It is this Muharram. There is no sectarianism in Gilgit," he said. I thought of the buffer zone down in the bazaar, and of Murtaza's story and his sad sigh, "Where can one go for peace?" I must have looked a little sceptical.

"I mean, before this massacre. But this Muharram, you know, anyone may join in. You may join in if you wish, if you share the sentiments."

For one wild moment I imagined the reaction if I did, indeed, join in. I nearly smiled again. "What are the sentiments?"

"To protest brutality!" he said, as though it was obvious and I some kind of fool.

"But the procession seems a touch brutal in itself . . ."

"No. It shows we are willing to protest brutality and injustice, even with our own blood. You will take tea?"

I'd long learned to take little in this town at face value, and I had my suspicions about Mr Khan. Indeed, despite the fact that he was keeping shop in a backstreet, he turned out to be a very eminent journalist, and father of the thoroughly modern friend of Rashida's. I enjoyed him. I enjoyed his explanation of the Muharram procession, because it enabled me to admit what I thought was an intolerable idea: that the parade, though bizarre and grim, was almost noble. "To protest brutality"—it suited more what I knew of my Shia friends, their mix of tolerance and passionate conviction, their perfect manners, their delight in conspiracy theories, their slight craziness. By devious routes I avoided the soldiers and worked my way back to Murtaza's. I heard radios playing, broadcasting the same singing chant from all over the Shi'ite world, and that night the TV showed pictures from Tehran.

Even in their Muharram, the women remained in seclusion. They were not shown on TV or seen on the streets. Rashida was hunkered on the balcony, her eyes red and tearful. She gazed unseeing over the flat huddled roofs of her neighbours. Round her arm she wore a strip of black cloth. Jamila was ashen, Salma distraught. She too wore a black cloth of mourning, and sobbed to herself. I went to my room and felt my own throat tighten, tears begin to prick my eyes. I dashed them away, annoyed with myself. As they went about their day they patted their hearts in time to the chest-pounding of their men, which reached their garden over the rooftops.

"You too will come to understand the tragedy of Ali," said Rashida. "I cannot explain."

The unusually cool wind had been a godsend, but by afternoon the heat began to rise—so too did the fervour, the exhaustion and the thirst. For hours they continued, making the slow circuit of the Shia quarter. In making its long way back to the mosque, the demonstration would actually pass our gates.

The tenor changed, the chanting became disconcerted and exhausted. Still the lashing continued, but more and more men fell to the wayside, where they beat their chests in time and left the blood-letting to the youths. An ambulance brought up the rear of the procession. By two o'clock, they turned the corner into our street. They were coming this way, listen! The girls forgot to grieve and grew excited. The clamour beyond their garden swelled and grew. Hundreds, thousands of half-clad men were going to press against their gates. I went outside to watch—me and little Hina, who alone could cross the threshold with impunity—and behind us, behind the closed green gate, the women waited.

The hot sun beat down on the bloody and exhausted men. Hina looked up at me, her eyes ablaze. She patted her tiny chest in time, like her granny and her aunts indoors, as the menfolk filed past. Now the fervent young men were spent; they'd stopped exhorting each other to greater and greater excess, but supported one another, arms round bloodied shoulders. It was brotherly, almost loving, a bad job that had to be done . . .

The women had organised a supply of ice-cold water, and as the first of the throng arrived they brought from the fridge jugs and dozens of tumblers. But they could not pour the grateful men a drink, it would be *shame*.

Murtaza appeared and stood in front of his gate like a cockerel. The gate opened a chink, a jug and tumblers were passed out. Murtaza took them and closed the gate behind him, firmly, with his foot. Again and again the jugs were sent back within to be refilled; again and again they reappeared. Not a glimpse could be afforded. The gate would open a crack, female hands with bangles push out a jug and the gate clang closed. The men tramped past, chanting, tramping their feet like an army, and the gate clanged and clanged. I knew the women were all huddled behind the green metal, because I could hear their muffled sobs.

It was like a dreadful accident, a pit fire or a train crash. There was an extraordinary sense of collective endeavour; men crowded round, reaching out for water, crying for water, and I too began to pour and disperse water, handing glass after glass to the outstretched, grateful hands.

Now the men were thronged around their gates, the seven women, firmly closed in, were crouched to peer through the little chinks at the hinges. I heard a hiss from Jamila: "Move over, we can't see!"

There was the Major, sweating and blood-smeared as though he'd just ridden off a battlefield; there the boy Mohammed, and there, to my surprise, a friend from Rawalpindi, who broke from this Muslim madness to make that most Western of appointments, a dinner date, before he joined the bleeding mass again. A white horse clipped by, decorated. I knew the white horse had something to do with Fatima, daughter of the Prophet.

"I cannot explain," said Rashida.

•••

Then it was over. The men, purged and weary, began to drift home. Big brother came in, trailing a megaphone, and leaned against the wall. He and Mrs Shah dragged gratefully on cigarettes. Someone made tea and we congratulated one another on a difficult job well done.

"You like our Muharram?" said Rashida. Though I said nothing, I was pleased with myself; I was beginning to understand. Or so I thought, for then she said, "This little one. In forty days, big one! *Then* you see some blood!"

The bazaar returned to normal. I sheltered on a tea-house roof during a brief and silly gun fight. A curfew was hastily imposed and lifted again. A consignment of UHT "Pakmilk" (copyline: "like a buffalo in your living-room") turned out bad and its cartons appeared heaped in every vacant lot. The peaches passed and the fruit stalls filled with small sweet apples.

Often I went walking. Through the "villages": the agricultural lands around the town. Or out to the Buddha. It was strange to think these people were all Buddhists once, a thousand years ago. All that remained was a carving on a rock a couple of miles out of town, and some manuscripts.

The rock-carving was a strange one. High on the corner of a rock where two streams met was the figure of the Buddha, standing up. I was weary of the town the day I went there. Weary of constraints, the constant monitoring, the surveillance. Where have you been? Where are you going? And from strangers: "Where is your husband?" I thought I might refresh my mind with a pleasant walk among the gardens and fields, and think appropriately Buddhist thoughts with this icon to gaze upon. But as Murtaza would have said, I knew no peace. Two brothers contrived to place themselves in front of me, whichever way I turned, like some evil two-headed demon. I walked east along an irrigation canal; they came towards me and blocked my way, calling "Siss-ter, Siss-ter," like snakes. They hissed like snakes when I turned back, hissed to the right and left of me until I could have murdered, Buddha or no.

I was coldly furious, my day spoiled. "Why do they do this?" I railed at Rashida. She intoned: "It is because you do not wear dupatta." And if I wore a thousand dupattas, they would still molest me, and it would still be my own fault. On the way back a little boy ran up to me and I snapped at him, but he only wanted to offer me some almonds, fresh from his family's tree.

As I got to know the family better, I still felt pretty displaced, but not so much in place or culture as in time. Life was simply old-fashioned. My friends understood my impatience with purdah. A double standard operated—in my favour. I began to learn a little Urdu, as the lingua franca. "Where are you going?" they'd call. "To the bazaar!" You could stand on the family's balcony and throw a stone into the bazaar, but they never went there—such a dirty, rough man's place!

To understand their culture I found myself making analogies with my own, and it wasn't difficult. Was Mrs. Shah so different to my own grandmother, who speaks a fine Scots, and left school young for a life of menial tasks; for whom Pakistan is as remote and unimaginable as is Scotland for Mrs. Shah? My grand-mother can't drive or speak a foreign language, has never crossed the threshold of a college; does not smoke, drink, swear or wear short skirts. She rarely goes out without a scarf. She'd get on well with Mrs. Shah. They'd talk about their gardens. Some of the wealthier Gilgiti families have the most glorious gardens, which they tend with expert and passionate care. They could no doubt exchange views about changing fashions: rising hemlines and shrinking veils.

Murtaza often talked about danger. Women of purdah-observing families are protected from a violent and dangerous world out there beyond the gates, by men who take this responsibility seriously, as a duty born of love and Islam. If their lives seem to us joyless—then what they enjoy is being Muslim. What we enjoy is risk. We enjoy, even when we don't, running the gauntlet of the wide world; and all the experiences that offers. Experience of loneliness, of worry, of insecurity, or loss and displacement; all of which transform into exhilaration and, if we're lucky, wisdom.

My friends had very little grasp of transformed experience—indeed, any experience—as most was vicarious. They'd pounce on news; when I went to Pindi for a few days I had to tell them every scrap about Pindi: the heat and plenty, the expense, the dirt. I told Mr. Shah I'd received a phone call from my mother—a minor miracle; and he roared in satisfaction and relief. "IT IS PROOF OF YOUR PARENTS' LOVE FOR YOU!"

Sometimes their grasp of the outside world is shaky. I was gone for five days, and they believed I'd been home to Scotland and back. They admire and pity me. I look at them and see the optical illusion of protection and oppression. They look at me and see the illusion of freedom, the terrible freedom of the lost soul.

The Northern Areas are frequented by mountaineers, who take unconscionable risk to climb the 8,000-metre peaks. When they get home, they put up with people's adverse reactions. They're told they're mad, at best foolhardy, selfish. Mostly they're met with incomprehension. Why take that risk? Stay at home, be secure, have a family. And when my Shia friends look at me, this is on the tip of their tongues.

One night I came home late. I'd been talking with some Westerners at the Golden Peak; one was very ill and shivery—an Austrian whose thin tattooed legs stuck out beneath a Hindu dhoti. What these Gilgit people think of us I don't know. We thought he might have malaria and I found Dr. Noor for him. When I turned up at Murtaza's the gates were already bolted against the terrors of the night. Very embarrassed, I called to be let in. No one replied. I tapped the metal gates and called again. It was dark, there were strange noises, and I was quickly angry and scared. Shadowy figures assembled from nowhere to watch my antics. Two police stopped beneath a tree and stared at me, their truncheons in their hands.

There was a back way in, so I crept through the little lanes until I found it, but that too was locked and I was decidedly uncomfortable; the lanes were so narrow that a single man would block my exit. So I returned to the street, and thumped the gates. I was angry with myself, and angry with the gates for being locked; angry with them too for resounding so loud in the night, although it was I who banged them.

I had resolved to go back to the hotel and stay there, when a neighbour appeared and also began rattling the gates, and calling "Murtaza! Murtaza!" through the crack. There was no escape. Then the bolt scraped and Murtaza appeared, in his nightclothes. He was less than happy and began at once: "Kathleen, I want to talk with you. There is some danger behind you."

Involuntarily I looked behind. The two police still stood in the shadows, light glinting on the buckles of their uniforms. Did he mean I was in danger, or the cause of it? As a woman, I was probably both.

"I have sense of humour," said Murtaza. I thought, "Murtaza, you don't."

He meant sixth sense, a hunch. Something was up. He took me inside. "Where were you?"

"Golden Peak."

"Tonight is come one man, he is looking."

"Looking at?"

"You. But you are not there. Salma saw. We are watching drama on TV and Salma say, who is that man?"

I thought, sourly: you watch too much drama on TV.

"He is inside the gate, watching you! A man! He is looking at you, into your room, like this!" He leaned over and wrapped his hands around his eyes, like one peering into a darkened room. He wrung his hands. I wanted to pat his back and say: It's all right, don't fret, just some old nonsense, but he was very agitated indeed.

"It is better tonight you stay in the hotel. Yes! Go! Go now!"

The "intelligence" had been watching me.

"Intelligence!" Jamila laughed. "They are teasing you."

"Intelligence!" said the Major, and rolled his eyes. Only the next day I was going to the police station to get visas and permissions to stay, but they had pre-empted me, and dared enter the family compound to stare through the window, hoping to see this strange lone foreigner, who gave out water at Muharram. Murtaza was deeply distressed. He said a lot about rape, and responsibility.

"If—God forbid—something happens, you are female, alone . . . this is great responsibility for me. I am behind bars!"

The women showed a lot less distress than their menfolk. The Major showed no distress at all. When I told him I had removed myself back to a hotel, and was leaving for a few days until things simmered down, he merely thumped his desk until the rock samples jumped. There was another man in the office, obviously of some rank. They spoke quickly in Shinas, then the Major bawled down the street to the tea-house, and then he turned to me. "I told you, any problem and you come to me!"

"It was my own fault. I'm very embarrassed. I should have gone for the papers sooner . . ."

"I am not a layman, you know. Not a *commoner*."

He stood and began to pace about, then wheeled round and cried: "I have found out who this bastard is, this snooper who did watch you, this bloody man!"

Again I said I was very embarrassed and sorry for the trouble I'd caused, but he was well away.

"I have asked the Highest Authority, who is this bastard who did disturb my guest! AND I HAVE RECEIVED AN APOLOGY FOR THE TRAUMA YOU HAVE SUFFERED AND I WILL CLAIM COMPENSATION. I AM *NOT. A. COMMONER*!

I whimpered, and was still. The lawyer, who had sat throughout this outburst, began to speak: "There are fifteen intelligence units in Gilgit."

"Fifteen!" echoed the Major. "KGB, CIA . . ."

"No, Pakistani agencies."

I looked surprised.

"Gilgit is Centre of Intrigue."

"Centre of intrigue."

"KGB agents also . . ."

"Russia, this Wakan Corridor is very close . . ."

The agents, I asked—are they local people?

"Yes, of course, foreigners would be too obvious."

The Major was driving a pencil at speed around his desk.

I said, "I suppose the government has a right to know who is in its country and why . . ."

"Of course."

"Every right."

"There is China, India, Russia; many countries wish to destabilise this area."

"It's after this Afghan war; now we have so many mix of people."

"Surveillance is necessary."

"Fifteen agencies . . ."

"They are watching . . ."

"BUT WHY THIS BASTARD DID DISTURB MY GUEST? IT IS *MY HONOUR*!!"

Explanation came from diverse sources. It concerned Israel, rape, and what Mohammed called Make-abomstone.

"What?"

"Make-abomstone!"

I puzzled over that one for a while, until I remembered the Major's command: "*Don't touch that, it's uranium!*" I put my head in my hands and laughed.

Two days later Mohammed brought before me a shaven-headed youth I'd often noticed skulking behind trees. "This police!" he announced.

This police was about nineteen. He shuffled his feet and began a mumbled apology. He called me his dear sister, but I felt more like his long-suffering mother. He refused tea, refused cake. He'd nothing to apologise for, except perhaps his jumper, an orange-and-purple-striped affair unusual in a surveillance unit. At least I tried not to smile. Mohammed Hussain showed no such restraint. He laughed like a drain for days.

The summer ended with a terrible air crash. On cloudless days a little Fokker Friendship heads down the Indus to Islamabad. Somewhere around the terrible snowy bulk of Nanga Parbat, which soars above the little plane and for minutes fills its windows, they lost radio contact and it was gone, with fifty of Gilgit's best on board.

Distraught families gathered at the airstrip. The poor people huddled over their radios for any scrap of news. Notable shops in the bazaar remained shuttered, their owners dead.

Mountain villagers, mountaineers and the army all searched to no avail. The rumour went round that the plane had been hijacked by India, last seen over Afghanistan. But the winter snows were coming and what chances they had of finding the wreck were gone till spring, if not for ever. It says something about the Karakoram landscape to know that they never did.

Still I felt displaced in time, but which time? I thought I could detect several, interfering with each other. There was the ancient time of warring clans who poured down the brae upon each other, but they arrived courtesy of Land Rover. There was the early-Victorian time to which the girls belonged, remaining modestly at home until their mothers arranged a good match. Over their needlework, though, they discussed the merits of their female Prime Minister. There was the modern time, too, of air crashes and telephones. These were all laid upon each other, like those children's pictures composed of several leaves of tissue paper. On each are drawn a few meaningless scratches. Only when all the leaves are laid on top of each other, and the marks seen as one, does the picture show through.

I left Gilgit on the Pindi bus one damp autumn day. The weather was turning. Summer, as Rashida said, was in his last time. Low grey cloud shrouded the hills and brought down a cool breeze. The cold in my bones reminded me very much of home.

2 Shia Girls

On a grey winter's morning, months later, the postman brought to my Edinburgh flat a green envelope from Pakistan. Even the stamps were covered in flowers. There was no other mail for me, apart from some standard communication from the Inland Revenue. I turned on the gas fire and huddled in front of it. Rashida wrote:

> *Your lifestyle is very strange and very difficult to us, because you know, we are purdah-observing. We live in home and safety. And you know, how much we are happy and full satisfy. We have no problems, and difficulties. We live a simple and Islamic life. I am very surprise to know you are living in a flat with your friends without your parents.*

Now, what is your planning? Here I want to give you a suggestion, if you don't mind. I am giving you a proposal. I want that you live with us in our country for ever. If you want to marry here, it will be good. If you want, you write to me and we shall arrange your marriage. I assure you, you will be very happy here. Your life will pass in peace and safety. But remember, you'll live like us . . .

I got up to tend the kettle and stood shivering at the kitchen window, looking out at the driech skyline of a city full of strange and difficult lifestyles. Dear Rashida. Did I want to marry and stay in Gilgit for ever? Of course not. But I could picture so clearly the flower gardens and the sparkling irrigation streams, the deep shadows cast by a relentless sun. For months my stomach had been clenched against the cold, and if I went to the Pakistani shop on our corner, the smell of the spices intoxicated me.

By the Islamic calendar, the year had just turned 1410 when I arrived back in Rawalpindi. A full year had passed; again it was the month of Muharram. The *Pakistan Times* was carrying exhortations to the ulema, the clergy, not to stir up trouble. They printed a cartoon of clergymen with crazy turbans and rosaries, skulking behind a wall. On the wall was a poster urging peace. "Do we get more outa peace?" asked the mullahs.

The office of Masherbrum Tours was a card table erected beneath an umbrella, on the platform of the bus station. A fat man sat with a book of tickets and a rubber stamp. "You are lone? In our country this is most unusual."

"So I can go at the front of the bus?"

He cocked his head. "Bus, 2 p.m. going."

"Ticket 2 p.m. say: Pakistan, 4 p.m. going," said one of the waiting men. "You are lone?"

At his side a snake-charmer set out his little baskets and began tootling on a pipe. Horns blared and boys bawled their destinations.

The drinks vendors cried, "Boteli-boteli-boteli!." I was offered a flannel; combs, hair restorer, fruit; the bark of a certain tree used for cleaning teeth; chewing tobacco called pan; scarves, shawls, toys, fans and sandals. A child with a set of bathroom scales contrived to insert them beneath my feet every time I took a step, and so earn a wretched rupee. A holy man, with painted symbols on his fine naked chest, threw things at me—a toffee, a banana peel—but I think it was meant in jest.

Hidden between a fly-ridden tea-shack and a tower of mangos was a waiting-room of sorts. Here was a transit camp of women surrounded by children and bulging baggage tied with rope and blankets. All were veiled for the journey, so they too resembled so much baggage. Outside buses were shunted and loaded, and belched black fumes into the already stinking air.

Mine was a de-luxe service, which doesn't go any faster, God forbid, and is still pretty uncomfortable. It meant that the mighty Bedford bus was even more heavily decorated. They are magnificent. Like heavyweight boxers dressed as clowns, the merry carnivalesque paintwork and chrome can't disguise the solidity of the thing. A horn blared and I went out to see my bag swung up the ladder on to the roof. There was action; the passengers swarmed, fussed and boarded, climbed over the seats and found their places. I was indeed ushered to the front, one of the "privileges" accorded us because of our sex; here, in the dead of night, one is to some extent safe from the wandering hands and toes and elbows. Plenty of welcome breeze blows in; a front seat is well worth having.

We were loaded and ready. The driver's lad had covered the luggage on the roof, wiped the windscreen, polished the mirrors, chosen a tape (my heart sank), performed all the pre-flight checks, ensured there were sufficient dangly toys and waving hands, prayers, stickers and plastic flowers and even started up the engine and dusted the seat before the driver, like the world-famous conductor of some magnificent orchestra, strode towards his vehicle. Here was indeed a

Bedford of a man: a shaven-headed Haji with a face hewn from Karakoram rock. His beard was dyed orange, his thick and bullish neck rose to a head covered by the woollen cap of Gilgit. He climbed in. He didn't even glance at the Hindu man who stood in the doorway imploring something of his passengers. He wanted to move, and wanted this heathen tramp off his bus. As though he had lifted his baton, there was a moment's hush as he selected a gear. He released the brakes, and the bus emitted a shuddering growl. We were off, we veered towards the road, the poor Hindu crying, "*Driverji, driverji, tairo,* please, driver sir, sir please, stop!"

My body remembered this, fourteen hours' worth of discomfort and ache. I don't know whether you grow more used to it or less. We left Rawalpindi, horns blaring, crossed the railway line and were gone along the Grand Trunk Road—just one vehicle, but a big one, among the trucks and cars and camels and wobbling bikes. The conductor had perfected the art of climbing out of the nearside windows, up atop, traversing the roof and re-entering by the driver's window, at speed. He sat on the hot cover of the gearbox, called me his sister and gave me an apple. I was glad to have him near; I felt nervous alone among all these men and, though frightened of the long night ahead, I longed for it, and the cool breezes of the hills.

At dusk we stopped.

"Pray stop!" said the driver's lad.

"You pray," I said. "I drink," and jumped out of the window.

"I drink," said the lad. "Nobody pray. Quick pray. Drink!"

If no mosque is near, a line of men forms at the roadside. They cover their heads with scarves and handkerchiefs, spread mats, and kick off their shoes. Side by side, they bow in prayer. Strangers to each other. How it must bind people, I thought, watching from a distance.

By dark we had picked up the Indus and were turned north on the Karakoram Highway. The hills began to grow into mountains.

Flickers of lightning illuminated the summits in a gentle show. We roared on and on. I stuck my bare feet out of the window; the scents of flowers and shrubs wafted in. Nothing, so far, had gone wrong. When it grew cool, I wrapped my shawl around myself, away from the sly gaze of some of the men at the back, the better to enjoy and dream. At Besham, which is a waspish and frenetic place even in the dead of night, we stopped for tea. At the roadside were sleepers on charpoys. They seemed not to heed the din. All through the night the tea-maker sat above his fire, boiling great vats of the stuff. Hurricane lamps hissed from the cobwebby rafters; and a swarm of bugs crawled around each.

Now the river began to twist and with it the road, blasted out of the mountainside. Above us rose great banks of rock and scree; on the offside the slope fell sheer to the thunderous river below. The Haji shifted the gears, and hauled the wheel round in his mighty hands. We thundered on. I knew we would stop again soon enough because ahead was dacoit country: bandits. There would be an army checkpoint with tents and beds at the roadside. We would stop, and get off to stretch our legs in the soft darkness, waiting until enough vehicles arrived to form a convoy. Then an uneasy soldier armed with a sub-machine-gun would jump on to the running boards, and the convoy would move on.

I fell into a doze, and woke as the driver cursed and brought the bus to a halt. In his headlamps I saw a few jeeps and trucks, and some people milling around on the road. It wasn't a convoy forming up, or a checkpoint. An accident maybe. If you look down the precipice to the river below, you often see the axles of trucks upturned in the river, helpless as beetles. Like the others, I jumped out on to the road and looked ahead. A mound of rubble and stone, as high as a house, had spewed down from the hillside above. *Road is block.*

So final was the block that already passengers were climbing on to the roof of the bus and throwing down their baggage. I secured my own, and did as the others did—sat on it. They formed small grumbling groups at the dark roadside.

"Ticket?" said the driver's lad, standing before me in the dark.

"You want my ticket?"

"Refund. Gilgit, no going. Road is block."

All around us, rumours and accusations. The road began to take on that characteristic look—a war zone, a relief station. People squatted at the bumpers of their immobile vehicles, spreading rumours. It was the first of two, five, nine such blocks. The downcoming vehicles, similarly blocked on the other side, were one, two, ten miles away. However many blocks there were, all were agreed on this: the last was the biggest. It was this government! Where was the money to repair the road? Gone in their back pockets!

No money in the world would stabilise this road, blasted out of rock and mud. We were halfway to Gilgit, I received half my fare, as was just. Among the litter of vehicles shrouded figures wandered. Some were bedding down to sleep for the night. A family lay in the dust beside their jeep, shrouded like corpses from some dreadful accident. I began to feel nervous, in the strange dark night, and wondered what was for the best.

A thin voice called to me from the roof of the bus: "Sleepee here!"

"No," said the conductor, "you go!"

Go where? I wondered.

"No go! Sleepee he-re."

People were slipping away into the darkness, taking their baggage with them. I walked down to see the roadblock. People were swarming up it like ants, with their attaché cases and boxes on their shoulders. Some wore flip-flops. One mile, two, ten? The darkness was green-tinted with moonlight. The moon had risen above the jagged shards of mountains and, for a brief while, would illuminate the gorge.

I pulled my shawl, a man's woollen one, around me. If I stuck with the gang already mounting the heap of rubble and mud, I'd be okay. I began to climb, using my hands to haul myself up. At least it was stable, but with one ear I listened lest more should pour down from above. I rounded a corner, but could see no one. The only light was the eerie tint of the moon. Away below, the river brawled. It was very loud, the sound trapped between the rockwalls that rose all around, darker even than the sky above.

"Yes!" said the thin voice. "Yes!" And he was beside me, a voice in the darkness, the voice from the top of the bus. *Sleepee here!* We were entirely alone.

"Go?" he said.

"Go." I moved on.

He moved with me, as I chose my footholds on the rubbly heap. I crossed the ridge of the landslip, and began to descend again to the road.

He said, "My friend are?"

"Of course."

"Love me?" he said.

"I love everyone."

"No!"

Another heap of rubble and mud rose immediately. Nine such slips, the rumours said. There was a trickling of water.

"Love me? Five hundred rupees you love me?"

I looked at him for the first time—a thin, slant-eyed youth with a scarf tied round his brow. He was groping about in his clothing and my heart clenched, but no, he was taking out a 500-rupee note, and holding it up to the moonlight to prove to me it was real. Two weeks' wages. Eighteen quid. Suddenly I wanted to laugh. What, right here? On the middle of this landslip? What would you do if I snatched your money and said all right, come on, all you've heard about Western girls is true? Run away screaming, no doubt. But there were voices coming: a party from the other side of the landslip was approaching, I could see their tin boxes glinting in the moonlight. More were coming behind me, going my way. I joined them. The two groups passed like parties of pitiful refugees, slipping across some remote border, with just the moon and the river to guide them. The thin-voiced youth disappeared, taking his fantasies with him. The rumours were all rubbish, his and mine. Only below, round a bend so you couldn't see the lights, the road was clear, and the vehicles were arranged like a mirror-image of those we'd left behind.

Nothing was going to move till morning. Only then, having exchanged passengers, would the vehicles turn and go back the way they'd come.

I chose a huge friendly-looking bus, propped myself against its tyre and took a swig or two of brandy from the illicit supply in my rucksack. Then I rolled myself up in my shawl, and slept on the road until dawn.

We got on, all the rounded-up passengers. The driver began an eight-point turn on the narrow ledge. At the third point, when his back wheels were sending stones and crumbs of earth down into the river, we all jumped out. But he didn't fall off, of course. When the bus was pointing north, we climbed back on board. This bus carried an entire replacement gearbox, just in case. Please God, I thought, don't let it break down. Don't let us have to wait at the roadside for five hours while they drop in a new gearbox.

We ground on and on and the heat grew greater and the rock brighter, and I was thinking about my friends. I was wondering why I got into these scrapes, and I was thinking about Rashida, the way she could glide into a room, silently. About the way all would draw their chadors over their noses and tuck in the corners, and would never, ever travel alone on a bus like this. Now the sun was up, the strangeness of the night was banished. Was it Murtaza who said, "It is very risk"?

We stopped for tea at a row of shacks. Some mangy dogs ambled about on the roadside. There was a puncture repair outfit and a long tea-house. The driver went off to a secret drivers' place and I saw him climb on to a platform hidden from view, then the smell of burning hash wafted down. The men sat round tables and drank little cups of sweet, sweet tea. There was a woman on this bus. She remained aboard when we all got off. She was fully veiled and sat behind the driver. Her husband or brother flanked her, but he'd jumped off and gone into the tea-house. She had a headache, she said. I asked, wouldn't she like some tea? She gave that charming gesture of refusal and thanks, a sort of turn of the head and crinkling of the brow. I could just see it under her veil. Her husband was indoors with the rest of them, tearing bits of chapati up to eat with his tea. Didn't his wife want some?

"No! She is simple womans. Islamic womans. Water only."

And I was thinking that the lightness of my friends, their feminine graces, their quietness, their quaint old-fashioned charm, was delightful, until it became profoundly irritating and I wanted to say: Stop it now. We're friends now. Be real. Beside them I felt rough and ungainly. I felt as if I had stubble. And I was wondering what difference it would make were Rashida British. How would she be? Still "feminine"? I doubt it—she had far too hard a streak in her to do that all day. And Jamila. She would stay out all night, and give her father fits.

We'd set off again. I fell asleep, woke and watched the barren mountains go by. Then I saw a leg in front of my face, outside, climbing down from the roof. It wasn't the bus boy's, it was dressed in tight denim even in this heat, and it was seeking one of the bars across the windows. We were doing fifty on an overhanging ledge. I couldn't look. A hand came down, with long painted nails, then another clutching an expensive video camera. It was a woman with a big nose and short black-hennaed hair, in an expensive-looking cut ravaged by the dust and wind. She held on to the bars with one hand and raised the camera, panned the valley and the river behind us. Italian, film-maker. Huh, I thought. Then she began berating the back of the driver's neck, in Urdu. The driver's shoulders tensed and he slammed into another gear. The conductor joined in the shouting match and a few men at the back added their tuppence-worth as she clambered through the driver's open window. She sat down on the gearbox and ran her fingers through her hair.

"God, these people! The conductor was getting funny with me, on the roof. Did you hear me shout? The more I said slow down, the faster he drove. DIDN'T YOU!" The driver flinched.

"I didn't know you were up there."

"They only picked me up a few miles ago."

"You're not Italian, are you?"

"No. Pakistani. Half Afghani. Now I live in London. They don't believe I am Pakistani." She turned round and bawled out a man at the back of the bus. "Did you understand? He says if I am Muslim woman, I should wear modest clothes. God, these people! The conductor was on the roof with me. He was getting funny, you know. I said to the driver, slow down, I am coming in. He didn't. No. Ugh, terrifying. How long to Gilgit?"

"Another four hours or so. Inshallah."

"Inshallah. God, this *country*."

Our trials were not over. In revenge the driver selected a tape and put it on at full distortion. A sort of subcontinental *Goon Show*, as far as I could tell from the silly voices and gales of laughter. Then that stopped and the now familiar tedium of the Muharram chanting began. He turned up the volume yet more. The speaker was at my ear. It went on for a solid hour. Then came a raving mullah. The very speaker seemed to jiggle and spit as the mullah worked himself up. He screamed like a soul in torment, screamed as though his very flesh were burning on his bones. The bus travelled on. As the mullah raved, passengers closed into a sombre or sullen hush. From the roadside, goat-herds turned to look at us, and village girls turned their backs. The mullah was all agin someone, and that someone was you. The London Afghani woman came back. She had been conducting a theological argument with some of the passengers on the back seat, about women, clothes and Islam.

I took my hand from my aching ear, the one the speaker was screaming into. "D'you understand this?" I asked.

"Shias! So what if he sacrificed his life for them, there's no need to make such a fuss. The whole thing's beyond my comprehension. Have you got a tissue?"

She tore two strips, rolled them up and stuffed them in her ears. Now why didn't I think of that?

On the outskirts of Gilgit we had to stop at a police tent to sign the ledger that purports to log the whereabouts of foreigners. There was a brief argument among the passengers over whether the Pakistani woman should sign or not. She wore immodest jeans, had short hair and argued; *ergo*, she must be a foreigner, she must sign the book. But she argued in Urdu and had a Pakistani passport; she was one of us. Confusion. And then, at long last, came the sign reading "You are now entering Gilgit Cantt." I thought I had never seen anything so welcome.

Fast food is no novelty in the land of samosa, but it had none the less reached Gilgit. At the corner of the chowk and the barracks stood the "Tax Burger" stall. What, oh what, was a tax burger? I thought: I'll prove to the Inland Revenue that I'm still alive, I'll send a photo of a tax burger. Little else had changed: the old hand-painted sign "Stop for cold drink, cock is it!" had been delicately removed, and one shopkeeper had installed glass windows behind which an array of ladies' shoes were displayed, but he was alone in his innovation; still the shopkeepers lounged about in their open-fronted boxes. And all around, above the street and its little shops, the ochre-tinted imprisoning mountains.

It had been a long journey, I was filthy, and the day was intolerably hot. It was, they said, the hottest summer for forty years. I wanted only to wash and sleep, and made for the Golden Peak. The boy Mohammed would be there, it'd be good to see him. Maybe he'd take me for a jinni. I laughed to myself, remembering the incident last year, when there came a very tall German man with spectacles so strong his eyes were magnified behind them. I'd collided with Mohammed as he fled towards the gate, crying, "Jinni, jinni! You look his eyes! Oh, is jinni!" leaving the poor German standing owlishly on the grass. Good old Mohammed. He'd make me some tea in the old pot held together by string. Dr Noor and Mr Latif would be discussing ailments in the shade. I was thinking of the wrought-iron chairs, the cool rooms, the wallpaper, as I stepped through the old gate.

A cement-mixer stood open-mouthed where the garden had been. There was a row of half-built concrete shacks. No grass grew where the builders daily tramped about; all was dry dirt. I swallowed hard. A trench, for water or somesuch, tore through the parched and broken lawn. The Golden Peak itself still stood, almost eclipsed by the brave new world growing around it. The old mosque was demolished and its madman dead, gone. In its place a concrete watchtower had been built and painted orange. And Mohammed's kitchen—where was it? Torn down. A concrete tourist unit replaced the smoke-blackened lean-to.

The office still stood, and I wanted Mohammed to appear from within, grinning all over his face: *It is joke!* I wanted him to show off his manly stubble, and make contemptuous remarks, but when I called his name, no one replied. I thought I might cry. I wanted to turn and go, but Mr Latif was here, he'd remembered my name, was shaking my hand. I could find no pleasantries to say to him, but blurted, "What have you done?"

"It is good business," said Mr Latif.

"You think so? Where is the garden?"

"After finish, again garden, inshallah."

"Inshallah! Where is Mohammed?"

"He is . . . in another place." He walked like the Duke of Edinburgh, with his hands clasped behind his back. A small smiling boy appeared, and fell into step beside us. Mr Latif said, "He is my son! I am China going, soon, some days' holiday, inshallah. He my son is manager. He is eight years."

Manager, eight years. Despite myself I almost smiled. Not everything changes at once.

The room at the back of the Golden Peak was damp, and grotty. That much remained the same. There was a rug of local goats' wool and a wooden fire surround, green-carved lintels on the door to the washroom. The washroom was so damp a minor landslip occurred during the night, and a bucketful of ceiling arrived on its floor. Huge drowned centipedes floated in the gunge of the blocked sink, white and ghastly and four inches long. I looked up "insect" in my Urdu book but could find only "animal."

"Animal!" laughed Mr Latif. "This is very funny! Animals in sink."

Mohammed's replacement was an elderly Nagari man, huge and silent. He wore a woollen cap and a shy smile, always. All the men who come down from the villages wear both; the shy smile because they are unused to foreigners, women especially. He set about the blocked sink with gun rods. A large rat poked its nose through the drain and vanished fast when I banged the pipes. I thought: this is a disgusting place. It should be torn down. I wrapped myself up in a shawl against the bugs, and fell into a sad but welcome sleep.

Mohammed came bounding out of a tea-shop calling my name. There was no hugging, no exclaiming. This is a Shia town, and I'd done my restraint training in Scotland. We reached for a polite handshake and suppressed our voices into whispers, because the cobbler cross-legged at our feet had stopped sewing to stare, and a small crowd was already threatening to gather.

We went into the hottest tea-shop in the world, a concrete garage with pictures of fat film stars on the wall. Ten minutes in that place and they could have sweated themselves sylph-like. There were no windows, no fan. The kerosene stove chuffed and kettles steamed. Down the back of the knee the sweat ran, down the throat, the armpits, breast and brow. Mohammed Hussain had spent the winter in the south in Multan, cooking for Germans. "Yes, they are tourists. They go safari."

Mohammed Hussain cooking for Germans on safari in Pakistan. I began to smile again. "So you don't work at the Golden Peak any more?"

He screwed up his face. "It is bad, this Golden Peak, you have seen? Where is the garden? Before, you know, all mens are coming, take tea, talk. Now, no! I don't like this, you know? Now I am at Riverbank Hotel. Nagari people."

"Did you have an argument with Mr Latif?"

"No argument. Small argument." He scowled, laughed. "Now there is this small boy! I do not like this buildings. It is very business. Mir of Nagar, you know, he sell Golden Peak. Now very rich Nagar man he has bought, he is making very change."

"Would you go back?"

"No! It is too hard work. Always work. Now there is this old Nagari man, you have seen? He is very very nice. If he stays I go back. If I go back, Mr Latif will send him away." He drained his tea. "Mr Latif is China going!"

"So he said, in two days. His small boy is manager."

Mohammed gave a very pained look. "When he is China, I will come. Okay? Now I am cook! Dahl, chapati, subzi. Come there."

I suppose that to know someone or something is to see them

through change. Poor old Golden Peak. The balancing act, so well maintained, between the needs of the local men and the foreign visitors was now destroyed. The rich Nagari man had come down heavily on the side of the tourism encouraged by the opening of the road to China. Now where would they present the polo trophies, if not on the lawn of the Golden Peak? Tourism had long joined that list of words, like "headmaster" and "bank," that produced in my stomach a slight weariness and dread. It is, indeed, very business. Mohammed's business. He had left the village and turned the full force of his scorn upon the army; so all that remained was tourism, the "very business."

Poor Mr Latif was so looking forward to his trip to Kashgar. His passport and visa he checked over and over again, his small bag was packed and waiting days ahead of time. When he left, it was with a jaunty click of his heels, but he returned within an hour. "Road is block," he said, and shrugged. It is the nature of the beast.

Then came the rumour that the border was for some reason closed, and then at last he was gone, he and his friends, leaving the hotel in the hands of the eight-year-old child and the silent smiling old man. This dear old fellow made tea so willingly that I came to feel bad about asking, and quite missed Mohammed's kicks and scowling assertions that there was "no tea in Gilgit."

I had a plan about Rashida, and the whole clan. I would surprise them. Unannounced, I would put my head round the green door and call her name. I was so looking forward to it, and could picture them coming pouring out, down the stairs, from the kitchen, from the sitting-room. There would be hugs and tears and admonishments—*why you no write?* I even put on a black dupatta over my shalwar-kameez, to please them.

First I went to the Major's office, and collided with him coming out. He was in full uniform, a beige affair, an impression of medal ribbons and shiny buckles and epaulettes.

"SO! KATHLEEN, YOU ARE IN GILGIT!"

"You are in uniform!"

He slapped my back till I choked. He ignored it. "It is this Gulf, this Kashmir. I am a reservist, of course. Today, I have Appointments. So, tomorrow morning, you will come to this office, we will take tea, we will DISCUSS!"

Rashida's father was just where I'd last seen him a year ago, shooting the breeze with the keeper of a shoe shop. They occupied the benches intended for people trying on shoes, but no one ever did. Only men sat there, gossiping. He gave me the nod and I climbed through the gate.

There was a cow in the garden, eating a rose. Women's voices came from behind the curtain. Jamila came out, making for the kitchen. *Too much work!* She looked different, older. She saw me and we laughed, and here the restraint of the street was lifted; we were among women and family. We hugged, and again I was overcome and almost in tears, such was their warmth. My hair was showered in kisses. She pushed me back and looked me full in the eye. "Two days you have been here! Why you didn't come? In Golden Peak! What you think, this new construction?"

"I meant to give you a surprise! I thought you lot kept purdah?"

She shook her head impatiently. "*Everything we know!*"

Rashida was married, only ten days before, and moved to her new home. Now she lived beneath the roof she used to spy upon last year. It was a stone's throw away. Someone sent for her and while we waited for her to arrive, there was lunch, and Salma's new large-eyed daughter to admire.

"We call her slow-motion baby," said Jamila, lifting the ample child up into her arms. Indeed, she did move like an astronaut, as she was dandled from auntie to auntie. It was a full house—

another sister was home from Lahore, with her husband and her two kids. A house full to the brim of sisters and cousins following Rashida's wedding.

We sat on the floor around the cloth, as plates stacked high with chapati arrived.

"Plenty of company," I said to Jamila.

"Much work!"

"But tell me about Rashida. Is she happy?"

"*Happy!* With her Hussain Ali, *very happy!*"

"What's he like?"

Jamila flexed her arm. "He is very big—You like?"

"Yes, I like a bit of muscle."

She screwed up her nose. "I like small, small. This other sister she like Big! Why you laugh?" She tugged the dupatta over her hair. There came the familiar china cups—one for Mother, whose welcome was genuine and effusive, and one for me, and one for the husband of Fatima, the Lahore sister. He had a pot-belly and was served first. With him in the room the women were different, less talkative, slightly impatient. He'd just been on Haj, and had brought back from Saudi a present of toys for the children. They ignored the toys and were squabbling over the wrapper, but were hushed so he could hold court and describe the Haj, the terror of being in a crowd of two million people in an area, he said, the size of Gilgit bazaar. Two million! *Das Lakh!*

"So!" the pot-bellied husband declared, helping himself to rice. "Your friend Rashida is married. This Hussain is thirty, very old. I too was thirty. She . . ."—pointing at Fatima, a plump, tired-looking woman—"She was fourteen! A baby!" He stuck his thumb in his mouth and made sucky noises. "A baby! For one year she did not look at me!"

She wasn't looking at him now, but listening. I was sure she was understanding more of his English than he thought. He pulled an imaginary shawl over his face and simpered. Fatima gave an embarrassed little smile.

"Her first pregnancy—she was seventeen—she cried and cried, "I will die!" Ha ha!" He amused himself with this memory for a moment, then announced, "We have seen London!"

Fatima said, "Yes, London. Very beautiful."

"How long were you there?"

"Five days only. Very expensive! But I have noticed these things: in your society, women after marriage have boyfriends! Yes? And are fond of Negroes. Well, Negroes are human too. And old people are Sent Away."

I was aware of an embarrassed shifting among the women—those who understood. Mrs. Shah had no English; she was merely delighted to have us all gathered and conversing in her home.

"In Islamic culture we are permitted four wives! But economic conditions prevent. The father of Rashida's husband had six wives, two died—very rich man. They quarrelled! Ha ha! You know, one Pakistani girl said recently, "Why should not a woman have four husbands?" Everyone laugh at that!"

I wondered who that woman was. "Why did they laugh?"

"It is not Islam. You know, Shia people, we have system of temporary marriage. You know about this? No mullah is necessary. Man and woman agree, by mutual consent, and marriage is dissolved. My brother-in-law did this thing with a widow from Skardu, and never told his wife! Ha ha!"

In the best room, with the heavy furniture and a maddish frieze of camels, there is a huge print of the Ayatollah Khomeini, almost smiling. Jamila took me there. We sat on the sofa and played with the babies. Rashida, she should have gone on the stage. (*This is not possible*, I can hear her say, *we are Shia girls*.) Her entrance was silent and effective. She drew every head, even in her own home. Gone was the workaday plait, and the plain outfit. She was in rich turquoise, her heavy hair was folded into a knot at the nape of her neck. As we hugged, I sensed a faint perfume. Her eyes were made up. She wore lipstick, jewellery (*"gold!"*) Her bearing was straight and strong. And something of her aura had changed, that over-devoutness. I didn't want to say that here was a woman who had ditched her girlish virginity, and now enjoyed some little power in her own home, but it went through my mind. Her English was rusty and she knew it. Because she learns from dictionaries, her vocabulary extends to outmoded and archaic words like "mirth" and "hapless," charming because so rarely used. She hugged me and looked into my eyes. Was she happy?

Yes. "Now I am married girl! Why did you no write to us?"

"Rashida, I did."

We went to Rashida's new home, a few doors away down the narrow wynd. I don't understand the etiquette of chadors and dupattas, but just to run a few yards down the back lanes, no chador was required. Dupattas are always required, or it is *shame*. As we entered another, smaller courtyard, Rashida showed me through a door which led directly into a bedroom. There was a double bed, and two dressing-tables. No room for anything else. Two little girls peeked in on us; Rashida sent them to fetch water for squash. She served the squash in two new matching tumblers of pink frosted glass which stood on the dressing-table, on a matching tray. I was glad to note that other people's wedding gifts are as frightful as our own.

We sat on the edge of the bed, spread with a pristine counterpane. I looked around the tiny room where Rashida was mistress. There was not a speck of dust; every glass ornament and boxed-up Chinese tea service was in its place.

"Well!" I said, for want of words. We wondered why it was that so few of our letters had got through. I didn't even receive the invitation to her wedding, which I would have accepted at once. "It is very strange," she said. Ah, innocent flower, who can't even pop down to the post office, who must entrust her mail to a range of brothers and cousins! But she was bursting with news and change. Change, change, it was a word she used over and over.

"What's he like, your Hussain Ali?"

"Very good man. Since January he has got a job, welfare officer. With Women's Literacy Projects. Yes, He wants me to continue with my education. If we go to Pindi, inshallah, I can attend college."

Women's literacy projects! I felt very happy for her, hugged her. "So now you live with his family. Your mother-in-law."

She snorted. "She is foolish! Everything she does wrong, but I am new girl, so I must respect. My life is very change. Look!" She stood and made for the other door. "This is my bathroom. I say to Him, I must have private bathroom, I do not want to go in the house, you understand? So He build for me." A new toilet, a washbasin, an old-fashioned upright washing machine. She touched it. She touched everything, the novelty. "My washing machine, my parents gave. And this is my shoes. Twenty-five shoes!"

"Twenty-five pairs of shoes?" There was indeed rack upon rack of the things.

"Yes, I bring. Also: fifty dresses. In here."

She left the bathroom behind and hauled a heavy suitcase out from under the bed; inside were yet more shoes. In another, shalwar-kameez and fabrics: summer weight, winter weight, flowers, polyesters, some horrid crimplene plaids. She even patted the blue carpet on which she knelt. "This my carpet. Room only is His, but everything—mine!" She was mistress of all the gifts, the glasses, flasks, tea sets, the shoes and carpets, the washing machine.

"But what is it like, living with his family?"

"He has brothers, so I want my own bathroom. I am shame. Hussain Ali is rich, He has two jeeps, He did inherit his father's lands. He is building a house in the village. He wants me to continue my education. My wedding clothes are here."

She pulled out a red shalwar-kameez decked with gold braid, like a Christmas cracker. The trousers cut so wide and flared that they moved like a dress, a sari. A seventies pop star might have died for it. And jewellery: beaten silver set with tiny chips of ruby. Dangly earrings like inverted cups. Chains that linked nose and ear.

She opened box after velveteen box. I thought it all vulgar. "This gold! This ruby!" She drew back her hair and showed her earrings. "Gold!" "He"—"He" applied to no one but Ali—"He is graduate of mixed college, in Karachi, but I am not jealous of these girls. He was pious at college, and waiting for me. Nine years He has waited! He tells me the stories of His college days and sings to me romantic songs . . ."

"Really? Jamila said so . . ."

"What! What she say?"

"That he sang romantic songs to you, nothing else."

She took a little pink booklet from a crowded drawer. "My diary, you may read. Yes, read. It is written in English. It is my feelings. He said: "Write your feelings, your life is very change." I write in English."

"Does he speak English?"

"No."

"No one can understand this diary?"

She lowered her eyes. "It is for practice. The English, when I am not speaking every day, is . . ."

"Rusty, like old iron."

"Read! And tell me the mistakes."

Rashida had nothing to fear from anyone finding her diary. Again we sat side by side on the bed. She read it, aloud: " "It is the last two days in my parents" home; tomorrow I am *dulhan*"—*dulhan*, it is meaning bride—"What my feelings for Hussain Ali?

What His thinking to me? We will become two bodies, one soul; and after almighty Allah He is lord to me. This is my wedding day, I am very nervous." This"—she turned a few pages—"This is after I am come here. Read!"

" "Their way is different, and I must make efforts to fit with Ali's brothers, and His mother. Today I am shamed." Shamed, Rashida? You often use the word."

"Often I feel. I am not accustomed . . . The first time we drive in the jeep together. *I am with a man*, you understand?"

"But he's your husband."

"First time for twenty-four years, I am without my sisters and parents. My feeling is very shame. My life is completely change."

I tried to imagine never having been alone in all my life. No solitary walks, no quiet evenings alone with a book or the telly, no cycling or mooching about galleries, no shopping, running, driving. Another curiously Western pleasure, being alone.

"Do you miss your sisters?"

"Very miss, Jamila. Now I go only as guest to my parents' home."

"Every day?"

"Twice a day!" she laughed, and read again: " 'After two or three months some couples get fed up with each other. Such has happened to this brother and his hapless wife.' "

"Who?"

She pointed through the window to another little door, firmly closed, and cupped her hand around my ear. "He beats her."

"What can she do?"

Rashida shrugged.

"Well, you can't just let her be beaten . . ."

"She is—how you say?—compelled. No one likes this brother."

I remembered meeting the year before a woman, intelligent, educated, with sunglasses and powder to hide the bruising around her eye. Compelled.

"Read! And tell me the mistakes."

"'Ali,' I read, " 'I am happy for you, you have fought and won what your heart desired.' His heart's desire. What's that, then?"

"Me!"

"Of course!"

"He did ask my father nine years ago. But Jamila was not yet engaged. It was not correct. You know, she is elder to me."

"Read! 'Today my sister is gone . . .'"

"Lahore sister, you did meet. For two days after my marriage she lived with me in this house. It is our custom."

I read on: " 'I must be used to unfamiliar people, unfamiliar house, unfamiliar . . . ' What's the blank?"

She patted the bed. "Sex! I have no experience!"

"What do you think?"

"I think he is very big and I am small. Still I am not used to this."

"But you like?" She smiled.

"You'll be having babies next."

"After one year. First we are enjoying. Family brings big responsibility. Contraceptive methods, no, this is not unIslamic. It means every child has much attention."

She showed me some poems, little Patience Strong homilies written at the back of her notebook; and some longer verse in Urdu. I asked her to translate. She worried at it for a moment. "I cannot."

She took the book away and sat again beside me. "What is your thinking of this diary?"

"Anyone who reads it will think you are a very good Islamic woman. You do seem very happy. I'm glad."

She nodded, and took both my hands in hers. "Kathleen, I pray to Allah that soon you will find your life partner, too."

She was pregnant within the month.

Of course there are no drinking houses in Gilgit; none in Pakistan at all. The corner tea-and-sweet-house is the nearest thing to a working men's pub. Certain older men in the cities remember the days of the first Bhutto as a golden age of liberalism, when there were clubs and drinking houses for those un-Islamic enough to want them. They closed under Zia. Now Benazir was herself in deep trouble; the newspapers rustling in the tea-houses talked of corruption and nepotism. Benazir's is a difficult place.

Needless to say, there are no women in the tea-house. There is a TV in a dusty corner. The rags that serve as curtains are tied in a knot, neglected and stained. Above the hubbub of conversation is the drone of the fans as they gently stir the cobwebs. There might be a couple of posters on the walls, gaudy affairs trumpeting the proprietor's politics.

After dark the police stop in for tea and lean their rifles against the wall. The tea is thick and sweet. A listing tower of *burfi* is displayed in the window, held together by its own stickiness. A selection is weighed and served on a chipped plate.

There is always a boy running back and forth with orders. Tea-house boys are not always the most intelligent of lads. Perhaps they would prefer to be out in the dark street at night with their pals and the stray dogs. Bats come out at night, and toads creep along the rough pavements of the bazaar.

News came that Benazir's government had fallen. The Cabinet had been dissolved by the President, and elections announced for the autumn. People either danced in the street, or wept bitter and angry tears. There was growing tension in the Gulf, and to many Pakistanis' disgust, their government had come out in favour of sending troops to the allied forces, the side of the USA, Saudi and Israel, their three great bugbears. "*The Americans say jump, and this government jumps.*" More to the point, closer to home and heart, there was trouble in Kashmir. I was to look at photographs of schoolboys: "This my brother, my cousin, killed! And for what, for walking in his own street!"

The Major shook his head none too sorrowfully. There will be war over Kashmir, again. In his office, at least, the world was being put to rights. He greeted me effusively; pumped my arm up and down, slapped my back. I thought: Maybe he thinks I'm a man. No, he complimented me on the black dupatta arranged artlessly over my breast. He pinched his nose. "What is your saying? 'When in Rome!' It is good, we are Shia."

I swear he enjoys this nonsense. I wonder how far he was over-stepping bounds by entertaining me, by ushering me into his office. I wanted to ask him questions, I wanted another run-through of the history of the province; the constitutional question in a nutshell. He was good at giving gloriously partisan accounts which made all of history sound like a particularly exciting polo match, and you were the puck. Why was India so determined to hold on to Kashmir?

"You see," he'd said patiently, "it is these rivers. Three rivers flow from Kashmir into Pakistan: the Indus, the Jellum, the Chenab. They are our lifeblood. Who controls these rivers controls Pakistan. Now India wants to ruin us. If these rivers are blocked, or diverted . . . Pakistan is starved. Yes! They are diverting."

Today, though, no one could talk of anything but Benazir Bhutto. On the wicker chairs of the office were two other fellows: one a neat dapper birdlike chap, in a blue safari suit. He was from Islamabad. The other looked so like a Scottish poet of my acquaintance that he startled me. Red-eyed and swollen-nosed, he looked as though he'd been on a bender for a week. There was much rising and bowing and dusting of chairs. The debate which I had interrupted quickly resumed. "Now, Miss Kathleen, what is the difference between Margaret Thatcher and Benazir Bhutto?" asked the red-eyed one. He wore a wool waistcoat over a large stomach. Faced with such a gentleman, always I thought of the burghers of Hamelin and their rats.

"Sahib, we are talking Global Concerns," growled the Major.

"Not this little fellow Pakistan. You must forgive him, this fellow, he is—what you say?—*diwana*, crazy!"

"Benazir crazy," the red-eyed one sighed.

"Benazir crazy! A Staunch Peoplist. He left his job for this PPP; now she is gone."

"A disaster!"

"We are not talking about this little Pakistan! This little fellow! Are we, Sahib?"

The man from Islamabad gave a diplomatic smile. "We can only sympathise."

"Sympathise! It's the *exact* word. Now, Sahib, please, your opinion of the status of the Northern Areas?"

The man from Islamabad cleared his throat. "It is my belief . . ."

"He holds Sensitive Posts in Islamabad . . ." said the Major.

"My opinion . . ."

". . . and believes this country is run by bureaucrats. Ha ha!"

The man from Islamabad nodded. "It is true all over the world."

"Governments come and go . . ."

"A *disaster*!" cried the Peoplist.

". . . but the bureaucrats remain."

"Quite. Now, if one consults the 1973 Constitution . . ."

"The 1973 Constitution! I have it here." The Major began rummaging about on his desk. The tea-boy came in backwards, gave us one wild look, left his tray and scarpered.

"I have it!" The 1973 Constitution, bound in unremarkable beige. "Here it is; one has only to read and understand!"

"Page one," the man from Islamabad persisted, "defines Pakistan: and I have consulted this and believe your case to fall under 2(b). Miss, please read."

I read, and concluded that anything and everything could fall under Section 2(b).

"Read, and *understand*," said the Major. "These lawyers . . ."

"What lawyers?" I asked.

"It is coming to the High Court, the case of the Northern Areas. Are we, or are we not, a part of Pakistan? These lawyers, all they have to do is read, and understand. It is not so difficult. It is written in Black and White. Read, and *understand*. I was a lawyer, an administrator of martial law."

"Martial law!" snorted the Staunch Peoplist. "Zia abjured this constitution."

"Amended!"

"Abjured!"

The Major sat heavily. "And she is asking me why there is no unity between Muslim nations!"

"I am?"

"Why not? It is this King Fahd, this USA!"

The man from Islamabad persisted: "It is because in your Section 2(b), it does not say 'Northern Areas' by name."

Staunch Peoplist took the book, and agreed. Nowhere was the Northern Areas mentioned by name.

"The High Court will decide!"

The man from Islamabad leaned forward a little. "In answer to your question. It is because the Muslim nations are underdeveloped economically, politically, socially."

Something in his accent made me wonder if he'd studied in England. "Please go on," I said. He drew breath, but the Major was on his feet, crying "Unstable!"

"This one man has the power to dissolve Cabinet!" wailed the Staunch Peoplist. "Is this democracy?"

"Pakistan at least has a written constitution," I tried.

"You have *Convention*."

"Enough!" cried the Major, and threw down the Constitution. "You will excuse us. My friend from Islamabad and I have an appointment."

"We will meet again," said that enigmatic gentleman. "I will explain many things."

The Major slapped my back once more. "Later, Kathleen, we will discuss, but not in this bloody place, this *office*."

Murtaza said: "Are you angry to me?" I said: "Of course not."

"Last year, it was a misunderstanding."

"On both our parts. Is Salma here?" She was, nursing her daughter, the slow-motion baby. She was plumper; her hand was soft. Murtaza and Salma grew ever more like Jack Sprat and his wife. Given her head she would be fat and jolly, he would become yet more dour and grey. They sat on the couch on their verandah, and their new baby ogled the flowers which grew all about, tall orange blooms I did not recognise.

"You have this flower in your country?"

"No, too cold."

"Ah, it is the hottest summer! Too hot. It is the first year I have this plant."

I was glad Murtaza had forgotten my promise to bring him some seeds, or was too polite to mention it. I had thought it a nice idea, then thought of the Scottish rhododendron, or the Australian rabbit. Visions came of some humble British flower, say the daffodil, introduced by me, spreading like wildfire through the Karakoram, jaundicing whole valleys, wrecking sensitive and unique ecosystems, sending species to the wall. Bird life decimated, families driven from their land by the golden host . . . What I really wondered was: Would I ever dare own up?

Murtaza was occupied with some calculations. Two big projects were under way: a school at Astore, a bridge on Gupis side. Work was plentiful, flowers bloomed, peace had reigned and a new baby was born, but Murtaza was as miserable as ever.

"Why do you people take no sugar in tea?" he asked as it was served. Here was a question I could cope with. Much whispering in the kitchen. *Separate tea for the guest, separate! No sugar. Sugar in a bowl, it's what they do.* We spoke amiably enough about health; it was a subject in which he could take a mournful interest. I said, "We believe sugar to be bad for the teeth, and general health." I was doing it again, lapsing into a sort of Pathé Newsspeak. Major Khan, General Health.

He stirred plenty into his own cup. "And so, still you are not married?"

"It's common, you know, among professional women."

"What is the meaning of 'professional women'?"

"Commonly, one who has qualifications. Women of higher education who, after attaining their degrees, spend some years at work in their chosen careers before considering marriage." That'll do, I thought.

He nodded glumly. "Thank you. You have Free Choice. I suppose it is a good system. In our system, our parents make the arrangements. My father says: You will marry with her. You have Individual Freedom."

"It can bring its individual problems."

"Divorce is common in your country."

"It is no great shame now, as it once was."

"But now you have your qualifications, and several years in your occupation. Now you can get married!" I looked at his eyes; there was not a hint of a joke.

"You have visited the Major, my cousin?"

"Yes, we were speaking of local politics."

"Ah, do you understand our problems? Do you know, here in Gilgit we have a Commissioner, for the whole Northern Areas. This one is from Peshawar. He, the heads of the various departments, even headmasters of middle and high school, are from Outside. Subordinates only are local, they can't speak with us people. We are like sheep, like colony of Pakistan!"

"I know, my country too."

"But you can vote."

"We are five million, against fifty million."

"After this Dogra regime we offered our services to Pakistan, and this is what we get, that the headmasters of our middle schools are from outside. Urdu, Punjabi, Pushto speaking. They can't talk to us! We are like cattle, like sheep."

"It is," I said, "so interesting."

"It's a mess! A mess! This question of language. My language is Shinas, it is Gilgit language. In Hunza, one side of the river, one language: Burushaski. On the other side, another tongue. Between Ganesh and Passu, another. Between Passu and Sost, yet another. In this Shimshal valley, another. In my village, in one village there is two difference of words, how do I say?"

"Dialect?"

"Just so."

"In my country," I said, "we are struggling to keep native languages alive. English has taken over everything." Like daffodils, I thought. We shook our heads.

"What's the solution, Murtaza?"

"There is no solution."

Up towards the library they were building more offices. Boys were swimming in the irrigation canal, their huge trousers inflated like crinolines. Another hot day in this too-hot summer. I wanted to go to the library because it was cool. I remembered the anonymous door in a whitewashed wall, green fronds tapping against the windows. The lane took me past the "Lady Shop." The Lady Shop was advertised by a large painting of a white-skinned woman giving a bright lopsided smile. She was surrounded by floating jars of cream and hairbrushes and nail polish, as if bothered by a poltergeist. I wondered if they have poltergeists, all these teenagers cooped up together.

The grass of the library garden was wet, and a pleasure to walk through. A hose propped on a stone spluttered out water. There was a gardener, squatting at the wall with his shirt-tails trailing in the grass.

Of course it was all still there, the studious quiet of the reading room. The librarian nodded in his tall and sombre way, like a flower, and unlocked the little rustic alcove which housed the local collection.

There was *The Travels of Fa Hsein*, the unassuming memoirs of a Chinese Buddhist monk who struggled over the Karakoram in the fourth century. Shelved next to that: *The Hunza Diet*, a cheap 1970s paperback which guaranteed that a particular mixture of fruit, exercise and meditation would produce appalling longevity. I chose an unbound book, a photocopy of an older typescript which had been bashed out on a Remington Rand. It was *The Autobiography Sir M. Nazin Khan KCIE, Mir of Hunza State (died 1938). Translated from the Burushaski into Urdu, Persian and English.*

This was treasure indeed. I took it to an easy chair beneath the softly turning fans, and composed myself by gazing at the photographs. A row of long-dead handsome boys looked down upon me, each with flying moustaches and a drawn sword across his knee. Did their spirits crowd around as I opened that glorious book?

Within ten minutes I was lost in a lost world of fratricide and hostages, of falcons, tithes and magic frogs, of British and Russian push-and-shove and the story of a gun cast of all the kingdom's copper. I was in clover; this is what Himalayan romance was all about.

At that time the Mir of Hunza controlled the passage between the British Agency in Gilgit and their outpost in Kashgar. Whether mail or messengers got through in safety, the Mir decided. He was therefore the happy recipient of astonishing gifts and sweeteners from every quarter. If merely to receive presents bored him, he could always go out and steal. There were raiding parties to enjoy; should he wish to stock up on horses, he merely rustled them from next door. The book progressed through a story of horrible complexity; of coups and murders amd power struggles. When the author was a small boy in bed with fever, with his faithful servant asleep across the threshold, there was a murder in his garden. He recounted the gory tale with complete equanimity. I got lost, couldn't understand who was murdering whom, who was married to whose sister, whose nephew was despatched to the Chinese court and why, but neither could the translator, for he interrupted the steamy narrative with an exasperated aside: "Note: I do not quite see what all this is about, nor is there any clue as to whom the people concerned are." I was mightily relieved, and grateful to him. It meant I could drop any pretence at scholarship and just get on with the yarn.

It opened when the author was a boy of eight:

Fond of riding and shooting, I went out daily on my donkey with a bow and arrow, and just before my eighth birthday my father presented me with a matchlock. In those days pebbles were used instead of bullets and in a very short time I became an expert shot. When I was nine my father let me select a pony from some he had captured on a raid on Ladakh, but alas, though it was as big as a Kashmiri pony, it was so lazy that it would not trot, so I sought counsel from Ghulam Naghshband who recommended a good beating each morning, a prescription that soon remedied matters.

So began a life of intrigue and raids, and court affairs so boring the Mir could hardly bring himself to recollect them. As an appendage to the book were written huge lists of grandiose names. These were noteworthy people whom the Mir had once met. There were dozens of dreary Rajas through from Srinagar;

there were Chinese officials bearing gifts of coin and silk; but it clearly bored the Mir to write of them. Here was a man who could remember vividly and with love the names of his father's horses until that gentleman was overtaken by age, "thereafter he used to ride a yak." Only after the list of horses come the Rajas, then the Multibars, but the names of his father's six wives escaped the Mir. He insisted, though, that every child was conceived in wedlock, and no bastards were left in his father's wake.

The treachery of the dread Nagaris filled the typewritten pages. For generations these tribes, who face each other across a wild river, had been at war. Occasional attempts at peace through inter-marriage between the royal families invariably failed. More years passed, more gifts of horses and weaponry were showered upon the Mir; these he remembered. He remembered being sent as a young boy to Gilgit; no three-hour trip on a wagon in those days. He was to act as hostage and so guarantee the safety of the British Agent, Biddulph, as the latter made his dangerous journey to Hunza. The boy was entertained here for the duration of Bid-dulph's stay. Only when Biddulph was safely home was the boy released, with his usual game-show shower of gifts. Other mous-tachioed heroes of the Victorian age are mentioned in the Mir's despatches: Younghusband, and Curzon. The latter distinguished himself in the Mir's memory by his inability to speak Persian, the lingua franca, above a single word: that for *very good!* which he repeated, parrot fashion, throughout the banquet.

The casting of the Hunza gun clearly fixed itself in the young Mir's mind. It entailed the services of one Adina, gun-maker to the Afghan Court, and no wimp, I'll warrant. He was persuaded to come to Hunza and set to work with one copper utensil from each household. (The more I read of this book, the more it felt like a Russian film script. How I could see the messengers riding from the palace down to the people's hovels, and demanding from the

peasants within a copper jug for the greater glory of the kingdom.)
Two-thirds of the Mir's own copper utensils were added to the
hoard, and Adina made a clay mould. The molten copper was
poured into the mould, but the cast was too big and the Hunza
clay different to that of Adina's native Badakshan.

So men were sent to Badakshan to fetch clay, and returned with
it, and another expert gun-maker. They melted down the original
copper, and rode farther afield to Ghujal and Mayun to scour the
land for more kettles and cups; and all was poured into the cast of
Badakshani clay. Forty men, it is noted, worked daily on the
process. The cast was broken after two days . . . but the gun was
one and a half handspans short. The gun-maker, no doubt wondering if he'd ever see Badakshan again, patched it. For a week the
gun was bored and polished, while another smaller Kohistani gun
was cast. "The secret of the gun's manufacture was kept from the
Nagaris." Just as well—they'd have split their sides: "at Dungdars
the Kohistani gun was fired for the first time and incontinently
exploded." What became of the expert gun-makers is not
recorded, but the big gun didn't let them down. It survived to fire
a welcome to Biddulph, on his arrival in Hunza. His journey from
Gilgit—from this, his very house wherein I sat—had been delayed
for two years while the road so desired by the British was
improved, and Biddulph's fear of treachery abated.

I got up, and began to look with renewed interest at the photographs—where was the Mir, where Biddulph? One of the pictures high and out of reach? There, though, was the last Mir of
Hunza. And here was a mad squinting photo of the first jeep to
cross the Shandor Pass; full of boffins and bespectacled engineers.
To take it the photographer must have lain on the bonnet of the
jeep, which was canted at an angle of 30 degrees. The film, at least,
had survived.

I sat again, and continued with the story of the magic sieve,
which began: "In the olden days, people were much troubled by

ghosts who would appear in villages with their feet turned back and one eye in the middle of their foreheads . . ."

Back at the Golden Peak—the palace of the enemy, the Mir of Nagar, the kingdom across the river—I thought: I would like to meet a Mir. The present Mir of Nagar is reputed to have a passion for Slough. Does he lean out of the window of his fairy-tale castle in the mountains, above the wheat-filled terraces and apricot trees, and dream of Slough? Are his nightmares full of friendly bombs? Was Slough the source of this wallpaper? And the children of Slough—whence do their fairy-tale images come? From the days when darkest Europe was like Nagar and Hunza: divided into innumerable kingdoms, each with palaces and princesses and ghosts with their feet on backwards. I thought how wonderful to have been here then; when poor Biddulph had to wait two years for his improved road. His track is still visible from the modern road, a hair-raising line sweeping and falling like a roller coaster up and along the rockwalls. At Nilt, it looks like the entrance not to another kingdom, but to another world entirely.

The next day was Friday, and the family were going on a picnic. I went to say goodbye, that I was going up to Hunza for a few days. They waited on the garden couch in a great display of finery. Each woman wore a richly coloured shalwar-kameez, with a yoke of mirror-work and beads. Rashida wore tiny jewelled slippers. Their perfumes were light, their handbags fit for an evening dance. A strip of jewels ran from Jamila's ear lobe into the folds of her hair, and enhanced her golden earrings. They had polished their nails. Even Mrs. Shah had used some lipstick. They were waiting for the men to show up with the jeep. Young Hina, in a frilly skirt with leggings, ran to the green gates and peeked through the crack looking for the jeep.

"Where are you going?" I asked.

"Naltar!"

"I thought that was a glacier."

"Very beautiful!"

"You're going on a glacier dressed like this?"

Jamila punched my arm.

"The jeep's here!" cried Hina. The women rose and processed towards the gates. Mrs. Shah checked through the crack to make sure. At her word each woman took a vast embroidered shawl and began to hide herself. Folds of cotton covered the jewellery, the mirror-work yokes, the wrists and bangles, the lipstick and earrings. The last fold crossed the bridge of the nose until only the eyes could be seen. I was standing in a crowd of ghosts.

I could tell Rashida was smiling, because her eyes crinkled up. She pressed her cheek to mine. "We are Shia girls."

One by one they lowered their eyes and stepped outside to walk the few yards to the jeep.

3 Karimabad Side

On the Hunza bus I met Ghulam, a man of maybe forty. He was gaunt-faced and thin. There was a crucifix round his neck; he is the only Christian in Hunza. Christianity exhorts us to love our neighbours; Ghulam delights in their downfall. There is something of the goat in the man: a demonic giggle, a Pannish mischief. He holds his atrophied left hand in his right, and consequently walks with a rolling gait, like an old sea-salt. He runs a café in Karimabad, which is the main township in the Hunza valley. The café is no more than a shack. Karimabad is now served by the Karakoram Highway. When poor Biddulph left Gilgit to reach the palace of the Mir of Hunza, the journey took a fortnight. Now a minibus will be in Ganesh, at the roadside, in some three hours.

Karimabad is suspended high above the road, looking over the deep roaring trench of the Hunza river to the Auld Enemy, the Nagar side.

We reached the township by leaving the highway and walking slowly up a dusty track, past apricot trees and the civil hospital, and the stooks of harvested wheat drying in the sun. On an alarmingly steep street, booths sell Hunza handicrafts and juice. Karimabad has become a tourist centre. Jeeps of tourists in scarves and dark glasses sweep up and down the track to the main road. There are several concrete hotels, and the foundations for more because the view is fit for a king; and the tourist is king. An entire realm is laid out at your feet. Bound by the white soaring wall of Rakaposhi, cleft by the Hunza river, there are green terraces and apricot trees, little flat-roofed houses huddled together and their fields around them. Around Ghulam's café are pastures of wild flowers, and Ghulam's familiar, his little black goat tethered to a rock. Goats feature a lot. At the roadside below, there are rocks covered in petroglyphs. Herds and herds of goats and ibex make their way across the rocks, older than Islam, older even than the standing Buddha carved on the rockface on the outskirts of Gilgit.

When night fell and the stars came out, I was watching the belt of the Milky Way reach over the dark wall of the mountaintops. The constellations and villages appeared like a mirror-image of one another, as if the patterns of lights of the villages below were reflections of the stars in a lake.

Ghulam crouched beside me, holding his arm. The wind was cool and fresh. Far below the river roared. Now and again a startling crack like gunshot echoed from the mountains. I'd learned it was not gunshot, but rocks falling; and the deep low banging and trundling was the river rolling rocks the size of taxis along its bed.

Ghulam said, "This Milky Way; in Burushaski language, we say 'Charkay Palash'; it means 'turn the world.' These Burushaski people believe that it is the power of this Milky Way that turns the world round."

The clear skies didn't last long; the next day clouds began to converge from Rakaposhi side, from Golden Peak and Spantic, and by evening the sky was thunderous and black. Behind Karimabad stands the mountain Ultar, whose basin is filled with cloud like a bubbling cauldron. Before Ultar, on a knoll at the top of the town, is the old palace of the Mir like a lone tooth. Its washed and stained walls gleamed eerily in the stormlight, its decayed balconies were held up by poles. Many storms had battered it, perhaps six hundred Himalayan winters. I went up the steep hill to the gates, where the gun-maker was brought to make his exploding cannon, from whose carved portals the old Mir rode out on his yak, through which entered emissaries and spies from China, India, Britain, and their plenitude of gifts; all was falling into ruin and decay.

The clouds darkened and darkened, a wind began to swirl about the mountains and glide down the glacier. It gusted hard and bowed the slender plane trees. Waves of dust blew up from the road into eyes, teeth. I ran blinded and manhandled back to shelter. Medieval figures scurried with sacks drawn round their features.

By the time I reached Ghulam's, lightning cracked the sky. It filled the Ultar basin with a bowl of eldritch light. Backlit, the palace on its hilltop looked like a mad Frankenstein film set. Lightning and more lightning began to leap between the mountaintops, and thunder rolled. We were bound on all sides by mountains, whose summits were picked by lightning to grin for a moment in a terrible light. Then the rain began. First it pocked the dry dust, and then it came down in sheets. Ghulam had pulled a bench on to the shelter of his verandah, and there we sat to watch. All over the valley, the electric lights went down.

Away below, in the pitiless, wind-driven rain, little trains of orange torchlight processed among the fields, as if in a carnival. A bolt of lightning flashed and for a moment lit the fields in grey, then darkness came again and the little torches moved.

"This very bad, very bad!" Ghulam called above the wind. "This villagers, you know, it is their harvest. Ruin!"

The lights ran back and forth. By the way they turned and twisted you could see they were following the edges of the fields and terraces.

"All is rain. Apricots, ruin. This wheat, soak." All the stooks that were cut and drying by the side of the road or in the fields would be soaked and smashed, the apricots drying on the flat-roofed dwellings would turn rotten by the morning were they not gathered in. And we were sitting on a bench like judges, watching sheet lightning bring out the summit of Rakaposhi, then fork wildly down the valley. The awesome rumbling of thunder echoed off the mountainsides. In the light of the flashes every poplar stood clear as day, in a chilling green-grey light. The lightning wrote some terrible message across the sky, the thunder applauded, and a new, reinvigorated deluge of rain followed on behind.

We said silent prayers for the villagers' harvest and, as the storm moved east over the Baltoro glaciers, for the mountaineers who would be camped at high altitudes, enduring a wrath of snow and wind we could barely imagine.

The rain fell all night long. Everyone—Ghulam, his cook, a friend, a couple of guests—slept fully clothed on benches inside his café. Mice scuttled about the roof, the rain drummed on and on. After the searing heat of the summer, I woke stiff and damp and felt at home. The cloud was still low enough to beard the hills, and fill the gullies and high valleys. When it lifted it revealed Rakaposhi plastered with more summer snow than anyone could remember.

Ghulam giggled, and with difficulty lit a cigarette one-handed. "My neighbour, he has a good hotel. His roof is leak! There is water coming!" He tugged a blanket round his shoulders and dragged himself, coughing and giggling, into the scullery. "Road is block," he called. "But harvest is okay."

If you ask the people of the remote villages their opinion of the road-building programme which will connect them to the towns, they sigh. They know there is much to be lost, but it means they won't starve in a bad winter. If a single storm wipes out the winter's supplies, there is always the jeep to the towns downside.

The day wore damply on, a day for drinking tea and reading what books could be found. When the sun broke through again, with it rose a high pungent smell—rotting apricots. By some mysterious means news came through from other parts, which Ghulam cheerfully relayed. Landslips had blocked the road north to China and south to Gilgit. Skardu was cut off because bridges were down. The road would be closed for a fortnight at least, because the men and machines to rebuild the bridges couldn't reach them until the landslips were cleared. Fuel would soon run out because the highway south to Pindi was blocked in ten, twelve, thirteen different places.

"But, you know," he giggled, "is good business!" It was very good business for hoteliers. Everyone was stuck.

Where jeep drivers were caught between two landslips they were making plenty of money shuttling back and forth. Travellers who, like myself, climbed the slips that kept them from their destinations paid good money for a lift to the next roadblock; there they put their luggage on their heads and climbed that; stopping to tell the poor souls coming the other way that they would find a vehicle waiting. So good business is done until that jeep too runs out of petrol. The more Ghulam found to relate, the more merry he grew.

"So! All is block!" He grinned.

Late that night, when all the cooking was done, Ghulam sat and let his friend massage his neck because his injured arm still pained him constantly. Then he whispered to his friend who stood, pulled a shawl round his shoulders and indicated that I should follow him. Ghulam said,

"Yes, go with him—he will show you something!"

I was led up a darkened lane, and shown into another small shack, no bigger than a garden shed. It looked like a kitchen, or a laboratory, with large pots and rubber tubes. Two other men were already there, young men from the village, who wore perfect white, despite the mud, and spoke in low voices. I sat on a wooden bench against one wall and watched as they worked by the light of a Tilley lamp. Around us on slanting shelves were piles of aluminium cooking pots, and a huge water filter. From a jerry can they poured a cup of liquor. At the very smell of the thin mulberry wine, all three men began giggling.

"Hunza water!"

"Illegal, you know?" said Ghulam's friend, raising the tumbler. "But this District Commissioner, this government staff: always drunk."

"They don't get arrested?"

"Of course not! The policeman who made the arrest would be suspended."

We took sips in turn as the tumbler was passed round.

"And if some little man is drinking and comes to court, does this Commissioner fine him, or imprison him? Of course! And then this official is every afternoon at the river, drinking, drinking!"

They set on the stove a pressure cooker of mulched-up mulberries, which had been left to ferment. They lit the stove. A pipe led to a bottle, suspended in the water tank to cool.

Now the still was set up, we drank, and told stories. One of the men in white said, "You did hear of this driver, next village, my friend? He was driving me, I was his last passenger. Only two days ago. He is come home, and is drinking Hunza spirits. This thing he is drinking from, this can, before was batteries. Acid. From lorry engine. Little little is in this can, it was not cleaned. Now he is dead. No problem. Drink! this can is clean, no acid."

It tasted nutty. There is Hunza water, a spirit, distilled from mulberries or apricots, and there is simple wine too, such as we were drinking. It tastes nutty, they said, because it's stored in stone boxes underground. Because the stone is porous, it's waterproofed with walnut oil. Again the cup of wine was filled and passed around.

Shaheen, one of the white-clad men, was a tour guide. He was one of those keen, engaging, young professional men whom a visitor will meet in disproportionate numbers, because they gravitate towards foreigners. These are the men educated or influenced beyond the scope of the village. Their college or travelling days have made them aware of many things beyond the mountains, but their culture holds them fast. They fall between two stools and are often unmarried, because if they reject their parents' choice, where will they find a girl-friend? They occupy a difficult place.

Shaheen held the cup up to the stormlight. "Tourism is good for people like me, but our parents talk of the olden days—before the British, the Mir's day. In the Mir's day, people used to make wine, apricot, mulberry. Like this, but now this is illegal! Now the government is strong. I will tell you: I am in Pindi, in Flashman's Hotel, you know? Buy alcohol."

I nodded; I had been there myself to sign the bit of paper which declared that as a heathen, I was entitled to a few bottles of weak beer. A sordid affair it was, but astonishingly tolerant. It is hard to imagine the British government permitting the sale of hashish to those whose culture or religion condones it.

Shaheen went on: "One police, he is watching. After he come to me and say: 'Have you permit?' No. No permit. He say: 'Okay, we talk about this, don't worry, come to the restaurant.' We talk, he say: 'I will not take you to police station; give me 5,000 rupees.' 'No!' I say, 'Take me to police station. I will stay two or three days. Is okay, I go.' 'No!' he say, 'Is no good!' Down he come, down, 1,000, 500 rupees. 'Okay,' I say, 'take it!' Two bottles vodka.

"Yes, in the Mir's day. If I have garden, apricots, grapes. You can come and eat fruit, take away. I no say: 'Why are you in my garden?' Now these people have business mind, selling."

I told how the making of whisky had been banned in Scotland, centuries ago, and the story from Neil Gunn's novel: how Young Art saves Old Hector's still from the excise man by dragging the stinking carcass of a sheep across the entrance. They laughed in recognition.

"It is your culture!" said Abdul. "I will tell you our culture. Hunza is fairy culture. In the Mir's day. Now, there are four seers remaining. Only. If a boy is a bit—crazy, you know?—his family know he is seer. This is what they do. The drums beat faster and faster, and the shaman is breathing this smoke—juniper smoke—and he is listening to the drums faster and faster and he is trance, in this circle of drumming, then comes—then he can see the fairies—on the mountaintops, and then he can speak with them. Quietly he is speaking to the drum, the fairies tell, tell . . . then a lamb is killed and the seer drinks until he is blood, all his clothes are blood . . ."

The cup was pressed into my hand and I took some more of the thin wine. I could believe in fairies, on such a night as this, in a little shack on a Himalayan mountainside.

Back at his place Ghulam showed me some architects' drawings, and a file of papers to do with purchasing land. The drawings were made by an English friend, and showed a modest three-sided building around a courtyard, flanked with those lollipop trees beloved of architects. On the roof was a Hunza skylight, a feature of local building. The plans showed four or five bedrooms, a couple of bathrooms. It was to be his new hotel.

"You are losing very much of your culture," I said.

"Tourism is good. We need more development," said Ghulam. "This is small hotel, not too big."

I thought: There'll be a funicular railway here one day soon, like Scarborough. You don't need a seer to tell you that.

"Haven't you enough? It's like Switzerland."

"USA, Saudi have! Why not Hunza people? Hotel-building is self-help. We need money."

"And if you make a lot of money, Ghulam, what would you do with it?"

"I would go to Karachi, maybe Europe, to get treatment for my arm."

In the late afternoon, when the sun was past its worst, I took a walk along the irrigation canal that runs through Karimabad and down to the neighbouring township of Alliabad. The water which irrigates the Hunza villages is saturated with mica, hence Ghulam's huge water filter. The mineral colours the water a deep unlovely grey, and forms unsettling swirling patterns, like shampoo. It makes tea taste funny, even if it's filtered. On one bank of the canal is a wide sandy path, overhung with apple trees and vines. Like in a miniature Venice, the balconies of little houses lean over the water. They are reached by a plank bridge and a ladder. On the quiet back paths one meets women, a spirited bunch and sharp on business. They sell embroidery and garnets and tiny flecks of ruby. Hunza women wear their hair in two long girlish twists, brought forward to hang on either side of the face. They're given height by an embroidered pillbox hat, usually covered with the ubiquitous shawl. A barefoot woman called Silma walked with me a while; she gave me apples, then invited me over the little bridge and up the ladder to her home. There was a lamp in the form of an unexploded shell, with a blue bulb. She was proud of it. She brought a child, some apples and pears, a blunt knife, and a stack of embroidered cushion covers. The child brought a handful of tiny garnets and rubies. They tried to entice me to buy.

I walked on, and fell in with a man called Abdul. Like Shaheen, he was a professional sort, you could tell by his clothes, his coiffure, his fluency in English. I could have walked a long mile with Abdul. Our conversation was constantly interrupted as he stopped to pass the time of day with almost everyone. Women waved to him and smiled, little children toddled towards him, men climbed the stone walls to shake his hand. He worked for the District Commissioner. I asked: Would he like to be District Commissioner? He said, Of course! He had studied downside, political science.

He asked, "Scotland is colony of Britain, no? Like Hong Kong?"

I tried to explain the Act of Union, humbled by his knowledge.

He growled. "I don't know why these peoples cast their vote for Margaret Thatcher. This Mr Kinnock, no one is casting his vote for him?"

We passed a crooked old man, walking the same crooked mile, who shook Abdul's hand joyfully.

"This man, he is to leave for Islamabad to receive an award for his help in rescuing an injured tourist. There is another, he rescued a drowning man from the river, he too is to receive an award. They are very happy. All these Ismaili people, very happy. We are not Shias, like these Nagaris." He gestured to the hillsides opposite. "You know this Muharram? When they beat themselves with sticks and chains, for the same reason we beat drums and are happy that Ali sacrificed his life for us. Nagar side wail and are in sorrow. Ismaili people makes music and dance—it is the same occasion."

Ismaili. He pronounced it I-smiley. These I-smiley people, cheerful, I-smiling men and women. It was hard to reconcile them with their reputation as muggers and highway robbers, who controlled the pass and looted the caravans.

There is a huge school in Karimabad. Karim is the Aga Khan's name, and the Aga Khan is the spiritual leader of the Ismaili people. The school was provided, like so much else, through his Foundation. All the way up the Hunza valley are little green signs indicating some building or project, some school or clinic or irrigation system sponsored by the Aga Khan; for of all the Ismaili people to whom he is the glorious Imam, he loves these Hunza people best. It is requited love: on impossible scree slopes high on mountainsides above the villages, messages are laid out in white stones. They are visible for miles, visible from a helicopter. In Urdu and English they cry "Welcome, our beloved Imam! Welcome, welcome!" A visit from the Aga Khan is quite an event. His photograph is ubiquitous. He is everywhere framed in shops and homes, he is made into key-rings, he dangles from the mirrors of Ismaili minibuses and jeeps. And everywhere he has the same benign, rather overwhelmed expression, like an unassuming bank-clerk presented with a retirement gift. Little does he look like a playboy and racehorse keeper.

Our return path took us past the academy, a modern building which, as chance would have it, would be seen to best advantage by the Shia Nagaris on the other side of the river. From our path we could see the sunbaked playground, where a dozen girls were playing volleyball. Girls in school uniform, a simple sky-blue shalwar-kameez and white chador. The shawl was tied firmly about their middles for the game. It is a sight you never see in downside Pakistan—girls playing in full view, running, shouting, laughing. These I-smiley people, a one-time powerful offshoot of Shi'ism, the sect of the dread Assassins.

Abdul said, "There can be no Islamic state. There is no unity among Muslim sects. Without unity, Islamic state is not possible." This was near-sacrilege, denying the possibility of Pakistan. And then: "You know this Salman Rushdie? Rushdie did disturb the world. You have this book? Please, next time, bring for me. I would like to read. In Pakistan, it is not possible to find."

I'd taken a dry whitewashed room in a hotel, one of a row of rooms built into the hillside like caves. My door opened to a grey irrigation stream, which spilt down into the yard of the building below. Every day an old man came there to do washing. Several times a day another cheerful old codger walked by tugging a goat on a rope. Sometimes the water ran, sometimes he diverted it with a shovelful of grey earth. I fell into a sort of lethargy, and remained in my room for four days. I read a novel by James Baldwin, and marvelled at the articulacy of the characters. I marvelled at the amount of drink they consumed—every page contained drinks, gin, ice, fridges. The storm had long passed and the summer temperatures climbed again. As the day outside grew hotter, I heard the ice I read about chink into tall cool glasses. I saw cold tonic sparkle over that ice and cover the gin at the bottom of the crystal glass. The ditch outside my door flowed grey and swirling. As Baldwin's people spoke and drank and drank and talked, I lay on a hard bed and read them. The sun reached its zenith and fell, mercifully. I learned the wooden window-frame, and the red quilt. By day I kept the window and mesh closed against the heat, but opened it at night to catch any passing breeze. From my bed, therefore, I could see the valley, moonlit. It stood still and expectant like a stage. Ridges of mountains came in left and right, like painted scenery. I read the graffiti on the wooden beam of the roof: Shazaman Aziz 1986. Olam Lahore.

On the second day, five army helicopters came, circled the basin, futtered away south again beyond the mountains. I saw my reflection in the glass window, and could see where the lines would form on my face. Washing was difficult; a bucket of silt-saturated water was all one had to clean the dust from skin and clothes. Every day, in the stream outside, the old washerman swung wet sheets around his head and beat them rhythmically against a wall. A spate of open jeeps with "Pakistan Adventure" painted on the side daily roared in and out of the township. Each jeep had two bright tourists with naked fleshy arms. Our bodies are lumpen and our clothes unflattering. There is a big sign at the top of the hill, near the fort. It says, in English: PLEASE, WEAR LOOSE CLOTHING.

Above the rooms was a café, favoured by gangs of dusty porters who would slam the screen door as they piled in, tired and hungry, to settle round a long table. Before them were set chapatis, and huge amounts of rice and dhal. Because they had just been paid off, they were good-humoured and rich as any oil-workers coming on shore. They were Balti men from Askole, two kingdoms and two languages away, who'd been carrying for trekking groups over the Hispar Glacier.

"No-good members!" they'd cry, and the commonplace porters' complaints were aired, between huge mouthfuls of food.

"Rupees, no!"

"No-good food!"

"No-good members! American memsahib, pah!"

The road has brought tourists, and for them it has brought thousands of plastic bottles of mineral water, which are stacked in crates at the door of every hotel or shop, or laid to cool in the grey silty waters pouring from the mountainside. The empty bottles are still being absorbed into households for various purposes, but once each household has a plenitude of bottles, what then will become of the empties?

On the morning of the fourth day there was a banging on my window: "Miss! Miss Kat-line!" A nose squashed itself against the pane. "Miss Kat-line. Come here!"

It was half-past six in a grey dawn. I opened the door. There stood Mr Durrani, shivering in his thin southern clothes.

"Miss Katline!" He turned and opened his arms to embrace the mountain scene before him. "Have you seen the Natural Beauty?"

Mr Durrani was a dealer in aquamarines from Karachi, with none of the dark guile one would like to expect in gem dealers. He had taken the room next to mine, and had shown me pictures of fabulous diamonds with names like racehorses. I looked blearily out at the steely dawn. Shreds of cloud wafted around the scree slopes.

"It looks like home."

"In Karachi is much hot." I realised I was feeling trapped by the Natural Beauty. Unless you manage to climb to a summit, you can go a long time without seeing far long vistas. I looked at the Natural Beauty while Mr Durrani engaged in some physical jerks and pulled the cold air into his lungs. It was indeed a far cry from Karachi. I felt a perverse longing for the desert. I wanted to see the sea, the long low hills of home. I wanted a sense of ancientness, emptiness, mourning. Water-light. But you can't describe the Himalayan mountains; all you can do is pour adjectives and superlatives like libations at their feet.

We took breakfast in the hotel restaurant, at a collective table pushed against the window. The red-and-green curtains, never drawn, hung heavy with years of dirt and grease. A big, handsome, cross-eyed man in brown ate *paratha*. Local music beat from an old cassette deck; a music of percussion and pipes without the flying strings that set my teeth on edge. On the wall were a silver-plastic-framed photo of the Aga Khan and a Chinese clock. This latter evinced all the glory that is Chinese design. A plastic-gold horse reared over a gilt-laced clock face. On the tip of the minute hand was a plastic butterfly, which alighted upon each passing minute. Our lives are as a plastic butterfly's, but a fleeting moment. Stuck to the walls were photos torn from a calendar. They showed idyllic scenes of Hunza with a pop or film star superimposed in a corner to suggest that the overweight and over-made-up Karachi singer really was crouching guiltily in a field. But, surrounded by the glory of Pakistan's manhood in the form of film heroes and pop stars, I couldn't take my eyes from the cook-boy, a shy and furtive youth. He had the most extraordinary face, round as the clock's. His eyes and mouth were round, his ears pointed. He never smiled as he leaned against the doorway, but looked at once harmless and angry, because of the two deep, deep lines between his round and heavy eyebrows. I knew I'd seen that face before; but where escaped me. Not a person, but a painting. As he stood in the kitchen door and watched me eat, it came to me—I'd seen the cook-boy painted fiercely wild and blue on the walls of Buddhist temples. He was the spit and image of the Yamatondo, defender of the faith.

Nothing was going to Nagar; no jeeps, no minibus. I waited at the monument to the dead road-builders of the Friendship Highway. One life per kilometre, someone said. Under an awning a man stirred a great vat of chicken broth. Vehicles came and went, and the notion to be anywhere but here grew in my breast. At length a boy leaned out of a minibus and shouted Sost-Sost-Sost, and I thought: What the hell.

At Sost the air was blessedly cool. A breeze with a hint of snow on its back blew downriver from the high watershed of the Khunjerab. Donkeys grazed among the flat stones of the river-bank. The river here is slow, yet to plunge into the gorge. A different atmosphere prevailed. This is the frontier. There is the ennui of a border post, and the excitement.

I never did send the immigration officer his postcard, but he was no longer there anyhow. In the yard, a soldier sat guard on a wicker chair. A garden umbrella shielded him from the sun, a sub-machine-gun lay across his knee. He gazed at the customs shed, perhaps wondering what he had done to be sent to Sost. A few shacks had been hurriedly erected to sell tea and biscuits, Pakistani provisions and Chinese "varieties." In the no-man's-land of rubble between the shacks and the road sat a litter of jeeps. A smart hotel with a lavish dining-hall gave the first—or last—glimpse of Chinese decor. Formica tables spread with plastic cloths with pictures of a dancing Minnie Mouse. Fold-away chairs with a design of squirrels in a branch. Bamboo screens. There were piles of hot plates, and stacks of attractive blue Chinese bowls, but only dhal and chapati to eat.

There was no one around but a lone Kashgari man who poked about the shit-strewn building site next to the hotel. A row of concrete boxes was being built to serve as motel rooms. The old man was an illustration from a fairy tale. His boots were black, his coat was long, he held his hands behind his back and nodded his thin grey beard. On his head was a wheel of black velvet and fur.

The sky is wider here than at Karimabad, and I went to the river to sit quietly. Still I had that longing for space and desert, water, plateau, steppe.

The quiet was torn by a convoy of seven Chinese trucks which rolled up to the barrier. The drivers gathered to lean against the radiator of the first truck and looked into Pakistan. They were Han Chinese, each in a scruffy utilitarian blue suit, shrunken, with the trousers turned up at the ankle to show their little high-heeled shoes. They wore dishevelled white shirts and blue caps. One squatted on the ground and concentrated on spitting between his knees. They drew on cigarettes, made comments on the scene before them: a typically Pakistani scene of amiable disorder. Beside the Chinese the Pakistanis looked even more clean, coiffured, well-dressed. The Chinese faces revealed nothing. They watched everything cool as cowboys.

The trucks they were bringing into Pakistan were Japanese. Isusi. Three were huge and laden with unmarked containers. Ropes lashed down the cargo, and to prevent the ropes fraying on the metal edge of the truck they were cushioned by old Chinese slippers. The four smaller trucks were blue, with "Sinotrans" painted on the door. On them were boxes and boxes of "Fine China, made in China."

It's hard to imagine two more disparate cultures bordering each other, though Sost is hardly Pakistan, nor Kashgar China. On this side of the barrier the Pakistanis are neat, dapper, mill about with shawls thrown over their heads in the unaccustomed coolness. They have not the quite frightening efficiency of the Chinese. To get their enormous packages through customs may take some doing. In a tea-house, one merchant sat unhappily on a bench reading and rereading a scrap of paper stamped by the customs people. It said—in English—"Confiscated: 4,000 very tiny pad-locks." Beside him sat a majestic Sindhi man, with a pillbox hat and curly-toed slippers. He had, he said, come back from a three-month trip from Karachi to Shanghai, Beijing and Hong Kong. He bought mechanical parts and shipped them home by sea, but he himself endured the journey overland.

"So I come home with several thousand!" He laughed. Several thousand what? Tiny padlocks?

"Oh, you know—tourists, tourists, business, business!"

The Chinese trucks were given clearance, and rolled off into the Hunza valley. It's all downhill from here. Tomorrow they would be in Gilgit, bringing to Pakistan gas meters and fire extinguishers, tea sets, silks, pencil sharpeners cunningly disguised as pink pianos, nail clippers in the form of green plastic elephants. The trucks followed each other out of sight: past the spate of new hotels celebrating the old trading—the Marco Polo Lodge, the Silk Road Inn, and the bank—a huge safe at the roadside.

As ever, a few steps off the beaten track and life moved more slowly undisturbed by the business of the border post. On a plateau overlooking the road is the village of Nazirabad. Its track leads steeply off the road. Now the day's business had been done, the trucks had passed and, the Gilgit bus long gone, a rural quiet again fell upon the place. The river roared and the flags fluttered. A man cycled hard to keep up with the white-eyed mule he chased along the Friendship Highway. I laughed, he laughed, the mule took its chance and veered off towards its mates at the river-bank. The dust-track up to Nazirabad petered out at the Aga Khan school, where a red motorbike, perhaps the teacher's, waited. The village was flat, not banked up on a hillside. New houses peeked between apple trees, whose fruit grew fat and heavy. But for that, it could have been a Highland village, with the quiet road as a spine. As in the Highlands, the road had brought its own detritus: beneath the trees a couple of knackered vehicles stood on stones. As in Highland villages, new bungalows shone beside the old croft cottages which began to fall in and decay, their roof-beams gone. The new buildings had chimneys and electricity.

I walked across an apple orchard and through the village. A woman was flailing the crop of beans; she offered me some, they were hard as bullets. Chickens pecked at the grey gravel. A girl offered me a huge rosy apple, and a man some butter-tea in a Chinese bowl. In his home was a baby swaddled tightly in blankets, asleep in a cradle hewn long ago from some venerable tree. It had rocked for generations and accumulated a plenitude of charms, talismans, ribbons and beads. A solid-looking object wrapped in red cloth was tied to the cradle's end: the Qur'an. The little packages worn by children to banish night-fears dangled from its handle. A huge cowrie shell on a string, beads and bows, to keep the sleeping baby safe.

I left, full of apples and tea, just as school was coming out. Washing was spread on the briars to dry. The enormity of Pakistani trousers, and vast shawls. Children spilled around me, girls and boys mixed. This village is divided from the next by a deep ravine. I walked down the twisting footpath, met no one, and crossed the little plank bridge into the next village. At the mosque there, children were sitting outside for a lesson. They were supposed to be singing, or chanting, but the girls gave me shy stares as I passed.

That night, after dark, I sat on the doorstep of my hotel. Inside several young Germans, who were going to China, pored over guidebooks. A young man rode up through the dark on a bicycle entirely without lights. He was in fatigues from head to toe. I recognised him as the man I'd seen in the green verandah of the mosque, leading the girls in their lesson. He was very young, scarcely older than his eldest pupils. We sat on the step of the Mountain View and looked at the stars in the northern sky. We talked about China. When he wasn't teaching, and sometimes when he was, he dealt in silks. He'd been to Kashgar, Urumchi, for them—the first time in 1986, when he was seventeen.

He looked up at the black mass of the mountains which surrounded us. He said, "My father, mother, at this time are in the high pasture; it is in Khunjerab, 50 kilometres from here."

"For how long?"

"Three months."

Three months up in the high pasture. It sounded like bliss.

"What do they eat?"

"Food!"

"There are no fields."

"They take from here. Eat animal food: meat, butter, cheese. Now they are fat, and soon come down."

"What do you do in winter, when the Pass is closed?"

"Nothing!"

"Nothing?"

"Sleep. Twenty-four hours. Winter is marriage season; dance, sing. But I no marriage. I do not like winter. I go to Karachi, Peshawar. This road is difficult in winter. I don't know the story of this place, but our grandfathers came from Tashkurgan, and this Wakhi is also spoken in Afghanistan."

He talked about teaching—he'd studied way down south in Karachi and came home to the northernmost tip of the country, back to the village. It was a good job, he said, a good thing to do, to help the village.

There was little transport south the next day. The bus had gone, and in the yard which housed minibuses, only chickens pecked. Over the wall was a midden, and round the back the plumbed-in toilets of some new commercial enterprise just spilled their contents on to the rocky river-bank, to dry stinking in the sun. On the reddish pillars of rock through which the road has been cut, there hung the shadows of choughs.

A minibus eventually appeared, was repaired, and did a few turns up and down the road, drumming up trade. The driver leaned out of the window, persuading all and sundry to go to Gilgit. Without eight passengers he would not go. You never see a vehicle in this country less than jammed full. There were few takers, though. The restaurateurs and customs men had their own thing to do. Four fellows with enormous boxes were involved in an argument in the customs shed. A soldier emerged from his tent to lift the barrier for a tractor adorned with tinsel. When it had gone and silence fell, you could hear the calls of the women in the fields. They never come down here.

The minibus stopped for the umpteenth time outside the tea-houses and the driver called to the assembled shopkeepers. It was a waste of time; no one would come, there were no spare people. I resigned myself to another day in Sost—but no, there was a con-floption, and there emerged from a tea-house a very old, thickset gent, a Uigur, with a green Kashgari skullcap on his bald dome.

Several people helped his progress. He walked slowly, leaning heavily on his stick. He had a Parkinsonian shake. The sliding door was opened, and slowly, with infinite shaking progress, he was ensconced, the stick between his knees and his old head nodding over it, for the journey to Gilgit.

The driver, the old gent and the cluster who had assisted got involved in a heated discussion, until the driver's friend said "Chelo," and we at last set off.

Though the journeys are long, you get used to them, and even still I feel a huge exhilaration driving around the Northern Areas. Though you ache and are bored stupid, you've thought every thought, dreamed every daydream, but some corner will turn and the river thrashing below or the soaring mountain above or the sheer wild beauty of a village will remind you why you came. Sost is a charmless collection of breeze-block buildings and tents and shacks, but cool and refreshing. I was happy to head back to Gilgit. As buses go, this one was underdecorated, just the poor Aga Khan dancing about from the mirror as we veered round corners. Now he had sufficient passengers to be in handsome profit, the driver gloated: "*You are my passengers, it is my luck!*" There was the venerable old Uigur man, the driver, a mysterious friend of the driver (there always is—"he is my onegoodfriend" means he is my friend, or I owe this bloke some favour, or I can't see a thing in these specs so he must sit on top of the gear lever and direct me). The day was turning hot.

By the time we left town we were half full. "*It is my luck!*" cried the driver. The old man fished sweeties from his pocket and sucked in a solemn grandfatherly manner. The friend of the driver, who wore a dashing Jacquard jersey, turned and said, "This Chinaman, he is come from Kashgar to Saudi Arabia! From Saudi Arabia he is coming to Kashgar, but his visa is not correct, and now he must go all the way back to Islamabad, and then all the way back to Sost."

"He's come to Saudi and back, and they won't let him cross, a poor old man?"

"It is his visa."

"But he's obviously a Kashgari, they should just let him in."

"What can he do?"

The poor old fellow looked very calm about this disaster. He would have to lean shaking over his stick for forty hours of bus.

"He is travelling all on his own?"

"Yes!"

"No family?"

"Lone. Like you!"

For a moment I understood the consternation that met lone

women in Pakistan, the same concerned astonishment I felt for this poor old trembling man, nodding his old cap over his stick, being mucked about by customs guards far from home. The driver turned and had a word with him; he gave a monosyllabic grunt. I admired his self-possession.

The road turned and turned, following the river. Now we passed a couple of abandoned buildings, strangely affecting in their barren surroundings. They looked on us with skull-like staring windows. The single telegraph wire, the river and the empty road all journeyed together. We passed squalid villages which the road seemed to have done little to improve, where shawl-swathed girls averted their eyes and cows lolloped out of the way. We had to slow down where the snout of a glacier had simply bulldozed the road into the river; you could lean from the window and touch the grey-gravelly ice. There was a twig bridge over the river, and an alluring path propped up by slender tree trunks led round a rocky bluff and on to some remote valley, days away. The road passed through deserted wastes, bound by mountains. These are places which in my perversity I find more affecting than all the gardens of Hunza. Derelict buildings, empty oil-drums, bare rubble, so far from the "Mountain Trip Soup Hut" and the fruit stalls of Karimabad. On high scree slopes, the message "Welcome, our beloved Emir!" Men flagged us down, and every time a deal was negotiated, the passenger clambered in, the driver giggled: *Is my luck!* By the time we reached the township of Passu his luck had brought him quite a throng: his onegoodfriend, the poor old Uigur, an English carpenter, assorted hill-farmers with sacks of potatoes on the roof, two smiley Japanese students of agriculture, and a wandering Sufi mystic.

I'd always wanted to meet a wandering Sufi, and had in my head some image drawn from dervishes. I imagined long conicular robes and a tall hat. This one was wearing loud golfing trousers and a tweed jacket. He looked like an eccentric Bavarian entomologist, but he did have a grey beard, and sunglasses. We had stopped for a cup of tea, served on a rustic bench beneath a shady tree. He appeared like a vision by the bumper of the bus. He was alluring. I went to see what this extraordinary figure could be. He grabbed my hand, pumped it up and down and clapped my back; he cried "Welcome to my country!" and I realised he was no Bavarian, and had no teeth whatsoever.

"You are from . . .? Ah! I like Scotch whisky! I had an English professor. Now I am going from here to there teaching on Human Rights!"

A small crowd surrounded him. He took the Japanese students in a warm embrace from which they tried to extricate themselves, smiling and smiling.

"Human Rights?"

"Why not! We cannot solve the problems of the world like this . . ."—he crashed his fists together— " . . . but at the table! Sufis . . ."

"You are a Sufi?"

He inclined his grey beard. From the corner of my eye I saw the bus driver and his onegoodfriend exchange glances.

"Sufis say: If there is man, I am holding him in affection, I am speaking my heart to his heart, he is my brother, and he . . ."

"What about she?"

"Ahh! My dear!" He took me in a great bear hug. "Sufism knows no distinction between sex, old age, big, small. Human Rights I am speaking! Also I am palmist, you know, telling fortune, and also I am head of Acme Insurance Company, Lahore."

I wanted to know how such a fatalistic people bothered with insurance; but it was time to pile aboard the bus. The driver looked uneasily at the several hundredweight of potatoes on his roof. Apricots were past, now it was potatoes. Every lane or track that came down from the hills to join the Highway was piled high with potatoes.

We set the Sufi down at the next village, there to talk on Human Rights. As we pulled away, he shouted to one and all: "My second daughter is to be married in Lahore in four months. Should you be in Lahore, you must come to the wedding celebrations! Goodbye!"

We left him standing by the roadside, smiling away to himself.

"Carpenter?" said the driver to the carpenter. "I was also carpenter, in Saudi."

"That's how you speak Arabic?"

"Yes; you see I speak with this Chinaman. Also he is speaking Arabic."

"You speak Arabic and English."

"And Wakhi, it is the language of Sost."

"Also Urdu," said the friend. "And Pushto."

"Stop!"

"I can understand this Burushaski, not speak. I have a degree from Karachi, in Arts."

"And you are author?" he said to me. I said I was, of a sort.

"Also my friend is author." The friend asked: "In your country, who earns more, author or carpenter?"

"Carpenter."

The author sighed, as if this confirmed some terrible suspicion. We fell into silence amid the shouting throng of the tea-house, and ate our potatoes. The poor old Uigur man chased a piece of potato around his tin plate with a scrap of chapati. It was too painful to watch; his hands shook so much he could hardly make the journey from plate to mouth. Over and over again he dropped his potato, and splashed fat on his clothes. I was having some sort of Proustian experience with mine; the taste of the mutton-fat made me think of Scottish Sundays, broth, Sunday School, uncomfy skirts, my nana shelling peas. Out of the window the sun blasted on the earth and stones, too harsh to look at. There are places so hot the stones have turned to glass.

"Why are you driving a bus up and down to Sost? You'd be a professor in my country." Then I thought of all the graduates I knew, waitressing.

"This is a private bus. I have luck, many passengers!"

"You've got a degree and umpteen languages."

"I also have a shop, but no problem, someone is there today, I didn't want to go there. And it is my luck! When I came back from Saudi, I bought this wagon, a shop, and a flour mill for my village. From Karachi."

His luck held. At Abbotabad he was turning away sacks of potatoes, but with bad grace accepted a simpleton, whose father was in some state of concern lest he forget where to get off again. Two glaciologists piled in, and a silent threesome.

"Teef!" hissed the driver. "I do not like this persons. Look your baggage, they are teef persons!"

A woman in full billowing black burqa stepped down from a Suzuki and walked straight into our path. He missed her by inches, directed a well-aimed spit at her back, and shouted something foul in Arabic. A boy on a man's bike warranted the same treatment when he wobbled from a track on to the road. No concession for villages was made. No one was killed, it was his luck.

On a bridge was graffiti'd: KSO. Nationalism is our aim. Karakoram Students' Organisation—We wants kill you. KSO! You are our enemy!

An itinerant storyteller had appeared in Gilgit. He was not of these parts, but dark-skinned and plump. He sat on a rock outside the ammunition dealer's, and drew crowds of woollen-capped boys and men to hear his swooping voice and dramatic flights on the squeeze-box. A row of wagons had rolled into town, and were unloaded by Dark-Age figures in hessian shrouds. On their backs they carried sacks of sugar and flour.

To touch one of these trucks was like touching a remote and

fabled creature, slightly unpredictable; an elephant, perhaps. The doors of these majestic Bedfords are carved like the portals to a castle, the cab within lit bordello-red. The running boards and footplates are wrought iron or shining embossed chrome. On top of the cab is a howdah, for the truck is surely evolved from the elephant. In the howdah travel the boy, tarpaulins, and perhaps a goat. The front of the howdah is raised like a tiara, painted with scenes of fighter aircraft, or a busty Fatima on a white horse, or rivers and trucks. There must be an entire guild of truck-painters, masters of the kind of art we see only on travelling fairgrounds. The wagons' high sides are a bestiary, an aviary, an aquarium of beasts and birds. Many of the images are religious: mosques, the Kaaba. Some are decidedly secular—a passenger liner, a tropical island with palm trees, a spread eagle, gold and blue.

Above the cab, but beneath the Neanderthal forehead of the howdah, there must be some crowning glory, say a whirring windmill. The wheel arches and window surround shine and gleam with mosaics of chrome. I like the names best. In *Jackie* magazine there used to appear an advert—hands with long nails typed this cryptic message to teenage girls: "f u cn rd ths msg y cn bcm a sec & gt gd jb." I could read the message, but never did get a good job; instead ended up in Pakistan amusing myself in tea-houses by translating the calligraphy of trucks. They used the same strange shorthand, so as to cram the words in. In gold, green, red, jewel colours they read "LHR RPD GLT FWD AGY." Lahore-Rawalpindi-Gilgit-Forwarding-Agency. "SWT GDS TPT COY RGD G. MDI RPDI." Sometimes a list of the driver's favourite things: Disco Rado Bed Ford. F1.11.

With their frequent appeal to discos I began to wonder if trucks didn't enjoy the slightly risqué reputation suggested by the red lights of the cabs at night. I had a lift in one for a slow mile or two, an old-fashioned one where the doors were of carved wood—none of your chrome. Behind the driver was a panel of mirror-work.

Pinned to the ceiling, magazine pictures of this year's film stars. A sticker showed a saucy girl in the act of winking, with her finger pressed to her lips: *Shhh!* Do not disturb. Fixed to the centre of the dashboard was a specimen vase with a spray of plastic mimosa. An astonishing number of people inhabited the truck and climbed around it while in motion, like trick riders at a circus. A circus! At last I had run away with the circus.

Jamila was making chapatis on an outside fire. She pulled the soft dough up on to her forearm, making perfect circles. She didn't look up when I came in through the green gates. "Why were you in Sost?"

I said, "How the hell did you know I was in Sost?"

She said, "Rashida, her Ali's one brother was also there, he did see you, he tell Ali, Ali tell Rashida, Rashida tell me."

"Nothing's secret, is it?"

"No!" She laughed. "No secrets!'

4 Askole by Night

I smelled goats' shit and woodsmoke, and realised that, high on icy glaciers, there are no smells. We'd dropped to 10,000 feet; the air was heavy with oxygen. I walked up a rough grove lined with injured trees, like one entranced. Tiny fields were creeping towards harvest. From deep inside a crop of peas, I heard a woman cough-cough-coughing. A filthy child clambered up a dry-stone wall, and said, "Alo Alo Alo Alo." Then she stuck out her tongue and flicked it with a forefinger. Sweets? Got any sweets? Then I was through the fields and in the village proper, following a stream up between stone-walled homesteads. A pall of blue woodsmoke rose through holes in their earthen roofs.

The path took me beside the mosque. There was a lamp burning inside, and the murmur of prayers. Through a house window, I saw a candle burning. It lit the wooden stalls where the people slept.

Then I was in a strange little room, one of a group like figures in a Rembrandt; sculpted faces in unlikely headgear, lit by a single oil lantern. I didn't know why I had climbed the rough ladder and entered this room. Someone had brought me here. Food was being prepared. There were some young men in caps, bandannas, very tattered anoraks. One began a polite conversation about marriage practices, but I was too tired to connect. Did he tell me he was twenty-five, and had three children by his fifteen-year-old wife? He brought servings of goaty dhal, and said the Haji was away on an ibex-hunting trip. In the corners of the room shadows moved. I thought I remembered being here before, on my first visit to Baltistan in 1984. It was the home of the village elder, Haji Mahdi.

Descriptions of Askole have been written by Europeans for a hundred years: "A poor village indeed, and certainly one of the dirtiest in Baltistan." That was in 1904. It hasn't changed. The first explorers reached for the same words as I did now: mountain walls, detritus, disintegrating rock, torrents and oases. De Filippi wrote: "Few communities are so cut off from the world as this little population of Askole. Before them lies an infinite extent of glaciers, behind them a desert valley, which for eight months of the year is absolutely blocked."

The walk down from Snow Lake, on the infinite extent of glaciers, had taken three days. The glacier was stable, so at night my two companions and I had pitched the tent, secured it with ice axes, and slept there. There seemed no point in hauling ourselves over the mounds of moraine into the ablatial valleys, for the sake of a scratch of grass. Although the Biafo Glacier was three miles wide, you could see every stone strewn on it, every bird's bone.

The air was as razor clean. We walked, ate the little we had, slept fully clothed: balaclavas, gloves.

Where the crevasses were too wide to jump, we had to walk in wide zigzags to avoid them. The glacier swept on, in its deep silence. I thought: Far in the future, when all is done, the M1 will look like this: a swathe of ice as far as we can see. It will serve us right.

The events of that morning already felt like an age away. We overshot the route off the glacier, and spent hours retracing our steps on the narrow ridges of moraine. We were in the spoil-heap of the world. The air was so clear that distance and light played tricks: greenish slopes that seemed close enough to touch were a day's walk away. The grass looks pitiful, but the local people bring goats up here to graze. Time was when the Nagari men would race across the Hispar and Braldo Glaciers to raid Askole. I didn't want to know. What they could do in hours took us days, and still we missed the cairns that showed the way off the glacier and on to the loose mountainside where a path would—inshallah—conduct us over a col and down to the river Braldo. At its snout, the glacier was no longer icy but black under a burden of rubble which it slowly conveyed to the river. These were the rocks which trundled and banged their way downstream. I thought we would never get off that hideous moraine. "Askole by night!" had become our rallying cry, what we said to each other.

We climbed the col and dropped down, by the narrowest path, to the riverside. It was like being readmitted to paradise. It was a desert. From ice to desert in one day. A lizard on a hot rock, a dog-rose bush, a bird, were like miracles. The Braldo river, a grey mess of glacier-melt, roared in its channel below. In the future, the strange glacial forms, its pillars and wind-sculpted plinths would figure in my dreams; but for now, I wanted only to reach the village.

The path was but a beaten way between rocks. It dropped through a steep nullah and I stopped to drink and wash and just throw water about in sheer exhausted exuberance. The sun caught the water-drops and sparkled them. The path rose through boulder-strewn plateaux. Around the next bend I'd see Askole . . . the next . . . the next . . .

I walked on. We straggled out, Paul and Janet and I, glad to be out of danger and off the ice, glad to be at a lower altitude, and able to walk alone. On the glacier, we hadn't dared stray more than a couple of yards from each other. Once or twice we even tied ourselves together with a rope.

Often now I rested my pack against a boulder at the side of the path, then carried on a diminishing number of yards. I was very tired. Every bend, I thought I'd see the village, its fields and trees, but every bend revealed new obstacles. Now the path stopped at the foot of a buttress of rock. High above, where the rock was sheer there jutted out man-made galleries of flat stones and thin tree trunks. They looked as if they'd grown by themselves like fungus on a tree. I began to climb the polished route, was conducted around the bluff, high above the river, and gingerly down the other side. Now lowering sun was shining straight into my eyes. When I turned to look back at the tower I'd just descended, the word "rookery" came into my head.

I was so tired—past tired now—that strange images and dreamlike notions floated into my mind, but dissolved again, like snow on water. I kept on through the boulder-fields, boulders the size of cars. Up and down nullahs. Far away, on the opposite side of the impassable river, there was a smear of coarse pasture. By now I could walk only a few yards at a time. Surely, around the next bend I'd see Askole.

In the middle of a boulder-field was a short stone wall. It divided nothing from nothing. Cut into the wall was a gateway of such simplicity it was almost holy, two uprights and a crossbeam of untreated wood, just trunks of slender trees. Then, round the next bend, I was there. Eden, tucked in among the mountains.

Tiny terraces and water-ways and poplar trees, the sudden colours, and earthy smells, a woman in a field of peas, coughing.

It was very dark when the others arrived. Where there is no electricity, the people go to bed at nightfall. It might have been 8 p.m., but it felt like midnight. Another European, too tall for the door, dipped his head and entered. He wore a bush hat with a scarf tied round it. His clothes had once been pale, but now took the hue of Askole dust. He was speaking in Balti. When a snarling dogfight broke out in the yard outside, he too could join in the laughing and swearing. He said his name was Ken, a Canadian. He was an anthropologist. He had been here this summer and last. This sounded so interesting, but I couldn't think for fatigue. When I asked Ken if the food we had received was a gift, or should we offer to pay, he raised both hands and intoned, "I am here to observe, not interfere." I took that, and what I recalled of the Haji's business ventures, to mean "pay."

Later, I lay beside the others, in a sleeping bag, in the schoolyard-cum-camp site, far too tired to sleep. In my mind, the stars, which were shining brightly, got confused with the schoolyard where I lay. I thought of the stars as children, tumbling out into the playground. I tried to think of new names for the old constellations: the smoothing iron; the Volvo. Still sleep would not come, but instead two village dogs. I pulled an ice axe close.

I must have dozed, because in the dead of the dark night, when the village turned in on itself and coughed, someone was abroad. He had a strong torch and was shining it full in my face. It penetrated my sleep, and I swam back to consciousness alarmed and ready to yell—what the hell was going on, who was shining that thing in my eyes? But I woke to realise I was challenging the moon.

•••

Because it was summertime no boys came to the earth-walled classroom at the bottom of the yard. The yard was much bigger than before; a bigger camping space. I think that was when I began to feel uneasy, when I saw the little camping yard had expanded three times. Not a blade of grass grew from its packed earth. All this I noted from my sleeping bag, which I couldn't bear to leave. I tried to find the exact word to describe the way my feet felt. *Cambozola.* That did it. Now I wanted food. Cheese, fruit, fresh green vegetables. Toast, butter and marmalade. In Skardu, at least there would be egg and chips. But though Paul and Janet were pressing on to Skardu, I opted to stay just for a day or two. Unlike them I had no job, no particular place to go. Later, I walked with them to the edge of the village, along the little earth path between the terraces, and there bid them farewell, watching for a while till they disappeared round the next bluff, then I went back to the village.

Under the single tree in the middle of the schoolyard was a sagging khaki tent. Written on its side was *POLice-POST, ASKOLi*. In a corner where two mud and stone walls met, a little fire burned. The policeman was preparing his breakfast.

A village man climbed the stile into the yard. He wore layers of ragged clothing and an old cap. His face was wizened, his teeth were small and brown. He held one of our tin plates; a dog had stolen it. "Doctor?" he said. He pointed to his foot, in its little toe-less rubber boot. Another man was already climbing the stile, with a lacklustre girl in his arms.

"I'm sorry."

"Doctor, no?"

None the less, the first in this pathetic queue hunkered down in the dust and began to unwind from his grimy ankle a collection of rags, polythene and leaves, to reveal some open sores. Then came the little dull-eyed baby, in her anxious father's arms, and a boy whose wounded foot had been treated with the traditional poultice of fresh dung. On the house-roofs, and washing in the stream, were blind old women with goitres at their throats, and I knew that within the homes, with the chickens and the smoke, were those with leprosy and cerebral palsy, who do not come outdoors.

A couple of handsome girls in full Askole attire walked up the lane with spades over their shoulders. They stuck out their tongues and flicked them lasciviously. Give us a sweet! Go on! The man with the bad foot threw his old pus-stained bandage into the stream the people drink from, and grinned.

In the summer, when the paths are open, the Western trekkers come, like another bright summer crop, and the village men go for porters. Askole is the last village on the Braldo Gorge, before the mountains. The Baltoro Glacier, the long Biafo-Hispar system leading west to Hunza, K2, Broad Peak, The Gasherbrums. Trekking groups and mountaineering expeditions pass through the little village, sometimes stopping to erect their tents in the schoolyard and buy a goat for the porters to eat. At dawn, they leave again, the porters dwarfed under the weight of their loads, their legs like rope. Village economies have shifted from subsistence to cash. They make money, but people get tense. I remember seeing a latter-day Italian photographer, some eighty years after de Filippi, being pelted with rocks for photographing women unawares; for jumping on to the flat roofs of the houses and photographing women. The rumour is that the women get it bad, especially down at Chilas, on Nanga Parbat side. The expeditions bring porters from other villages. The men get wary of these off-comers eyeing up their women, and the women are prevailed upon to stay even more out of sight, across the too-short summer.

The village is like a three-dimensional snakes and ladders. Little tight lanes wiggle like snakes between the dry-stone walls. This is the animal layer. Goats look out from windows like gossiping neighbours. So they keep warm the people in the layer above, who reach their homes by ladder. The summers are spent out on the roofs, looking at the mountains, the villages on the other bank of the river, the yellowing terraces. There are summer bedrooms, and piles of drying fodder. The whole village can communicate by means of its roofs, and ladders.

It was strange to be alone. I walked the quarter-mile uphill to where a wall topped with a tangle of briars marked the border of the village. On this side of the wall were grasses and wild flowers, butterflies and dragonflies. There was a copse of trees where the stream entered the village lands in a sparkling sheen. One could worship this laughing water. It is the font of life.

Outwith the wall is a blank face of rock which grew to tower above the village at its feet. It was glorious to wash in the fresh spring water, but I didn't stay long, because I felt uncomfortable, odd and displaced without the others, yet to grow back into my own skin. It must be how Rashida and Jamila feel on the rare occasions they are alone. From several fields away a man waved to me, cheerfully. He was working with a spade to maintain the irrigation channels. I took care to stand on no crops, but to follow the tiny paths as best I could between the little terraces, stepping from one to the next, following where they led. There were peas growing, fodder choked with wild flowers. Butterflies and bees. In some fields the irrigation stream was running, in others it had been recently diverted and the path was fresh mud. I didn't feel comfortable wandering between the fields. I felt I was being watched, and rightly: they weren't mine to wander in.

In the middle of the day a party of Americans arrived and began to pitch tents. They chose to sleep not in the camp site but in another place, where the village petered out into desert. In the camp site they had their cook and guide erect a mess-tent, and there appeared picnic chairs, stoves, kettles, eggs, fruit. They had tarpaulin, polythene: hard currency in the villages. A small and wondering crowd gathered—of boys and ragged men with babes in arms, and a miller's boy floury from head to toe.

In the evening Ken came over. "Do you know who pitched those tents?" he asked. "They're in the graveyard. The people are upset, eh? This is the camp site here. They're trying to contain the problem, provide a camp site, and what do they get? Tents in the cemetery."

Ken lit a cigarette, and sat beside me. A village man leaned over the wall and made some raucous comment. The people had taken to Ken. So the trekkers were a problem to be contained?

"What do the people think of Westerners?" I asked.

Ken laughed a hollow laugh. "That's been kinda fun, watching the interaction. Let's just say there's misunderstandings on both sides. I'm picking up the language. I learned some when I was here last year. I'm looking at Indigenous Risk Management. I'm looking at these people's strategies for reducing risks. Every risk, from inbreeding to crop disease."

As you enter the villages little boys try to sell you a small embroidered pouch, a glorified version of those they wear round their own necks. It is a talisman against evil. They clutch their throats, roll their eyes, fall writhing to the ground, pick up a stone and play at avalanches: a pretty good mime of the awful things that can befall a traveller. For immunity from these dangers, they offer this nicely embroidered talisman. Five rupees. I guess that's what we think of as Askole Risk Management, at a glance.

Ken needed litle prompting. His own relationship with the trekkers was as uneasy as the villagers.' They brought company, news, a drop to smoke or drink, and at times some decent food.

"There are three hundred souls in Askole. Four extended families," Ken said. "One of the families is an off-comer, they've only been here a couple of centuries. Their name has some connotation of mental deficiency. They might be right. It's taboo to marry within the village, you know that?"

Ken said the village was older than the people themselves believed. "The Haji says it's only three hundred years old, but it was mentioned in some Persian manuscript in 1450."

When the sun began to dip behind the mountains, making pink billowy veils out of the clouds, the mountaintips turned gold. It was inexpressibly beautiful. That sort of optical illusion was happening again. It was paradise until you screwed up your eyes and saw it as a filthy collection of disease-ridden hovels. Ken waved his hand towards the fields, the hundreds of tiny terraced fields. "For weeks I was trying to get to understand who owned what. It's all to do with the question. You've got to ask the right questions, the very word. The exact word."

"How collective is it?"

"Not as much as it used to be. I wanted to know how the fields are divided between the families, good fields and bad. How the risk of bad yields is managed. But could I get the word? I just couldn't trigger it. It was as if no one wanted to tell me. Weeks and weeks I tried. Then the other day I was walking up the fields with this guy, and suddenly he started to tell me. Just like that."

I had a sudden image of the irrigation systems: how by the simple lifting of one critical stone, the right question, the streams begin to gurgle and flow, splashing from one growing field to the next and the next.

"And crop disease. How they control that. Diseases are variety-specific, yeah? So to avoid total blight they plant three varieties. Three kinds of peas, for example. The overall yield is less, but if there is a disease, you don't lose the whole lot. It's rationale. There's such a rationale. That's the thing with development agencies, they come up here and say: You can improve your yield by doing this or that. Get them to plant this strain of wheat or that. They just don't appreciate the rationale. These people have survived here for centuries. They've got to know something." Ken's voice veered between a laconic North American, through excitement, to a sense of urgency.

"How many fields are there?"

"I tried counting. I'm mapping them all. But I'll tell you this: each one has its name. Every one of the tiny fields has its name. And the names are so old, no one knows where they came from or what they mean."

In the soft evening light, the harsh shadows had gone and one could look about in comfort. Many Askole people have closed-up squinting eyes from so much sun, and the smoke. But in the evening it was beautiful. A goat bleated; the clouds turned mauve, the peaks golden above the darkening valley, and I felt as if Ken was describing a poem. Ancient names and exactitude. Rationale and the precise word, as if the village were as tightly managed as a beautiful poem, so well crafted you could not see the joins, so assumed, wrongly, that there were none, that it was all a happy accident.

People came in from the fields for their evening meal. The Americans camped in the graveyard sat at their table beneath some trees. Ken was going to override the "observe, don't interfere" principle and have a polite word. "Might get supper, too," he said.

In the morning he called over the schoolyard wall: "Come with me, I'll show you a photograph."

He led me to the place we'd eaten the first night. Women looked down from their rooftops as we passed below, bones and dung crunching under our feet in the narrow lanes. Though the men had taken the shalwar-kameez, the women kept traditional homespun tunics and hats. Balti people are of Tibetan descent; they came as nomads in the ninth century, and no doubt they brought their costumes with them. The women wear their hair in many tiny plaits, the way Tibetan women still do, but the Askole hat is a wonder. All that glisters is attached to the upturned peak: shells, date stones, broken zips, buttons, foreign coins are all arranged pleasingly and sewn on. Their tunics too. We stood aside for two women with creels of fodder on their backs. One had a resplendent display of ring-pulls stitched to her shirt. Her companion wore a deep beaded necklace over her tunic. They smelled of woodsmoke. In Askole, there was none of the coy turning away of the purdah-observing women. Maybe they are too much with the beasts and the seasons. Without their work in the fields, the village would surely starve. As she passed, the first woman looked at me, then Ken, and made some raucous remark that needed no translation. A clove of garlic dangled from her hat.

"I like to think they're reluctant Muslims," Ken said. "Do you know, they smashed their musical instruments, fifteen years ago. It was a collective decision, but the Mullah had a lot to do with it."

I told Ken about the last occasion I was here, six years ago. It was the end of Ramadan, and the end of the fast and the heralding of the Eid would occur at the sight of the new moon. It was a cloudy night, not the best for watching the skies. The village schoolmaster stuck his radio to his ear to hear the official confirmation, the way we mistrust our own watches at Hogmanay and feel we must watch Big Ben on TV. But I remembered seeing some village men, hunkered on a mound, looking up at the sky. And when it came, they greeted the sight of the moon with an eldritch cry, like wolves, a howling and baying like wolves. It made my hair stand on end. Then in the morning, to break the fast, the Haji brought us a dish of sweet noodles.

"They're very hospitable people."

"Overburdened?"

"Totally overburdened."

I tried to imagine the reaction if a bunch of Baltis turned up in an English village, pitched camp in the graveyard, wandered around the village peering into folks' houses, making comments in some weird tongue. At Christmas, to boot. The poison chalice, because rumour was they could cure your ailing children, and give you rope, clothing, batteries. The Mullah probably didn't like them, but did they like the Mullah?

We reached the house. "A bit more stucco on the wall and it would be a Mexican café," said Ken. "You want any cheese?" Here the village headman kept a shop. He dealt in mountaineers' requisites, buying from one trip and selling to another. In the spare room were extraordinary things: tins of sauerkraut, packets of chocolate mousse, the flotsam left by a retreating tide of trekkers. I was glad to buy a tin of Swiss cheese, and wait in the gloom as Ken disappeared into his lodging and fetched the photograph.

I looked at it by the light of a little stained-glass window. It showed Askole: a few flat-roofed buildings, some trees, and the omnipresent mountains.

"Taken in 1909."

"Nothing's changed."

"Everything. That's the point. It's not there now. The whole village has shifted. See the hills? I went to the exact place he must have taken this picture. I could line up the mountains in the background, yeah? These buildings are gone. It's all gone."

I couldn't explain why that was so strange, and interesting. Why Ken felt it too.

"Are you going to stay here all winter? Down among the animals, four foot of snow on the roof?"

"Hell, no, hey, I like my car and my computer, you know?"

Ken told me a strange story. He wanted to look at conceptual and perceptual differences. To explain, he pointed to the mountain on the other side of the river which dominates the little village at its feet. "One day I saw a strange star thing there. We all saw it, all the village. It was just hanging there. And then it moved, that way, fast. The people were asking me what it was, but hell, I was as freaked as they were. But we got talking about stars, and I started to talk about the solar system and all. What did I get? Blank stares. It's not ignorance. They perceive things different. I want to find out how."

A new respect for the villagers was growing on me. Before I'd felt for them a wonder that they survived at all in the most inhospitable of places, but now I was learning how tightly screwed down it all was, how managed. Every tree, Ken said, was spoken for, every shrub and bush belonged to someone. The stream of trekkers and climbers and porters and all was a problem to be contained. And one of the problems with the trekking parties and the expeditions was that they were far too big, far too much of a burden. The incoming porters, hundreds of them, cut the villagers' trees for firewood, even if the Western boss tried to stop them. And people preferred to go behind rocks rather than use the village latrines. And they camped in the cemetery.

The old men, and a few of the young ones, were sitting in the shade of the mosque. It was a crèche. They held the babies in their laps while the women worked the fields. The babies were grubby and wore little canvas helmets. The old men were making rope from goats' wool. In the villages, the simpletons are given work. Often they wander the lanes, spinning with a distaff. Grinning and spinning, spinning and grinning. A cloud of grey wool foamed at the feet of the men at the mosque. Backwards down the lane the spinners walked, beside the stream. Chickens fluttered under their feet. They held weighted handles, like football rattles or prayer-wheels, with an end of the wool attached. As they swung the handle, the wool twisted tight into rope. Every other year they replace the bridge across the Braldo, which connects Askole with the village on the other bank. It's a swooping affair, made of twisted twigs. Three cables of twigs: one to walk on, one on either side to cling to. The whole tips to one side when you put your weight on it, and the thrashing river below upsets your stomach and your mind. If you fall off, you are dead. Therefore you stay on, and shake for the rest of the day.

That evening the Askole policeman emerged from his tent, stretched, scratched and shambled towards us. The Americans had a guide, a big bearded man from Hunza. He'd packed his charges off to bed and sat with us. The policeman came in plastic flip-flops, a notebook in his right hand and a fag in his left. He had two days of stubble on his chin and a striped waistcoat over his shalwar-kameez. He looked like the air-raid warden in "Dad's Army." He addressed us all, threw back his head and began a great long story of complaint. With his cigarette he pointed north, the notebook he waved towards the south. The story wandered east and west, arrived home, and began again. Anwar the guide understood it. He spoke Burushaski, the Askole people Balti, and between them, Urdu. Anwar made conciliatory noises, and nodded a lot, and tried to interrupt. The complaint was about people who go where they are not supposed to go. Who wander up the Baltoro Glacier without permission, without the required permit to enter militarily sensitive areas, who dodge him, the policeman, and get him into all sorts of hot water. At length he shambled back to his tent and Anwar spat. "Police! What do they do? They disturb the people and take their money."

"Why do they take their money?"

"Because they are Muslim! Muslim! All they want is money." He gave a sly look. "You like Benazir?"

He must have got the right answer because he stood to check his people were asleep, then said, "Come on, we have coffee, melon, biscuits . . ."

The cook lay sleeping in the mess-tent and woke rubbing his eyes as Anwar stood the kettle on the stove. Anwar looked about his makeshift kitchen and said with pride, "Now I am guide!

Before, printing works." He chopped melon into little tin bowls. It was unspeakably pukka. I understood the wonderment of the villagers. Melons! Coffee! Efficient gas stoves!

"I like foreigners. I would like to marry with European. Is possible? My one friends is marry with German girl. I like European girls. They are in smiling condition. You are marry? Boyfriend? Childrens, no childrens?"

"Would you like to go to Europe?"

He nodded his great bear head. "But I am only son. You understand? My parents . . . I cannot go."

It occurred to me that Anwar and Ken were like each other. Both worked in other cultures which threatened—promised—to absorb them utterly. Ken would have no problem readjusting to his car and his computer, but Anwar . . .?

"In Pakistan it is difficult to get a girlfriend. So I no married. My parents say: Why you no marry with her, with her? But I say no."

"Why?"

He shrugged. They were simple village girls, but he was no longer a simple village lad.

"I have someone, but she is lost. Married, you know. Gone USA. In Pakistan, for one night only is possible to get a girlfriend. Pay some money for a girlfriend, you know? No good. But you know what I think? I think sex is part of life."

He cocked his head. I felt sorry for him, a man between two cultures, two consciousnesses.

"You sleep lone?" he said.

"Lone."

I slept lone, thinking of all the things Ken had told me. Things before Islam. Of the winter tales, sagas of old Tibetan kings the people recite in the dark cold nights; of the suppressed mythology; of the one old man in the village with it all in his head; the smashing of the instruments, and the fairy culture that persists, especially in the high pastures, and the jinn—the jinni-mother who came to the village with her feet on backwards, who covered her baby in earth and vanished it. And that was only a generation ago; they could just about remember.

A dog in the village barked. I turned to sleep. With my ear to the ground I could hear the river-roar vibrating through the earth, resonant and deep.

I took some mail out for Ken, and left him in his village. In autumn he would leave for Ontario, and the people would prepare for winter. By then the day would have come when it would all be too late. The costumes, the rationale, the jinn. Ken seemed resigned. "I'll be sad to see them go," he said, and laughed. "I was born in the wrong century." In another month, the little community of Askole would no longer be so utterly cut off. The road-builders would have arrived.

The next was a fragile and delicate morning. Though it was still summer, the rosehips would soon turn a burning red. I walked out to the edge of the village by the little track which crosses the cemetery, where square graves are marked with white stones. Then, beyond the fields, there's a copse of bushes and trees. There are enchanting flour mills, fairy-tale stuff. Wooden gutters conducted the water from a stream on to the flat wheel that drives the creaking machinery. Once I lifted the latch of the little wooden door and peeked inside. It smelled of flour and earth, and a shaft of sunlight fell through the tiny window, and the flour-dust danced in its light. The rhythmic creaking and turning had worked magic on the miller, who lay asleep on a pile of sacks, flour in his hair and beard and ragged clothing.

There were two other walkers this morning, coming upriver. One wore a pink shalwar-kameez and a fine astrakhan hat. Teachers, they were, coming to begin term. It was just that sort of day, the end of the holidays. The teacher would climb the stile into the village; the holidays would be over.

So I reached the stream that led to Chakpo, another shitty little Eden full of thin hens and flat-roofed houses. There was a shout, and I turned to see an old man running behind, making gestures with his hands as if he was opening a book. I thought of the policeman and his book, and groaned. Was I supposed to sign something? He shouted again. There was a thick low wall just a few feet long; I waited for him to catch up. It was nothing to do with books, it was his hands.

"Doc-tor?" he said.

His barrel chest rattled as he breathed. He opened his hands as if in supplication; they were in a sorry and useless state. Once the skin had been as thick as the sole of a boot, and as dry; now it had fissured and split and peeled from the quick in strips, like old wall-paper. The flesh beneath wept pinkly. I thought at first it was rope burn, but he said not. A little inadequate handcream was all I could do. He wasn't impressed. He'd run for a mile to catch up, with his heart full of hope, and now he sat on the wall and looked unhappily at his useless hands.

Ken had said "the villagers don't believe in hot water." That means they don't come to the hot springs above the village. They don't strip and lie luxuriating in the hot smelly pools. They never gasp with shock and delight, after a hot day's labour. Or feel themselves buoyant, having walked for days. What a treat they miss! I wonder why.

For a hundred yards around the springs the turf and stones are crunchy with crystals, and at the pool itself there are bits of clothing and rags, dropped and turning to stone. On the air is a whiff of sulphur. The pools are on a slope and you may lie there, as if in a jacuzzi, gazing out at the snowcapped mountains and the clouds passing in a blue sky. Cleopatra, eat your heart out. Was it

she who bathed in milk? A yellowish spillage has seeped and hardened on the hillside in front of the pools, more eggy than milky,
but the story goes that in the old days this was a land of giants and
this, a giant's palace. But an earthquake shook it down, and turned
everything to milk. You can see strange forms poking through
the milky deposit. Earthquakes, giants, hot springs, and jinn.
The old man I'd just turned away—was he the one with it all in
his head, rags on his back and his mind full of giants and jinn?
His head full of lore and rationale, and his hands turning useless in front of him?

This village sits upon a ledge overlooking the river. There's a steep
mud-bank down to the water's edge. The water is a filthy grey
mess of glacier-melt, gravel and mud. Two girls with creels on
their backs were looking down as if over a precipice from which
they might just fall.

The girls were watching the old bridge across the Braldo, which is
a crate dangling on a pulley wheel. It was still there, but beside it a
team of labourers were at work, building plinths to take the steel
ropes of the suspension bridge that will carry the jeeps to Askole.
The girls who watched had undoubtedly never seen a vehicle, or a
light bulb. Road is coming! There was already a queue at the wire
bridge. An old man sat like an oracle on the rock the wire was
wrapped round. He wore an orange balaclava and sucked a cigarette
through cupped hands. He had a ghee tin full of black grease and a
paintbrush. Every time the crate swung back across the river to him
and its passenger clambered out, he assumed a very serious expression and dabbed the pulley wheel with grease.

The bridge was here because at this point the river narrowed and
the span was not so great—it's hard to say, maybe 200 feet. The
river's wrath was up, though, at being forced through this bottle-
neck, and at its edge you could be splashed by waves as if at the sea.
A land of giants indeed. We were dwarfed even by the river-banks.

Two by two people were ferried across in the dangling crate, until they joined the group of tiny figures on the other side. I'd heard a story, maybe apocryphal, of a French expedition who were there for ten days, conveying their thousand porters and equipment. A thousand porters. Ten days.

The box swung in and, madly, I thought of the sweet chariot in the song, coming for to carry me home. One of the floor planks was missing. I told myself it was like going to the shows—think of the fair, the Ferris wheel—and clambered in. To counterbalance me, a man piled in too and we hunkered together with our knees at our chins as the box was swung out over the dizzying river. Two men on the far side began to heave the rope, and the pulley wheel jerked out over the water. Once we were clear of the banks, a freezing updraught blew and we could hardly hear ourselves speak above the roar.

"I AM ENGINEER!" the man shouted. I could tell by his clothes and complexion that he was a downsider. He wasn't gnarled and his teeth were white and whole.

"FROM LAHORE WE ARE BUILDING THIS BRIDGE IT IS THE LAST BRIDGE."

The last bridge on the last valley in Baltistan.

"HOW LONG WILL IT TAKE?"

"ONE MONTH ONLY!"

I began to enjoy the ride on the last bridge. I had faith in the steel cable and the crate, and the strong men on the bank heaving away on the rope. We swung into land, and many leathery hands held the box steady as the engineer and I climbed out. The men around us laughed a lot and smelled strongly of goats. Here, on this side, the jeep track was already laid out. It had brought the bridge-engineers and their equipment. All that was missing was the last bridge.

I could see the old track, the precipitous narrow path that swooped like a bird across the faces of the mountains, which had served for centuries. I could remember walking to Askole by that way in fear and wonder six years ago, with the smell of wild thyme catching in my dry throat. I remembered the terrible heat, the dust and rocks you had to cling to with both hands. Three days it had taken to reach Askole; I thought it the most extraordinary place on earth. I thought at once of Skara Brae on Orkney, the prehistoric village. We had walked in from the then roadhead, at the top of the Shigar valley, where the gorge narrows. It was like walking into a funnel, upriver.

Now the road was coming, would the old path fall into disrepair? Fall out of people's memories, become a thing the old ones remembered, like jinn-mothers. Like how to play a pipe or drum. Like how to build a home-made bridge out of twisted twigs. I remembered Ken's unsentimental maxim: Observe, not interfere. But: if any youngsters remained in the village, after the road came to take them away, would they be told about the days before the road? Before the road, the hotel, before the electricity came and people stayed up at night. Before the girls' school, and the clinic?

I sat at the edge of the raw new road, looking across the river at the old path. I was beginning to torture myself about this business of implication. Don't interfere. Of course we interfered. Why were they building the last bridge, if not to bring the tourists in, in jeeps? *Was it built for my betterment? No!*

Janet had joked that one day, Balti women would have jobs driving tourists in jeeps to K2 base camp. But Ken retorted that we'd be able to beam ourselves around, like on *Star Trek*, before that day came. But Askole was on the brink of the biggest change. Had I done this? Had we all done this? And was it good? If you got the trekkers out of the graveyard and into a nice little hotel, and a regular shipment of kerosene, so the trees went undamaged, wouldn't it be the last word in problem-containment? I had a sudden mad image—of a trekker in full flashy gear, the kind of gear we think it necessary to wear in a land where the folks subsist in rags, climbing over the village stile, hand in hand with a black-swathed mullah. Here we are, we have arrived.

Now it was a short walk to Hoto, where the new road had already arrived. There, a scabby-faced lad was selling cardboard cartons of fruit juice, aggressively, from a wooden kiosk. The stumps of the trees felled to make the kiosk were still raw. The ground was already littered with cartons.

"Doctor?" he said, pointing to the sores. And what was I to do, wag my finger in his scabby face and tell him he shouldn't cut down trees to make shops, shouldn't litter his yard with used cartons, shouldn't harass people, shouldn't ... shouldn't ...? Because, despite myself, I bought some juice.

Four military porters passed, noticeably better dressed than other village men. They had fine moustaches, the coveted tracksuit bottoms, warm jumpers. In the afternoon, two army helicopters unzipped the sky. And I remembered it wasn't just the tourists who brought roads and opened up remote areas. There was a war on, the Kashmir face-off, up at the Siachen Glacier. There, it was said, more men died of frostbite than of enemy fire. They said a yak-track had been constructed up the Baltoro Glacier, for the army. They said there was a Pakistani woman up at Gasherbrum base camp. They said, "It is very change."

There seemed little point in hanging around. An engineer's jeep was leaving for Skardu, and I got on. For hours and hours we drove down bluffs and rock, round switchbacks. We could see on the other side the villages where the men were less than pleased about the road. If you could drive to Askole, their services as porters would no longer be required. They would be thrown back on their tiny fields and herds of goats. And without the expeditions, the trekkers and the military, there would have been little portering in the first place. For a century it's been part of their lives; for the last twenty years, their mainstay.

The jeep passed gangs of navvies, with flat dishes of rubble on their heads, and officious-looking gaffers with hennaed beards. Down the track, in the miserable village of Apolygon, there was a crate of Coca-Cola cooling in the irrigation stream.

I can claim the uncertain honour of being one of the first people to have travelled from Askole to Skardu in a single day. I can't claim to have done it in style, but lying on the back of the jolting jeep. This was culture shock. The glaciers were far away; instead there were smells of the town in the smoky darkness; fumes, and fairy lights. There was a grainy TV in the hotel, showing loud reruns of the World Cup, and adverts for cigarettes and soap. To be in a room with harsh electric lights was so uncomfortable I had to go and stand out on the roof, under the stars. The walls of Skardu were daubed with signs of dubious welcome. *Down with Israel! Down with USA!*

5 In Baltistan

From the flat roof of the Karakoram Inn, you can survey Skardu's bazaar. It's made of wood. Wooden booths with awnings propped up on poles stretch down the hill. There is only one colour, like Plasticine all rolled into one, the lunar brown of the mountains. It's a dusty place, sand-devils whirl there of an afternoon. Unlike Gilgit, Skardu has an end-of-the-road feel. There are few Chinese gewgaws to be bought, but the stuff of life is constantly loaded into jeeps: tea chests and flour sacks, sugar and soap, the things the villagers need to supplement their crops. The sky is a deep clear blue, the winds are strong and saturated with dust. Particles of asbestos from the rock around account for the people's coughing. The men of the bazaar look as though they too have been dressed by a strong wind; shirt-tails and waistcoats, caps and shawls. There are roadside cobblers and sellers of gemstones chipped out of the mountains. The cobbler outside has a huge owl by his side, staring at the bright sunlight. The owl makes me think of the Ayatollah poster in Rashida's room.

The Karakoram Inn itself seems popular with Pakistani businessmen, and groups of downside youths—no girls—in their holiday duds. Most Western mountaineers stay at the K2 Motel, at the edge of town, and use its lawn to sort out their mounds of food and equipment. The Pakistani holidaymakers are not so adventurous. They sprawl on their beds playing cards all day. They comb their coiffured hair, shave and trim their moustaches. They are perplexed by the hairiness and scruffiness of the Westerners they meet—wealth warped into a denial of itself. This hotel promises hot water, an unheard-of luxury. It offers an extensive menu of Pakistani and Chinese food: eggs, soups, vegetables, Chinese fried rice. I asked for them all, but the waiter replied, "Eggs, soups, veg-e-table, no. Skardu, all bad eggs. Chapati, dhal only."

The hotelier was a silent type. He wore his shawl all the time, draped over his left arm. The arm must have been injured or disfigured, because he never revealed or used it. He stood behind the desk in the restaurant and dispensed keys. There were Western-style toilets. I discovered that by standing on the seat I could see out of the tiny window into the yard of the mosque. The mosque is an extraordinarily gaudy affair, all yellows and pinks like icing, which might well have arrived from outer space; or out of a cornflakes packet. Five times a day the call to prayer sounded over the town.

There is graffiti everywhere. These are a passionate people. BSO! ISO! Baltistan Students' Organisation! Islamic Students' Organisation! There are subgroups, youth wings and factions. "We want commission!" PPP! "Education is a right, not a privilege!" I thought a lot could be gleaned from the graffiti, and pestered for translations. The people laughed. "Is saying, 'Hotel, cheap, and clean, on this street,' or 'Buy our very good eggs!'"

Horns blare and engines roar, but the Skardu cows, thin, docile beasts, amble up the middle of the road and eat cardboard from the red-painted oil-cans which serve as litter bins, and command USE ME. On the arid patch of waste ground between this hotel and the next is a short flight of steps, the kind used to get on aeroplanes, which has been dumped with the same incongruity as our own supermarket trolleys. The yard behind is occupied by a scrap dealer, who flattens ghee tins with a rock, then weighs them on enormous scales.

I have never felt as easy in Skardu as in Gilgit; there is a different atmosphere. Visitors are tolerated. Just. Apparently some of the Urdu graffiti reads "Would foreigners dress with decency." They should put it in English, French, Japanese. Men or women in shorts cause scandal and distress.

At the beginning of the day, about six, I took a chair and sat overlooking the street. Sometimes time weighed heavy. Smoke was rising from the little clay chimneys opposite. I could see the trees reaching above the little roofs and, in the morning light, the barren ochre mountains. Skardu sits at the junction of the Indus and Skyok rivers, where both slow down into a wide meander before pouring themselves down the gorge toward the Indian Ocean.

There is a large satellite dish on the outskirts of town, and TV aerials. The continuity announcer is a woman, still as a waxwork, with a dupatta draped over her head. Her voice is soft, supplicating.

The first Suzuki appeared, like the first wasp from a byke. I could see into the rooms opposite: the lodgings of a young mullah. I could see him in his black robes, carefully winding the white turban round his brow, and studying the effect in a glass. I decided that Skardu lacks Gilgit's inherent silliness. Too serious by half.

•••

In the evening, a man called Asghar sat beside me in the restaurant, leaning forward in his intense way, with clasped hands. Asghar is tall and thin, half Ladakhi. He seemed a gentle, caring man. He's a student in Islamabad, but in the summer comes home to do a bit of tour-guiding—good money. He was a volunteer in a Pindi drugs rehabilitation unit last year; he told me in hushed tones about the addicts and their families. There are plenty. The poorest lie on the streets in the shade of the trees near the grand hotels.

Asghar said he had a friend, a Shi'ite leader. "He is leader of this BSO. You want to meet with him?"

"That would be interesting."

"I'll bring him here. Please wait."

The Baltistan Students' Organisation initials shout from every wall in Skardu, every roadside boulder. Its leader, Ali, was an intense youth. He took a paper napkin and, as he spoke crushed it and smoothed it, crushed and smoothed it. He kept his head bowed, and spoke too fast for me. Like a small army he manoeuvred the saltcellar and container of toothpicks. What was the BSO? A students' organisation. Most of the time he spends in Pindi, as a student of engineering.

"They come to Pindi, Islamabad, smoke, drink, it is city. They are from villages, it is difficult for them to be Muslim. Also, we are for reforms." He shifted the pepper pot and looked up through his thick hair. "In Pakistan we are learning . . . we say over and over the same things. We want education, not saying the same things, you know?"

I thought of the girls and boys I'd heard chanting, chanting, in village classrooms. By rote. "Yes," he said, "It is not education."

"A Gilgit shopkeeper told me once: "In Islam, we may explore the works of God, but not question them.'"

Ali was drawing with his finger on the tabletop. He said nothing.

"I've seen it painted on walls: Education is a right, not a privilege."

"It is this mullahs," he said. "They are backwards. They are *professional*, make trouble. They make the young men crazy in their heads—they make the young men want fight! They are not Islamic, they are . . . professional."

"Tell me about girls. What about for girls?"

He glanced at me briefly through his hair. I don't know whether he didn't catch the question, or whether he chose not to answer, or whether he was speaking in some deep metaphor. He said: "What is this?"

"A pepper pot," I answered, but that wasn't what he meant. He was pushing it towards me.

"If I give to you this pepper pot, what am I doing?"

"I don't know."

"If I give to you this pepper pot, it is yours. I cannot say, 'Give to me this thing!' You understand?"

I glanced at Asghar stretched out in his chair. He was starting to smile.

"If I give to you this thing, I give to you!"

"I'm sorry?"

"It is this!"

Asghar gave me a friendly shake of the head. Ali shoved his hand into his hair, muttering. The pepper pot lay between us. Abruptly, he stood up. "Now I must go to student meeting. We must be quiet. This mullahs try to stop us, when we make reform. Goodbye, Madam." He left hurriedly, by the swing doors, narrowly missing the waiter.

Asghar leaned forward and clenched his fists.

"I've upset him," I said. "I'm sorry. I just couldn't understand this business of the pepper pot."

Asghar gave me a complicated look. "He is good man, little crazy," was all he said.

At the top of Skardu bazaar is a vast monument. A white obelisk surmounted by a ball and a flying eagle. It serves as a roundabout and meeting place. It is inscribed with a text from the Qur'an. Old men and young sit at its plinth. It was erected to the dead of the Liberation of Baltistan, 1947. That must mean the uprising against the Maharajah. I thought about finding a coherent account of the Liberation and wondered if there was a library, like in Gilgit. Skardu was no British outpost, so had less of the obvious influence. Its influences are much more Tibetan. The Balti tongue is an archaic form of Tibetan. They are proud of it, an oral language; all written work is in Urdu. Some of the buildings of the back bazaar have a Tibetan look to them—they lean and sigh, are jammed up by their neighbours, have eaves just nudging into the air. The backstreet of the bazaar is traffic-free. There are shops of aluminium pots, and a delicatessen with every spice and herb in glass-fronted jars, boxes of every sort of rice and tea, shawls and bales. Skardu is bigger than it appears; far from the bazaar are wide avenues, girls' schools, UNICEF health buildings, long-winded signs denoting clinics and projects galore, which point to offices, invariably closed.

There was indeed a library, the upper storey of a concrete block. The lower half was inhabited by a paint store. There was no apparent door. I went round the back, clambered over oil-drums, and saw a concrete stairway, which had long since parted company from the wall and stood alone, like the flight of aircraft steps behind the hotel. The library door was padlocked, and had been for a long time.

In the Sahadim café, where smoke billows out on to the street from the barbecue, a sweating man fanned kebabs with a bamboo wing. They serve good paratha. A loud conversation was going on between the proprietors and a strange figure, bigger than anyone else. He was bearded, wore a bush hat over his shalwar-kameez, carried a staff like Moses, and a little silver snuffbox on a string round his shoulder. His Urdu was so strange-accented, even I could understand.

"What is your country?" the Skardu men cried.

"I'm an American."

"How long have you been here, if you speak Urdu?"

"Seven years."

The boys behind the desk were Pathans. They seem to do a good line in cafés, Pathans, like the Italians in Britain. Posters of Zia still hung behind the desk.

"You like this Zia?" said the proprietor to me.

"Prefer Benazir."

"No! It is not strong government. You are British, I think. You know Mike Gatting? Cambridge?" He lifted his head and looked straight into my eyes. "It is difficult for our people to come to your country. Why?"

"The British government don't like to admit young men, because they fear you will bring your whole family also."

He contented himself with a withering look, then laughed. "Sometime is true. Is true! But here is no facilities. Much discomfort. Transport is very discomfort. Little money."

"I don't know what to say."

"It is because you have dollars. I have rupees only. It is Iniquity of Currency."

"May I pay for the tea and paratha? Three rupees."

"No! You are our guest."

"I'm a customer in your café, it is your business. Here, three rupees."

"No. Thank you. Welcome. You are our guest."

The American called himself Jungly John.

"Call me some other name, or something. I'm publicity-shy. I prefer one-to-one exchange, the old-fashioned way."

"But you keep notes?"

"Sure. Books full. Botany, history, language. One day I oughta sort them out."

It was dark, and we sat on the flat roof of the hotel. He asked after Ken, up in Askole. "He's an okay guy. Doing good work, before it's too late."

"Do you think it *is* too late?"

"Sure. Demographic changes, fundamentalism, tourism, defor-estation. Chitral—I could take you up places in Chitral, shit, they used to be forests. I was speaking to the new head of forestry. He was sitting behind his desk with his head in his hands. He knows. Same in California. There's a little bit of ancient forest left there, so the logging companies are saying: What the hell, we might as well have it."

I liked John. He said he'd been all over the Western Himalayas. He had the air of a Victorian explorer. He even looked like one. Even when the hotel had closed for the night and the staff wan-dered up on to the roof to sleep, we talked on. Medicine—he had books of notes on local medicine, which he favoured over Western, on the rare occasions he'd been ill. All the anxiety of change I'd felt in Askole I offloaded on Jungly John. We spoke a lot about travel, the ethics.

"It's all going down," he said. "Sinking under the weight of tourism. The cult of the objective. You know the worst are these climbers, these trekkers. All they care about is their Goretex. And their Objective. Always a fucking Objective. They've got no interest in the villages they drag three hundred porters through. Is it any wonder everyone gets stressed out and starts throwing stones?"

"This graffiti, someone told me it says, 'Westerners should wear modest clothing.'"

"Dress decent, can't they? These guys in shorts. That's Islam, though. You want to know about the pre-Islamic culture? The signs are there if you take the time to read them. You ever seen the shrines? With all the horns?"

Now he was talking. Again and again I'd seen rocks strewn with ibex horns. Ask, and you're told it's just decoration. I remembered asking someone who shuffled his feet and said, "This is very backward area."

"At home, we still stick antlers over the doorways and think it's decorative."

"And there's the *mani* walls. You'd notice them, either side of Askole. Ken thinks that's what they are, and I agree."

Buddhist prayer walls. I remembered the old man who laboured up behind me, asking for help with his hands—how we'd all sat together on the thick low wall. I thought it was a rest for the porters' packs. I said, "The little goats carved on the lintels in Askole, just the same as the petroglyphs at Hunza."

"Sinking fast."

"It takes a while. In Scotland, there are still a couple of seers, a clootie well or two. Healing wells, you know?"

"No shit?"

We talked about the villages and he told me how they organised themselves: the kind of work Ken was doing. The hierarchy. Headman, then four elected villagers responsible for co-ordinating collective work: mills, irrigation. Their performance is assessed, and if it is found wanting, they are fined. Rationale.

It was late, we were tired. John said he was off in the morning, to walk a little-used pass into Hushe valley. I was going to Hushe too, but by road. I could walk no more. He asked what people always ask, about travelling alone. I told him I was torn between staying with Westerners, in purdah, no worries, safety and seclusion. I can't fully denounce purdah because we do it ourselves, we go in gangs everywhere and keep ourselves separate, in a little cultural bubble. Because why? Because it's dangerous out there. I laugh at Murtaza's fears, then act as though they were true. If you want to meet people, student leaders, engineers, oddball itinerant Americans, you've really got to be on your own. So I was on my own. And I'd resolved to go to Khapalu, and then on to Hushe. After I'd eaten a lot more egg and chips. We set a date a week away and arranged to meet in Hushe village, inshallah, because I wanted him to tell me more. *The signs are there if you look for them . . .*

Over his tea the driver shook his head. "This Khapalu road, no carpet! No carpet! This jeep is coming like . . . sewing machine, you know?"

I knew. The tea-house boy threw more chapati on our table, and poured more water into the communal tumbler. Customers started from beneath their rolled caps. The walls of the tea-house were lined with grubby magazine pictures of the Ayatollah Khomeini, of Benazir Bhutto, and of President Gorbachev. From an upper corner, a yellowed image of Princess Di peeled off the wall. Outside, in the intense sunshine, tomatoes ripened beside the latrine. Chickens pecked on the road.

I walked to the river to stretch my legs. On a whitewashed wall beside a bridge someone had painted:

	Israel!
Down with	*USA!*
	Saudi!
	USSR!

The carpet was coming. We had passed the team of tarmac-layers about an hour out of Skardu, and merely drove off the road and around them. They had a log-fired tar boiler, and a kettle on a lesser fire. They wrapped their heads in paisley-patterned scarves and worked with hot tar through the heat of the day. I'd been sitting on the back of the jeep, on top of the cargo, and was covered in sweat and dust.

Opposite the tea-house was the village mosque, where two wash-houses had been fashioned by building a little dry-stone hut over the irrigation stream, which was heavenly, clear and cold. Inside the jeep were two passengers, a married couple. She wore an old-fashioned shalwar-kameez in red and green. It was baggy and shapeless. We sat together in the shade of the mosque's verandah. She told me they had been to the hospital in Skardu. She patted my pocket and asked for money. She wanted to swop her tin ring for my gold. She rubbed the cotton of my shalwar between her gnarled fingers and grudgingly approved. Then she tugged my earrings, and asked how many children? Where was my husband? Where was I going?

"Khapalu," I said.

There is a gesture: put out your hand palm down, and twist it quickly so the palm is upwards. It means: everything: Where, what, why why why? People do it from rooftops, from fields and roadsides, from windows. Where are you going? Why are you here, what is your country-name, where is your husband, why you are lone? The day was already wearing on, and we had a long way to drive. I don't like to travel by night.

I'd turned up early to that part of the bazaar where jeeps leave for Khapalu. Skardu is a sort of trading and clearing house for the valleys around. There was a particular supply house, from which the jeep would leave—oh, early. Eight o'clock. At five to eight I came from my hotel. "Nine o'clock going!" said the shopkeeper's son. At nine, "Twenty minutes please." By ten-thirty the jeep had been thrice loaded and thrice unloaded. Men grunted under sacks of flour and sugar and rice. They placed aboard pinkish lumps of rocksalt, boxes of soap bars and cigarettes, and a crate of empty bottles. The order of loading was discussed loud and long. Neighbours joined in. The jeep, emptied, drove away. Another older one arrived in its stead, and was duly loaded. Sleep while you can, I thought, and retreated out of the sun and the street into the back of the shop. A fan turned slowly and the shopkeeper, an old, old man with owlish spectacles, said, "Half an hour, going, inshallah."

There was a tower of sacks, huge plump sacks stuffed hard with sugar. Sugar is a little more giving than flour. I like rice best. Once, in China, I'd fallen briefly but wretchedly ill, and spent a three-day bus ride curled like a cat on a sack of rice. Thus was I hauled across the desert. Its smell penetrated my semi-conscious state and comforted me, like a mother's apron. In the back of this merchant's house I chose such a sack and sat on it. The shopkeeper wobbled his head and made a sleepy patting with his old hand. I lay down to doze. Around me were shelves of school-jotters and batteries, Red and White brand cigarettes. The flour sacks had a picture of a handsome Sindhi farmer, his head swathed in a scarf. The soap showed a leaping tiger.

At noon they declared they were ready. Then we had to travel twice round the bazaar, drumming up trade or passengers, each time arriving back where we had started. Some more passengers climbed on. The wise do not sit but stand on the back footplate, holding the bar the better to absorb the shocking jolts and bumps. You never see a jeep but it's got eight men aboard, with the tails of their shalwars flapping in the wind and the ends of their scarves held ferociously in their teeth. We set off, and reached the hospital. It was too hot to stop. People were milling about the hospital, families were encamped on the dry earth of its compound. Some errand was done and again we set off, past the satellite dish, past the fierce square prison with its watchtower. We drove out of town, across the bouncing suspension bridge, away to hills and beyond.

The river is slow and wide, with grey silt beaches. The road again is but a track through the boulder-field between the river and the terraces, which are beautiful, layered like feathers. Each tiny scrap of usable land is walled in with river-stones. Water falls from each to its neighbour below. It was harvest time. In the villages, shaded by trees and bushes, stood huge haystacks and threshing machines, themselves painted with flowers and beasts. The machines blew great clouds of chaff across the road. Now there is a road it is possible to bring in threshing machines, and the hand- or bullock-stamping days are gone. In the later afternoon clouds gathered and a wind blew up, bending the fragile little trees that lined the road. No scarf, however tied about the face, was ever enough to keep out the wind-blown dust, great choking clouds of it that rose like devils with every gust of wind.

We drove past strange riverside rock pillars, and barren tracts of land where stones had been placed deliberately, mysteriously, in long lines. No goat could graze in these lunar, empty stretches. Above, of course, the mountains towered, blocking out the sun for a blissful moment or two as the road entered an undercut. The dust storms were bad, but to get in behind one of the lumbering trucks was worse—the fumes wrapped and suffocated us in an evil black cloak.

Darkness fell; we bounced on. The little man who sat upon the spare tyre took his box and left, smiling and bowing. The blue signs with names of villages passed—still no Khapalu. "Khapalu, one hour more only near, not far."

The road was like a desert, ankle deep in soft sand and gravel. Ahead, behind, left and right, the full darkness of the mountain- sides closed in against the night sky. We stopped. Through the few trees to the left the river swept on its way. The driver jumped out. "Here one hotel, my oneverygoodfriend hotel." He approached a darkened single-storey building. There was no one there. "Hotel close," he reported. There was some giggling in the undergrowth beneath the trees. The moon was rising above the jagged moun- taintops and bathed us in an eerie light.

"My verygoodfriend, other hotel, new hotel, please coming." I jumped down, hauled my squashed rucksack from the general cargo, and followed the driver down a path towards the river, where a hurricane lamp spilled from a doorway.

There was something eerie about this spot. I think it was the proximity to the river. The hotel was built on the bank of an unlovely swampish eddy where the water stilled and grew stagnant. Bushes of a sort loomed eerily from the shallows. Now and again a fish jumped. The hotel owner emerged from a kitchen and led me along a candlelit verandah where, at a few rickety tables, a couple of men ate their dhal in silence. A cloud of river-bugs danced around each candle. Five identical doors led from the verandah into as many little bedrooms, each with two beds and a thick durrie on the floor. The hotel manager hovered about, unhappily. "New, hotel," he said.

"Very nice."

"Facilities, no. You understand? It is new hotel."

"Yes, new."

"Facilities, no. Electricity, no."

The jeep driver saw me throw my sack on the floor and stepped forward to shake my hand. He must go now. Now I was safely off his hands, he could go. The manager whispered, "Please, no facilities. *You take bath in field.*"

The problems for a woman traveller are largely offset by the advantages, save in this quarter. Toilet facilities are nil, especially on journeys. You may wander among the roadside boulders, among the evidence that you are not the first to seek privacy there, but such is the interest aroused by a lone woman, she is never left alone. If it's not a male fellow-passenger taking his chance to get acquainted—"My dear siss-ter, my siss-ter, where are you going?"—it's some deranged mongrel. I don't know how it's done. I did not relish the thought of taking a bath in the field, neither by night nor by day. Islamic women, like Victorian women, don't shit.

There was very little clean water. The silt in the river and the dust and grime of the journey combined into a sort of paste on my skin. The candle served only as a beacon to mosquitoes. I went to bed, and in the dark fastened the window against the swarming bugs, wrapped myself in my shawl like a parcel, and slept.

•••

A granny opened a high window and threw out an outraged chicken, which squawked and fluttered to the ground. The S-shaped bazaar snaked up a hill from its junction with the main road. Few shops were open. Rivulets of schoolgirls passed: "Whatiz! Whatiz!" "Whatiz" is a common greeting, short for "What is your name?," but folks just say it like "hello."

In Khapalu there are some fine buildings, some wealthy people whose high walls contain new homes with windows and gardens and chimneys and jeeps. But for the most part the homesteads are wooden, with gantries. Dark subterranean passages connect them, and little muddy paths. Cows and goats low from their night enclosures, behind fences of briars and rags.

I was plucking up the courage to enter a high green gate, guarded by a man in a chair, around whom an anxious huddle formed. Behind him I could see the roof of a modern bungalow, with solar panels lifted towards the almost perpetual sun. It was an L-shaped building; you could just see over the high wall. The solar panels were interesting, but what intrigued me was the name on the sign: *Al Amin Clinic. Dr Frazer.*

Rumour had reached me of a Scottish doctor practising in far-flung parts. A friend doing his elective in Skardu years ago had mentioned a compatriot working in the remote villages. I hadn't imagined a modern and efficient-looking surgery, but pictured a character living away in the hills, bearded to the knee, who alternated between tending his field and treating the sick. There couldn't be two. The doorman broke off remonstrating with an anxious-looking chap with a child in his arms and let me in. A family of women with the same look of anxiety were sitting on the steps.

There strode across the verandah a young woman of my own age, in a green shalwar-kameez. She stopped when she saw me. I felt a bit stupid; I said I'd heard there was a Scottish doctor, it wasn't that I was ill, I said I was interested and perhaps she knew my friend?

She waved aside this gabbling and with a Belfast accent said, "Come at 12.30, when surgery's over." She looked at me more closely. "You can have a bath, if you like. We've got hot water."

"Ach, come in! Alison said you'd be joining us. I'm Angus Paton." A large Scotsman with a prophet's beard firmly shook my hand. "One moment till I get rid of this fellow." Mr Paton shouted in Urdu and slapped the back of a man who, looking suitably intimidated, backed towards the gate. " 'May all your children live!' That's what to say. Dr. Frazer's on leave, you know that? My wife Morag is the doctor, and the very able Alison is nurse. Morag will be in shortly. She has a lassie in labour in the front room. Come in."

The house smelled heavenly—it smelled of bread, real fresh newly baked leavened bread. The dining-table was heaped with correspondence bearing stamps from every nation. There were bookshelves, and a huge fridge. At the window a wire fly-screen obscured the view to an arid little yard. It was a room which didn't know whether to be Scottish or Pakistani, and opted for both. The bread was in a small electric oven, fat and round. Mr. Paton followed my covetous gaze.

"The first for three weeks. We haven't had electricity for three weeks. This is my wife, the doctor." Mr Paton quite dwarfed the birdlike doctor. Both were grey. He had his fine preacher's grey beard and she wore her hair with an old-fashioned plait pinned over the crown of her head. Alison popped in to apologise for being busy and I thought how odd we looked, we women dressed in these strange garments, flicking these irritating scarves out of our way. I began to think of the Islamic shawl as a symbol for the entire culture; one I would on occasion wish to draw around me, and on others simply want to tear off and stamp underfoot. It was the oddest culture shift, suddenly to be among Scots and Irish people, with their accents at once so familiar, but very strange for being out of context. We sat at the table and swopped Edinburgh stories. As her husband spoke, Dr. Paton took a leather fly-swat and stalked the room.

"I studied in Edinburgh," he said.

"Medicine?"

"No, I'm no doctor. Theologian. Allow me to show you some of my publications." He leaped to his feet and came back with a buff-coloured booklet; it was in Hebrew. I held it and made interested noises, feeling a bit embarrassed. What could I say about a work in Hebrew? If indeed it was Hebrew. I thought it was in Hebrew. I wished he would say something to give me a clue.

"I came to it through Arabic, I studied Arabic at Edinburgh. Know what it is yet?"

Dr Paton danced about us, thwacked the fly-swat. Whenever he said something of import, she thwacked the fly-swat.

I shook my head.

He recited a few lines of something powerful and strange.

"Song of Solomon. Much of the trouble between Muslim and Christian is misunderstanding. Take the Holy Trinity. They think our concept of the Holy Trinity is that God knew Mary and Christ was the product of that union. A notion they hold as blasphemous. And so do I! Terrible Idea!"

It was only then I realised I was in the company of missionaries. I didn't want to ask. Neither did I want to ask why one should translate the Song of Solomon into Hebrew. If indeed it was Hebrew. Mr. Paton said, "I go to the bazaar, you know, and distribute literature, some of which I prepare myself. This little thing is the Gospel of St Luke, in Balti. Persian script, of course. Only two books in Balti. The other's a series of lamentations for Hussain, you know Hussain?" He threw back his large head and beat his chest, chanting the Muharram chant. *That* Hussain.

He stopped abruptly. "We may be interrupted. The superintendent of police may arrive with all due pomp and ceremony. He has spots on his neck."

"Minuscule!" said the doctor, and thwacked.

"We must keep on the right side of him; we're not supposed to be here at all, but we have been, for twenty-five years."

The door rattled.

"Fellow outside with a blister!" cried Mr Paton.

She said witheringly, "A blister."

"I told him I'd seen worse and to go away. We're not treating men."

"Why not?"

"No male doctor. Wouldn't do to offend local sensibilities. Well, I'll leave you two girls in peace. Goodbye." As swiftly as that, he left the room.

Dr. Paton put down her fly-swat, and cocked her head on one side. "Wad ye like to see oor clinic?"

We breezed into the next room where the expectant mother lay. I hesitated at the door. "Nothing happening in here?"

"Och, no, she'll be a couple o'hours yet. In ye come. She's been here since 6.30 this morning, she thought she was going to drop the baby there and then!"

A girl lay unhappily on the bed. A chorus of female relatives hunkered on the floor, like owls roosting on a branch. Their shawls trailed behind them. They turned towards us huge dark eyes.

"She's only seventeen, and kinda frightened." Dr. Paton passed through this little group. I padded behind. Another consulting room. "We do minor ops, deliveries, home visits. We have constant light from the solar panels. They run the lights so we can see what we're doing when someone arrives in the middle of the night, which they do. It's useful to see what you're doing, in the middle of the night. And this is our fridge, to keep the vaccines cool, and Alison's cartons of fruit juice."

She showed me the dispensary. Bags of commonplace drugs, for the shits, bagged and ready in appropriate amounts. Flagyl and aspirin and the like. Rehydration solutions. Beside the drugs was a dispensary of religious tracts. On a lone chair outside on the verandah was a man. All his limbs were somehow curled up and tucked into the tiny chair. Only his eyes moved to follow us, and the hand that held his cigarette.

"Is that the husband?"

"I think so." She asked him, in Scottish-accented Urdu. "No, it's her father, hard to tell sometimes, they marry much younger lasses."

They invited me to lunch the next day. Angus Paton declared that Alison was the one I should talk with. "She speaks Balti. Well, she has a young mind, she can pick these things up. We're not so young any more. We're supposed to be retired."

Heaps of tract and correspondence were cleared off the table and it was set for lunch with a cloth, and knives and forks. I thought I'd never seen anything so homely. Knives and forks. A tablecloth, chairs. Mr. Paton said grace and, treat upon treat, they served me chips, brought to table by their cook. Ravenous hunger got the better of me. Dr. Paton must have noticed. She said, "Normally we just have chapatis, but as you were coming . . ."

"Do you get many visitors?"

"Och, yes. We're in the guidebook. It says we're Austrian. I don't know where they got that idea!"

Angus was talking about snow leopards. It was Alison's turn to swat the flies that dared land on the table. They had seen a snow leopard while on a picnic above Khapalu, just there it was, right there. He had written to a naturalist friend that he'd encountered a snow leopard and was told that he and Dr. Paton were "two of the few Europeans still alive to have done so." Alison said she didn't see it. "I wouldn't know a snow leopard if it jumped in the window."

Involuntarily I looked towards the window. There was no snow leopard, but a squadron of ants was bearing away the corpse of one of her swatted flies. I said I would love to see one, a snow leopard. The nearest I'd come was a yak in Askole which had been mauled by one. And, depressingly, four pelts hanging on a street in Linjow, China, for sale at 200 dollars apiece, starting price. Angus told me about a nest of kingfishers he'd spotted near Skardu, the last time he'd had to endure the journey to Islamabad by road, and all because the new broom of a police superintendent, with the minuscule spots on his neck, had made trouble about visas and permits.

Dr. Paton excused herself after lunch for an afternoon sleep. "A habit," said Angus, "from our years in hot Multan. I took it up when I was a pharmacist in Edinburgh, working nights. Is that still there? That was when I was studying at New College—under the great Professor Stewart, but he'll be gone now."

I was overcome by mischief. I told Mr. Paton that my stint at New College was under an Irish Catholic. He stood up and roared, "An Irish *Catholic*?" He exhaled a great breath. I sipped my tea and thought about snow leopards. He shook his great head and left to join his wife.

Alison looked cool and fresh and calm and sensible. She wore a green shalwar-kameez, and dupatta, and her fair hair was tied back in a pony tail. Now we were two Western women alone together, our outfits suddenly seemed ludicrous. Why were we dressed like this?

She poured more tea, and I asked her something I hadn't dared ask Angus, in case he thought the notion blasphemous. "This is a Church of Scotland mission, isn't it?"

"Oh no, oh no, we are Brethren."

"*Plymouth* Brethren?"

"Others call us that," she said, with a hint of disdain. "We call ourselves Brethren. Do you know of us?"

"I have a friend who was brought up by Brethren parents. He's from Glasgow." I knew what David had told me of his childhood. No music. No TV. Now he adores music. He'd to sneak off to his granny's to listen to her scratched 78s. He filled his empty childhood by learning languages. Dozens of the things.

"Brethren are strong in Ulster, and in the West of Scotland, and in Africa."

"Through missionary work, no doubt."

"My great-uncle went to Africa. Died at twenty-six. That's what happened then."

"But you're a nurse first, aren't you?"

She rose to clear the tea things from the table. She said emphatically, "There's no question about it, no comparison."

"Medicine?"

"I don't care if I never saw another syringe again. I know almost nothing about medicine. No, it's the spiritual side. I am here to share my faith in the Lord Jesus Christ. My degree's in sociology. And after I felt I could make a long commitment to Pakistan, I went to Edinburgh to study nursing."

"A long commitment?"

"I imagine spending most of my life here now."

For a moment I was taken aback. Not at the idea of spending a life in Pakistan, but at that cool certainty of faith.

"Is it hard to go back home?"

"It's hard to go shopping. If I go to Marks and Sparks with a couple of girlfriends, and watch them paying £20 for a cardigan. *Twenty quid!* My husband's in school in the south. He's learning Urdu. And when he arrives, Angus can leave. We have to have a man around, you know!"

Morag put her head round the door. "I've taken her off the drip."

Alison nodded. "I like helping, especially the women. But—ach, medicine. Maybe I'm not compassionate enough. Getting up all hours of the night."

"Do you charge for treatment?"

"Five rupees. The people abuse it. They come for stupid things and at all hours. We do what we can and really serious things, we send them to hospital in Skardu. But it means I can show them the love of the Lord Jesus Christ."

The quiet of a siesta had fallen on the clinic. Alison sat at the table with her hands clasped in front of her. We were much the same age. Had we walked through Skardu bazaar together, we might well have been taken for sisters. Except, of course, that she had an unshakable Christian conviction. I didn't feel I could ask her straight out if she'd managed to convert anyone. To my untrained eye the people here seemed just to be coming to terms with Islam. In this valley, the people were neither Shia nor Ismaili, but kept an easygoing form of Sufism. I settled for "Are there any Christians in Khapalu?" and she understood what I meant. She said, "There are some who believe in their hearts, and I believe that they believe. I have contacts who tell me there are some believers—one family, he still goes to mosque on the appropriate occasions."

"But they can't 'come out.'"

"No. No. Oh no."

"What happens to people once they've converted? It can't be easy for them?

"They can't declare themselves. It's a personal crisis for them. It's a very hostile environment."

"So what do you do?"

"I believe that's God's work. Mine is to show them the love of Jesus Christ." She gave an ironic grin. "And anyway, I work with women, who don't understand Islam anyhow."

"So they can do what they like."

She smiled. "Well . . . call it going in by the back door. I have friends now, homes where I can go and be welcome. They're such gossips! I'm supposed to have a daughter in the Punjab. Why don't you bring your daughter? they say—no use insisting I haven't got one. And all their talk is of their children, and what's going on in the fields, but I'm such a townie. They ask what we grow in my country, but I haven't a clue. It's Morag and Angus who are the naturalists."

The afternoon was wearing on. Soon I would have to leave. But here it was cool, and although we were so different, I could speak with Alison in the rapid shorthand of two people of the same generation from the same place. It was language up to speed, we could even use Scots words and I realised I'd been missing it. Perhaps she had been, too, because she seemed content enough to talk to me. When she offered more tea and mentioned a cake, I couldn't refuse. She went to give instruction to the cook and returned to the table.

"What happened to that girl that was in yesterday, did she have her baby?"

"Two babies were born last night. Both boys. A good way to start, with a boy. It takes the stress off you. Proves you can do the required, so you're not going to find yourself divorced. Did Angus tell you we're renowned for infertility treatment?"

"Infertility treatment? No!"

"He says to the villagers, 'The best of men had but one daughter!' The Prophet himself. But still, infertility is the worst thing for a woman. You can have so many kids you're exhausted, worn out, but at least you're secure. It's simple what we do. A pep talk to reassure her nothing is wrong—it usually isn't. Something to regulate the thyroid, vitamin B, and an explanation about your fertile time of the month. They just laugh at that one. Mostly they're run down. And worried sick, which doesn't help. You have to explain that if your husband's away in the army, you don't have much chance . . ."

She shook her head sadly.

"They come a long way to us. Well, if you were about to be divorced because you hadn't produced, you'd come a long way. It's worse than being overburdened, these poor girls living their lives under all this stress and comment. But you know," she said, "sometimes these guys are really nice. They're fond of their wives, they might not want to divorce. But they've got their families on their backs, pressurising them to take another wife. Sometimes it happens, the husband takes another wife and keeps the first on, to save her the shame of being sent away. So she's got to sit there and watch this new wife produce kids, poor thing. There's one in the village now, like that."

"Men are never infertile?"

"Another laughable idea. And that men determine the sex of their babies. It's unacceptable. If a woman has four girls in a row— loud lamentations: 'I am sinner! I am sinner!' There's a woman here whose sons were all stillborn. Then she had a daughter who was hydrocephalic. She cherished that child for two years until it died. Her husband is decent and caring. When she became pregnant with that daughter we said: 'She will have to go to Skardu, to be looked after.' And he took her. There's many wouldn't bother. But she says to me: 'I don't think my husband has a bad heart, he is a good man, I don't think he is wicked, but he must be, mustn't he? Because all our sons are stillborn.'" Alison shook her head. "Kids. And once you've got them, you've got to keep them."

"May your children remain alive!"

"Sometimes they don't."

An angel passed. We sat for a moment in silence. Maybe we were comparing the villagers' lives with our own. In truth, I had been shocked by Alison saying "I am here to share my faith in the Lord Jesus Christ." Shocked and almost impressed. What it must be to know what your life is for. The inner certainty. She was looking out of the window, where the sun beat down on the arid yard.

There was no certainty in my own life. I could wander where I would. The terrible freedom of the lost soul.

•••

"Is it so awful to be divorced?"

"Not like it is in the Punjab." She laughed. "You wouldn't believe how common it is. As I got to know people here, I realised they kept turning up at the clinic with different partners! It took me a wee while to work out what was going on. Trial marriages—they might try it on for a year or two, and if they don't get on, or she doesn't produce the requisite baby, they can divorce and marry others. It's not like in the Punjab—ugh, I'd hate to be a Punjabi woman. You know, even the family of a divorced woman will shun her. Soiled goods. It doesn't have the same stigma here."

"Can a woman ditch a husband?"

"Yes, especially if her family have influence and she complains loud and long."

I wanted to ask Alison what the opening up of the roads had meant to the villages. All these tourists. She snorted. "It's not the tourists. You know where this road leads?"

"Skardu?"

"Iran. That's where. Islamisation. That's what they're complaining about. They get meddled with. That's what this new road's brought. The clergy cross the border to Iran, and come back full of Ideas. Iran gives money for development programmes, but there's strings attached. Guess who suffers? 'We want the women veiled.' 'We want the women to behave in an Islamic manner.' "

"What's that?"

"Not to make cheeky comments to passing men, as far as I can see. This one guy came with development money and suggested to the women that they might like to make some nice black veils in their handicraft sessions. But they'd have none of it. It's coming, though. They used to have a lot of singing and instruments, different songs for the changing seasons, but that's suppressed."

We finished the cake. Soon it would be time for evening clinic, when a hapless queue of villagers would arrive at the gates. Alison stacked the cups, and stood, flicking her white dupatta over her shoulder. I took it as my signal to leave, so stood too, and said my thanks and goodbyes. We shook hands, and as she showed me to the door, Alison said, "You know, what I'd like is to build a church here one day. One day. To build a church. But the time's not right. Not yet."

The track winds through the villages, twisting up and up towards the mountainside. Hidden in a high pass is the summer pasture, what Alison called the "brough." With her accent I took it for an Irish word, but it is Balti for the high pasture. That was why the town had such a somnambulant air, and the bazaar was closed. The people had taken to the shielings for the summer and left villages behind.

I followed the road with no real purpose. It was a beautiful summer's day, the kind you think you knew as a child, hot and blue and full of promise. Khapalu was gorgeous, a great lush tumble of yellow and green between soaring mountains. There were forty-seven distinct villages, so Morag Paton told me, in that one valley. I passed several wooden mosques at the roadside which, like that in Shigar, edged towards the Tibetan. Their eaves longed to fly, their strong doors were surrounded by carved architraves. From the fences dangled taviz and strings caught like the wool of sheep. Beside their homes, families of women washed clothes in the stream with the cakes of red soap on which I'd sat for the journey. Glad of a diversion, they rocked back on their heels to twitch their shawls and pass raucous comments about me. Someone had once asked the village headman of Askole how the people kept their clothes so clean. "We wash them," he replied.

An old lady passed, tugging a cow, and shouted. That gesture—where are you going? Flowers and fruit hung heavily around doorways, the trees were laden. The road went up and up, a dusty track from which wynds and alleys wound into the labyrinth of homesteads. Cockerels crowed. I went on until the hillside levelled off and half of the villages lay spilled out below me, and then I saw something astonishing. In front of me, in a neglected garden, was a Tibetan palace, four storeys tall. It was square, with that odd, almost nautical manner of Tibetan temples, like the grounded ark; square with little windows, a flat roof. Jutting out from the upper-most storey was a wooden half-moon balcony. Some windows still held a pane or two of coloured glass, red or green. Wash was falling from the earthen walls, but I could picture the white skirts fluttering above the windows that so lighten Buddhist temples. Wooden gut-ters emerged from the walls like oars, and on the walls the beam ends of logs which supported the floors formed a pattern. Maybe this is what made me think of ships, something to do with port-holes, oars and sails. I was enchanted. It was at once sad and won-derful and lost, a fairy-tale palace that had slept for a thousand years. It must have been a thousand years old. To imagine Khapalu a thousand years ago: before Islam, before roads, before anything; when, as the saying went, the bear sat in the bear's place and the lion in the lion's place. The sun shone brightly on the ancient walls, and the blue sky sailed overhead. Like a child in a story I was drawn towards the palace, to the garden fenced by a tangle of flowers and briars, round to the front, where a path led arrow-straight towards a great door.

No one was around. In the distance I could hear children laughing, as if in a schoolyard. I could hear goats bleat, and a woman call. There was no one on the dusty road. I dodged inside the garden and ran for the door. It wouldn't be deserted—nothing is ever deserted, despite appearances—but just one look inside?

The door opened into a dark, cold alley. It smelled of deep earth and cold stone. It led through the building and came out the other side. I could hear voices there, women's, children's. As my eyes adjusted I could see cracks and fissures in the walls. One day soon it would all come tumbling down. Only age held it together. A staircase in a corner promised to lead up into the other storeys. Then, in the archway of light ahead of me, there appeared the silhouette of a child. He saw me, and fled. Maybe he thought I was a ghost. Then a gang of them came, dark shapes in the intense sunlight, then a woman, and then a young man dressed in jeans.

"Please, this palace, not enter," he said. I felt suddenly very rude and stupid. I apologised—someone's private home . . .

"No problem," he said. "You are welcome. But this palace not enter, there are . . . problems." He began to escort me to the gate, while the gang of women and children closed in behind to wave and smile.

"This is your family home?"

"Yes. It is very old. Nine hundred years. My name is Arif Hussain Yabgo."

We shook hands. Then, as we stood at the archway of creepers which formed the garden gate, he said, "But there is another palace, the king's palace. *Badshar Mahal.* Shall we go there?"

"May we?"

"Why not? The king is my friend. And here are my also two friends, Raza and Hamid." Indeed, two more young men, sensing fun, had appeared from nowhere and came running down the dusty track towards us. Raza displayed his rank with a loud check sports jacket. Hamid wore a well-cut traditional shalwar-kameez. And so I fell into step with three merry young lads who had about them a quality I couldn't define. They were different. Maybe it was Raza's jacket. Together we walked yet higher on the path, leaving behind us the old palace, towards more fields, terraces and homesteads. We travelled with increasing merriment. I nearly burst into song: The wonderful wizard of Oz. We skipped along. We were going to the palace. Maybe we would have tea with the Mir.

"Do you live in that palace, Arif?" I asked him.

"Yes! Also Islamabad, also Karachi. I am customs-and-excise."

Raza added, "I am student in Islamabad."

"He is my cousin," said Arif.

"So you've come home for the summer holiday, is that it?"

"Holiday! Holiday!" cried Raza and spun round, his jacket tails flapping. We all laughed. It *was* a holiday.

"Polo ground!" cried Arif, as we passed the dusty arena. He thwacked an imaginary ball. "I am polo-playing!" Then Raza dropped his voice and gave me a sideways look. "You like Benazir?"

"Yes. Do you?"

"He is vice-president of PSF," said Arif.

"What's PSF?"

"Benazir youth wing."

"He is for People's Party."

"Aren't you?"

"I am BSF."

"Which is . . .?"

"For Baltistani peoples, who want to be Pakistan fifth side."

"But you are still friends?"

"Why not? It is Democracy!"

Arif pointed to the terraces we walked between, huge, beautifully tended. "This fields, very big fields. They are king's. Before is king, you know. *Khatam*, finish. Now is Democracy!"

"Democracy!" the others cried.

"Our name," said Arif, "is Yabgo. It is our caste name."

"I didn't think there were castes in Islam."

"It is king name, king only."

"Name only. Now is Democracy."

"So you're noblemen?"

They dropped their gaze, modestly. From the air Hamid divined a message. Perhaps he heard it from a passing goat, for there was no one else about. He announced: "King is on visit. Only his daughter is here."

"A princess?"

"Yes! Come on, she is my friend."

The white palace stood squarely within a formal walled garden. Beyond the wall lay fan-shaped terraces, bigger and better than anyone else's. Water fell in a sparkling sheen from one terrace to the next. The boys led me on to a cobbled lane, which took us to the palace gates. There was a lodge, built into the walls. Just outside the palace gates was a huddle of lesser buildings, still very grand. A little bridge, which would not be out of place in Venice, reached over our heads from one old stone building to another. Arif pointed: "This princess house, come on."

He led me up a stair and into a dark, low passage. Almost immediately we passed through a door which led directly on to the little bridge we had seen from below. It had red handrails. The bridge crossed the road and then passed over a stream, clear and fast, which served a tangled flower garden. I leaned on the rail and breathed the flowers" scent. "Come on!" said Arif. We stepped down from the bridge into a small orchard, and there, among the fruit trees, sat the princess. A princess mooning alone in her garden while all the kingdom lay at her feet. She smiled. She had been scoffing mulberries. The juice painted her mouth like lipstick, and the hand she extended was purple with their juice. It matched the fruity checks of her outfit, from which yet more mulberries fell as she stood to welcome us. She was comely, fair-skinned, and really quite plump. She was at ease with the boys, who cavorted around her garden and shook the mulberry tree with a stick to rain down yet more fruit.

"And some plums, Raza, you'll find a plate indoors. Wash them, won't you?" To me she smiled graciously, and we sat together eating fat sweet mulberries and the most wonderful plums, small as gooseberries, which the boys collected from the trees. The princess's name was Shah Jebeen.

When I could eat no more fruit, Shah Jebeen sucked the juice from her fingers and told the boys to show me the palace proper. A little bird hopped in the mulberry tree, eyeing the fruit we'd dropped. If it had opened its little beak and spoken to me in rhymes, I don't think I'd have been surprised.

We ran across the parched lawn of the garden. There were cherry and lilac trees. The old Mir had been a keen gardener, so Robbie said. I stopped to look up at a tall building on the right of the garden. Within, I could see the exposed beams of its ceiling. A child looked down mournfully from a high window, then waved. "Prince House!" said Arif. "Come on!" On the palace proper, the front door was grand and enormous, surrounded by an architrave with strong crude carving. Later, Mr Paton told me the door had been carried home as plunder from some other palace in some other kingdom, the spoils of an ancient war. Two flights of stairs led up to it but, led by Arif, we made for the tradesman's entrance on the south wall.

Although the Mir was on a visit, he'd left his door open. On the lintel was chalked NO ADMISSION WITHOUT PERMISSION. Arif read this slowly, then turned and laughed. "I am permission!" He danced inside.

That we should go immediately to the roof was obvious and unsaid. The Mir had taken the precaution of locking his living quarters with rusty padlocks. A silent decrepitude pervaded the building. Round and round a central well we climbed, on ancient dusty stairways. Each door was carved with geometric shapes. I stopped to feel them, smell them. I was quite transported. It was not utterly dark. We spoke in whispers.

"Arif? How old is this building?"

"I don't know. One hundred years."

"Two hundred!" said Raza.

"Three hundred!" said Hamid. We emerged from the stair into a pale diffused light. We had reached the uppermost storey. A ladder of sorts rose from the earthen floor to a trap door, which led on to the roof. The ladder had no rungs. Raza squirmed up it, but slipped and marked his jacket. He sat for a moment trying to look dignified, then decided he was having too much fun. We tugged and hauled each other up through the hatch into the sunlit roof.

I stood between earth and sky, and looked round. I couldn't breathe for wonder. I'd climbed a ladder without rungs and squeezed through an old trap door, and so clambered into heaven. Behind us the rockfaces of the mountains rose to remote and jagged summits, and before us fell a cornucopia: the villages of Khapalu. They tumbled in golden terraces and green trees down to the banks of the great river. On all sides mountains bound our vision. The sky was intensely blue. Though all that Alison knew was also true—that in the exquisite yellow fields, and among the groaning fruit trees and under the roofs of all the little houses I could see, there were people ignorant, sorrowful, superstitious and brutalised—it was a proper kingdom. I'd opened a book of fairy stories, and found a way in.

"Well?" Arif called. He had clambered on to a rickety wooden skylight.

"Oh, it's . . . wonderful! WONDERFUL!"

The three young bloods took up the cry, and whirled like dervishes around the roof calling, "Wonderful! Wonderful! Wonderful!" From her garden far below, the princess waved.

In winter, because the glaciers are frozen, the river Shyok is low and milky-blue. It can be crossed by a series of bridges. Now summer silt has turned it grey and even at the banks it moves swiftly. Out in the middle of the river the water twists together like a grey plait of hair. I was looking for the raft, the *zakt*. They said it was an hour's walk out of town. If I followed the road around a couple of bluffs, and kept looking down the steep rocky bank to the river's edge, I'd see the raftsmen. I set off early, to get a long way up the Hushe valley before dusk, because I knew full well that such a simple-sounding thing as a river-crossing can be a long time happening.

Two others were waiting for the raft: two men squatting on boulders at the verge of the road. I put down my sack and sat on it. It was early still, and cool. I kept my woollen shawl wrapped around myself and looked northward, out over the river. Here the Hushe river spread wide and joined the Shyok. An island, quite barren, rose out of the river like a minuscule Rock of Gibraltar. Beyond the island, perhaps a mile further, a line of green denoted a village clinging at the foot of the mountains, distant-looking in the morning light. Although this bank of the river was a sheer rockface, through which the road had been blasted, the opposite bank was a flat, swampish-looking boulder-field. On that bank was a biblical scene: two men, each with a long bamboo pole, were pulling a raft upriver, by means of goat's-wool ropes which they held over their shoulders with strong hands. Their trousers were hitched to the knee, and you could see the muscles working as they hauled.

Rafts are traditionally made with goat or sheep skins. The limbs and neck are sewn tight to make a leather bag, and the thing is inflated in a grotesque, if efficient, balloon. Half a dozen of these, with a platform of bamboo poles lashed to them, form a raft. Progress has reached the Shyok river in the form of inner tubes, but the principle remains. The raftsmen do not cross the river directly, but use its strength to their advantage. Having landed the raft on the wide mud-bank opposite, they haul it upriver a hundred yards or more, so the sweeping flow of the water will bring them down with it, to land on our steep bank. Then again they haul the thing upriver and launch it into the current, to bring it safely to beach again at the original point. Out in the middle, when the current is at its worst and racing hellbent for the Indian Ocean, there is some mighty poling to be done. Spare poles are carried for passengers to join in.

There was a shout when the raftsmen were ready, and we scrambled down the bank to the edge of the water and on to the raft. Our Charon was old and bearded, powerful as a smith and lean as a greyhound. He held the raft as steady as he could while we got on, kneeling. Of my two fellow-passengers, one was burly and silent. He was wearing a pink lacy lady's cardigan, and he carried nothing but a hatchet. The other was a tubby little man with a shopping bag on wheels. The crew pushed away from the bank and out into the river-race. Grey water slipped up between the inner tubes with an unpleasant slap. They began to pole earnestly, as the strength of the river took a grip on the craft and tore it downstream, fast. I held on. The man in pink looked at his belly and cherished his hatchet. The other, with the shopping trolley, took his chance.

"Madam!" He cried above the roar of the river. "Should you be encountering any problem with connection with your transportations and accommodations, my card." We flew downstream like a leaf. It is a charming Pakistani habit to present one's business card at the most improbable moment. Siachen Tours, it read. The ferrymen knelt at opposite corners of the raft and poled like fury.

"Transportations are all right, thank you!" The bank drew closer, and suddenly we were spat out of the main current and on to the shore. The ferryman leaped off and held steady as we crawled on to the land.

It was only 8 a.m. Already I'd been adopted and beguiled with promises of tea, and fruit. More plums, peaches, I was to come, take onecuptea with Mr Ali of Siachen Tours, whose home was very near, in Saling, this village. However tiresome it sometimes seemed constantly to be adopted, ushered, treated and watched over, it was worth cultivating a network of friends. Mr Ali found some poor lad to carry his shopping trolley, the wheels of which were little use on the putrid green mud. We made an odd caravan: the pink hatchet-man, the boy with the shopping trolley, portly Mr Ali and me. The raftsmen were already hauling their craft back upriver for the next crossing. On the far shore a waiting figure could be seen. Commuting, Baltistan style. The morning shadows were retreating fast as we crossed the last yards of mud and entered the village. Soon the sun would appear over the mountaintops and the heat begin to climb.

Mr Ali was true to his word. He led me through fields and orchards to his home. There appeared a flask of butter-tea, and tin plates of plums, peaches and apricots. Biscuits appeared as if by magic. Of course there is no such thing as magic, but many unseen female hands in the kitchen. There appeared also several other people known to Mr Ali through complex patterns of kinship, friendship or business. He kept his room with a masculine fastidiousness reminiscent of old soldiers, but then you never ever see an untidy room in this country. A single bed stood upon a thick, well-swept durrie, and beside it a silver-framed photograph of a young man, perhaps himself, a few years younger and more mightily moustachioed. There were trophies for polo-playing, and a rifle propped in a corner beside the wide window which looked on to a clustered flower garden.

On the wall were photographs of Mr Ali and friends on a glacier. They were wearing long embroidered coats, wrapped over like dressing-gowns. The room was tranquil, washed in a pale green. Cross-legged on the floor sat a man who looked like Mr Ali—you could tell by his waistcoat that he was a big shot—and another, a thin, very fit man with an anorak over his shalwar-kameez. This was Olam Ali Sher, who was on his way upvalley. Mr Ali had assumed complete responsibility for my welfare, no matter how I protested, and if Olam was going my way, then that responsibility could be safely delegated to him. There was an exchange between the two men, with many glances in my direction. So much for being on my own. Olam Ali Sher felt much the same way. Despite his sour mutterings to Mr Ali, the latter cried, "You can go with this man. He is my onegoodfriend!"

Olam Sher looked less than pleased with the arrangement, and I said so.

"He says you walk too slow," said Mr Ali, candidly enough.

"He's right."

"He is my verygoodfriend, and will extend co-operations to you."

"I'll be all right."

"No. Please, you are our guest."

Olam Sher knew he was on a hiding to nothing. He was lumbered. He drained his tea and jerked his head towards the door. Time to go. Mr Ali also stood, declaring, "I am come to saw you off!"

I tried to keep up, but he was a Balti. He was twice my age, and you could tell he meant to cover ground. He had a deep barrel chest, and a bamboo staff. He tied a red scarf round his head in a most dashing manner and I knew I was in trouble. "I'll take the jeep, there's one loading up, I saw it," I said, but he looked at me yet more piteously. He led me by back routes through the village, along the sandy banks of irrigation canals and between high homestead walls. We had covered about three miles before he relented. In that time he seemed to have decided that I wasn't such a bad sort, or that he might as well have some fun with me. We emerged from the shade of the village trees on to the dusty road. It was already hot. If he was going where he said he was, we'd another twenty miles to cover. The road, of course, was all uphill.

A cargo jeep came by, already laden with a cheerful gang. Olam submitted, and we were hauled aboard by a dozen village men. In the fields we passed whole families, threshing the old-fashioned way with bullocks. Two women piled on board the jeep, *upside*. They wore no veils, and tied their black hair in soft buns. Both wore behind their ear an audaciously attractive posy of wild flowers. One draped her arm around the shoulders of the man at her side. This valley was a different place. The women looked so

Tibetan I could picture them both in black hats, spitting sun-flower seeds. Even Olam Ali Sher began to smile, once he'd told everybody how he'd been sandbagged with this Westerner, who couldn't walk at the speed of light, who was going to Hushe—why? God knows.

It was one o'clock and very hot before the jeep got as far as it was going, which was a village called Brale Gone. We paid the jeep driver and crossed the Hushe by a fine new suspension bridge. Olam Sher had taken to talking with me. "One hour only, my village."

One hour only. Say, three. Three hours' walk. The new jeep track continued on the west bank but we had crossed to the east and took the old way, through the village and up on to the hillside, but not before Olam had stopped to chat with a dozen people. Women ran towards him, bareheaded and laughing. "She is my sister." "He is my friend." Then we were out of the village lanes and trees and again up on a mountainside. "Hot is it, your country?" he said, striding out with the staff.

"Nothing like this."

"Many wagons?"

"Yes. Very many."

"Mountains?"

"Nothing like this."

We stopped beneath a tree and drank a little water. The wiry Olam pointed with his stick down to a ledge of land which swept out into the river. "This is my village, Khane."

It was green with trees and crops in their tiny terraces. There were flat rooftops half hidden by trees, and on the roofs the orange stain of countless apricots drying in the sun. A lizard darted under a rock at my feet.

"It's too hot. Very hot." This from Olam Sher. "Let's go."

We descended a steep scree slope to the village edge. There was a gate, and a rocky stream which sprang somewhere high in the mountains. It was the font of all the life before us. Olam braced himself on his stick and ran the last few yards downhill, skirting round a huge apricot tree. His was the first house, and he was inviting me in. His house was surrounded by a high fence of briars and twigs. His gate was similarly defended. Against what? He ushered me in and closed the gate behind us. We were standing in an earthen court. In front of us was a white mud-walled building, shaded by the low branches of a walnut tree. A low wall on the right gave some privacy to the latrine. There was a washing line with some clothes, and a couple of homespun blankets with bright borders. Huge balls of spun wool hung like wasps' nests from the lower branches of the tree. Olam called out. A woman's voice replied from the house and a tumble of little children ran out to meet us.

Where I come from it's considered pretentious to be sensitive to anything, and not encouraged, so it has taken me a long time to acknowledge that I, like everyone else, can walk into a building and feel right or wrong. A princess's palace or a peasant's hut, it makes no difference; sometimes a place just feels right. I resolved to read about geomancy, what the Chinese call feng shui, or the art of placing a building in its most auspicious setting. I don't know what factors matter—the arrangement of light, water, trees, hills, the relationship with compass points, ley lines or whatever. Olam's simple home struck me as such a building, perfectly set. And be it cause or effect, his was a happy household. From the cluster of children around him he took one up in his arms, a smiling bare-bottomed girl of three. He gestured for me to follow, and walked into the shady passage.

The house was built of whitewashed earth. Wooden doors with primitive latches and tilting lintels led from this passage into its three rooms. At the farthermost door Olam took off his shoes and ducked inside, the child still in his arms. I stood uncertainly at the door. As my eyes grew accustomed I could see within a dark and smoky kitchen, where a little fire flickered beneath a pot. By its light I saw a young woman hunkered on a very low stool. She was in the act of ladling water from the old ghee tin that served as reservoir into the pot. Half turned to me, she smiled a huge grin and waved me in. The children waved me in. Olam waved me in. I took off my boots and entered.

The woman saw me settled then, with a strong high voice, she announced her name: Gulfam. GULFAM. She smiled an infectious grin and set me off. She tried to pronounce my name, but wrinkled her nose as if the very sound smelled bad. Harsh afternoon sunlight fell through the glassless window at my back, but was quickly absorbed into the gloom of the kitchen. I thought of Scottish blackhouses, the turf cottages without chimneys where the smoke from the central fire was left to find its own way out into the drizzling skies. This was a modern house, with a tin chimney poking through the ceiling. The ceiling was of logs supporting a woven affair of twigs and branches. There hung deep black smuts, like bats.

Two older children, a squinting girl of ten and her elder brother, were following Gulfam's orders and procuring from a suitcase a cloth which they spread on the floor in front of the window. On this I was encouraged to sit, with smiles and tugs. I tried to say the sackcloth that served for everyone else was fine for me, but none of it. Furthermore, I was to drink the tea which Gulfam was providing from the best cup, complete with handle, and saucer, while the others made do with chipped china bowls. Ah, God, the palaver of guests! The tablecloths, the silver cutlery, the wedding china, the never-ending, insufferable adult clack. Of course it was Balti tea: with butter and salt. I couldn't help it, my face twisted up, and they all laughed.

Gulfam tugged her shawl over her hair, which hung in two long thick twists on the front. Now I could see in the gloom I saw she was wearing a baggy old shalwar-kameez in bright blues and yellows, with an incongruous design of pineapples. Olam had set down the little girl, but drank his tea, also from a good cup, with a sleeping baby laid out across his lap. She was dressed in a cotton shift and an elaborate woollen helmet, like that of some medieval peasant soldier. Her face was very grubby but, nothing daunted, when the baby woke Olam swung her upright and kissed and crooned. The little girl was jealous and clambered over her dad's arms too. Gulfam laughed and smiled, and I soon came to realise that smiling was her resting state.

Immediately tea was over she began to cook a meal of potatoes and chapati. Olam left, patting the air to me to say: Stay, stay. Stay, stay, echoed Gulfam. They spoke about me—I could tell, because as Olam spoke Gulfam looked at me and smiled all the wider with strong white teeth, nodding and wrinkling her nose at me. She spoke to me directly and when I didn't understand, spoke again, slowly and loudly, with the strange song-like Balti syllables. Then, when her husband was out of the way, she rocked back on her little stool and let out a call that flew from the open door and windows. Like a yodel, it carried through the cluster of her neighbours' houses, and was answered by other women in other smoky kitchens or on other roofs, and one by one they all began to arrive.

A wonderment of children appeared first, to cluster round the door and stared at me. Led by Gulfam, we trooped out of the kitchen and into the best room, sunlit and rarely used. A bed stood against the wall; there was a stack of winter bedding and a few photographs. The jacket of a uniform hung from a nail in the wall. With extravagant gestures Gulfam bade me sit on the bed. Behind me she laid the helmeted baby, fed and lost in a milky sleep. The children followed, whispering and giggling: boys and girls, girls with babies tied to their backs, boys pinching and poking each other as they dared to approach me. Gulfam sat herself on the floor and, like a small class, so did the children. They were waiting for me to do something. Another woman arrived, and another, with shawls so long they fell from their heads to drag in the dust at their heels.

"Hadgee!" cried Gulfam, gesturing the younger of the women, a round-faced girl. Hadgee took her place beside Gulfam and gazed at me. I grinned, she grinned, the kids giggled. An old woman arrived and a *frisson* went round the room. This woman's hair was grey, her face was hewn from living rock. She alone was permitted to sit on the bed, beside me. For her alone, Gulfam fetched a cup of tea, in the good china. As she sipped it, straight-backed and dignified, she scrutinised me with hawk-like eyes. I avoided her terrifying gaze by counting the number of people now assembled in that small room: half a dozen women draped in shawls, and some twenty-five kids.

The boy who had spread the cloth for me was standing with friends on the threshold. He was playing with a little torch which he had concealed in the pocket of his blue shalwar-kameez. They were egging him on to something. Abruptly, and deeply embarrassed, he said in Urdu, "Sister!" and then in English, "Sis-ter!" He gathered confidence, and pointed to Gulfam and Fatima. "Sister!" They beamed at me. And in what little Urdu I had, translated into Balti for the benefit of the women, the schoolboy extracted from me crumbs of information which were held to the light like crystals by the assembled company. Names rained down on me: Gulfam, Hadgee, Fatima, Mustaq Ali, Maryam, Habiba, the helmeted baby asleep at my side, Musarrat, the girl who hovered ever closer to me as if at some strange animal at a zoo whom at any moment she might summon up courage to touch—that was Sajinn. The schoolboy himself, Anwar Ali, his giggling friend, Mustaq Mohammed.

What was my country, had I no friends? Gulfam said something raucous and all the women laughed. The boy turned crimson and fiddled with his torch. Sajinn took her chance and sat right up against me like a cat. "Leave the lady alone," said Gulfam, and she moved off an inch, only to crouch back. She smelled of woodsmoke and goats. A little boy, no more than a toddler, weed himself and was whisked from the room. Another knelt motionless and awestruck at my feet. I leaned forward and said "BOO!" His sudden scream of abject terror tore our ears and woke the baby, who cried and was passed by Sajinn to Gulfam, who put her to the breast. The boy's sobs subsided, and to my apologetic expressions the women made faces of reproach and sorrowful amusement.

The day's travelling and all the days before were catching up with me. I felt my eyes close, and began to feel oppressed by the crowd of people surrounding me, plucking at my clothes and asking questions I had no hope of understanding. I longed to sleep, like the baby Gulfam was again laying on the bed at my side. She gave a string of loud syllables. I smiled helplessly, but the women roared. At a single word from Gulfam, the children left the room like a flock of sparrows, and a blessed silence fell. Now we could get down to business.

"You!" Gulfam said, all in gestures. "No children?"

I tried a sad little smile. No children. The women shook their heads and chucked like hens.

"No tits either. Body like Sajinn's, hasn't she? A ten-year-old!"

Gulfam got herself to her feet and waddled about in front of us, pretending a huge pregnant belly. This is what you want! The women rocked with laughter. Sajinn frisked me. My already ineffectual bust had shrunk to nothing. I wanted to explain that I wasn't usually such a stick insect, but this is what a diet of rice and dhal does for me. That and wandering about on glaciers. But what can you do? Sajinn felt among my clothing for anything resembling breasts, but declared it hopeless. I was more embarrassed than they were. But Gulfam was a success—as Alison had told me, she had her children and chief among them the intelligent, formal, male

Anwar Ali. She was proud of it. She pulled up her shalwar and showed me her huge blue breasts, the reward of childbearing, as proud of these grand trophies as anyone else would be of silver cups on the dresser. She pulled one up by the scruff like a cat its kitten, and shook it at me. The other women nodded in approval. *This is what you want!*

"And if God isn't good, this is what you do." Gulfam hunkered in front of me, concerned, sorrowing. I was her sister and she would help me. She looked into my eyes, her own mocking and pitying at once. "You must pray to God, for a baby. Like this!" She beat her heart with her fist and lifted her arms imploringly to heaven: *Bismillah!* In the name of Allah! Bismillah! The shawl fell from her hair as she threw back her head. Fatima joined in: *Al-lah!* Sajinn smiled childish encouragement. The hawk-faced elder looked stern as an American Indian, then relented to give me a slight nod.

When I woke, the women and the baby were gone. Through the open window, I could see late-afternoon sunshine creeping over the mountains. I lay for a few minutes, enjoying peace. Children's voices reached me, and the occasional bleat of a goat. I noticed the river's rush which pervades every village, so constant and ubiquitous that you become unaware of it until it reappears at times of silence, like your own heartbeat. Another sound: of an axe thudding into wood. Softly, the door opened, and closed again before I could see who was there.

I was ravenous. I had been ravenous for days, no matter what I ate. In my rucksack, which was propped against the wall, were some biscuits and half a tin of cheese. There was a latch on the door and I turned it, locking myself in so I could eat without being discovered. Alison had said, half cynically, "These Baltis, they're not that poor," and she was right, but the burden of my ravenous hunger was more than I could inflict upon them. I ate the lot, then the few remaining apricots left over from lunch. "*Chuli*" in Balti.

It was the first word I learned, because they were everywhere. They fell from the trees and lay ignored upon the earth below, such was their plenty.

From the window I could look down on the village. It is so steep that although the room in which I slept is ground level from the back, it is the first floor from the front, and a cellar is formed beneath. The cellar is a byre for goats and cows, who have their own strange Tolkienesque windows and doors. Their roof is our floor. The axeing came from outside, and I followed the sound out into the sunlight. There, in a corner of the yard hemmed in by the fence of briars, was Olam, sweating as he axed a lump of greenwood into sticks. Above his head spread the branches of an old apricot tree. In the tree was Anwar Ali, with his hands and pockets full of apricots.

Apricots were the villages" work of the moment. Olam pointed to a rickety little ladder which led from the yard up on to the flat roof of his house. I climbed it and discovered, as in Askole, that the whole village could communicate via its roofs. Gulfam and Hadgee sat on the latter's roof, next door, which you could gain by just jumping the space between the two houses. They were stoning apricots, and a small mountain of the fruit was heaped in front of them. There were two home-made creels, one to receive the fruit, and the other the stones. The fruit was then spread upon the roof or on any convenient flat rock, and left to dry in the sunshine, its sweet high smell blending with that of goats and smoke to give the village its characteristic odour.

They were experts and could shell two apricots simultaneously, one in each hand, with a twist of their thumbnails. Sajinn was there, with all her plastic bangles and uneven teeth. Wrapped about her was a homespun blanket of grey scratchy wool, the kind I'd seen dangling from trees. Blankets are finished with a few embroidered flowers or a border of colours and pompoms. Leaning secured against her back was the baby in the helmet. Such was the work of girls of Sajinn's age. Sajinn and baby moved in close to me, and we worked for an hour until the apricots were finished and the afternoon was wearing to a close. Then, as they spoke together for a while, Gulfam took the grubby shawl from her hair and unworked the twists with her fingers so that her hair fell in greasy strands about her shoulders. Sajinn, eyes crossed myopically, worked her way through Gulfam's hair, crushing with a firm thumbnail the lice she extracted. The little bare-bottomed girl stamped about on chubby legs, and learned to love games of "This little piggy went to market," so every time I sat she would toddle over and sit at my side, and thrust her little feet into my lap.

"How old are you, Gulfam?" I asked later, when we all sat again in the kitchen. She was energetically working a thin wooden churn, like an outsize bicycle pump. She never stopped working. Anwar Ali translated into Balti. Gulfam cocked her head thoughtfully, threw a wild gesture, and grinned.

"She does not know," said Anwar Ali. "You?"

"Twenty-eight. You?"

"Eleven. This"—he pointed to the little bare-bottomed girl, who had exhausted herself with piggies going to market and slept where she had fallen—"This, three. This"—the baby looking around on Sajinn's back—"four months only."

Sajinn herself was nine or ten. Gulfam could be no older than me. Younger, maybe. She was again at her customary place to the left of the stove, sitting on her low stool, only an inch or two from the floor, with her knees drawn up about her shoulders. She leaned up and sighed. I offered to help, but realised that in entertaining the kids I was doing her a favour. They arrived in a little flock and were hugged and cuddled, then would abruptly leave again. Strange children would arrive, stay awhile, go. Neighbouring women came, stayed awhile, went. I rarely saw men. Right now, all the children were in. It was growing dark. I sat on the cloth and allowed Sajinn and her girlfriend to play with me like a giant doll. I lay down and they leaned over me, scruffy angels, asking soft questions. Their breath smelled strongly as they enquired, in Urdu, about my mother and father, about whom I could say only their names, that they were at home in my country and worked in offices; a set of circumstances so remote from this village.

I wondered what pictures, if any, my words conjured up. They seemed satisfied to know my country was cold, rainy, without mountains; that I had but one sister and one brother. They transferred from their thin wrists to mine an enormous number of plastic bangles, and then Sajinn uttered one of the few words of English she knew, which, oddly enough, was "pain." I was in no pain, but she and her friend began to knead my arms in an inexpert but delicious massage. "Pain?" she asked, laying her healing hands on my brow. "Pain?" on my calves and shoulders. I lay looking up at the smoke-blackened rafters, happy to allow them to knead away days of jolting jeeps and dusty trails, while Gulfam, ladle in hand, caught my eye and laughed. Two huge black hens jumped in the open window and began pecking about on the kitchen floor. Gulfam pushed a dish of chapati scraps towards them, and they settled to roost for the night in a wooden box in a corner of the room, beside a stack of suitcases sealed with little Chinese padlocks.

I woke at dawn, alone in the good room. Bedbugs had made a feast of me, but in the peace and quiet of the first light the feeling was of holidays, the first day of the long summer holidays, of waking up in a place both unfamiliar and wonderful. Olam was already up, and Gulfam too. They were hunkered on either side of the little fire, talking softly. Gulfam poked sticks into the fire. When the water boiled, the sticks were removed and saved until next time. She served Olam's breakfast of chapati and Balti tea, freshly churned. What remained she poured in the ubiquitous Chinese thermos, for the kids' breakfast.

The family slept outside under the stars, rolled up in blankets on the swept earth roof. Summer must be very heaven to villagers whose winter months are spent huddled with the beasts, under an insulating layer of straw on the roof, while the world outside, now so green and golden, turns to a barrenness of grey and snowy white.

Olam was again going down to Khapalu. The children appeared bleary-eyed at the door and Gulfam began to manage their breakfasts. Each child was closely watched, so that no one got more to eat than the others. Constant was the flow of hugs and smiles, from both Olam and Gulfam, who even found smiles left over for each other. I never saw them touch.

There is a shop in the village, and to reach it we walked little lanes and earthen alleys; above us the balconies of houses lurched drunkenly about, and people waved and called. More children scrambled down the ladders to join the throng which surrounded me. I was the property of Sajinn, who was wrapped in her blanket like an old woman, with the baby's helmet nodding on her back. She secured her hold on my left hand while half a dozen fought for my right.

At various houses Gulfam stopped and called, to introduce me as a poor skinny Westerner, and childless. They were concerned for me, would pray for me. Old toothless women, young smiling women with babies on their hips, women beating clothes on a flat rock at the side of the stream, they pointed at the heavens and reassuringly told me of Allah—it would be all right. I'd see. Now the whole village is praying for me. The children squabbled, and fell into the irrigation streams. Two boys played races in a wheelbarrow, and the kids showed off by teasing the village simpleton, a sorry-looking girl of Sajinn's age who clung to the walls with downcast eyes. This poor child obviously wished herself invisible and clutched a pair of plimsolls to her chest like a doll. They snatched the shawl from her hair and ran off laughing.

It was quite a crowd that entered the yard of the shop. The earth was bare, a depleted tree struggled to grow. The shop was in the cellar of the house. It was cave-like and secret. Within his dark domain the shopkeeper worked by the light which diffused through the thin curtain. Dickens could not have invented this man. He was one of the dirtiest I have ever seen. Behind him, fearsome shadows and strange shapes hung from the rafters. He didn't say much. On his head was a foul green skullcap. If I was a kid I would be scared of him; he would be a bogeyman. He kept sacks of rice and tubs of ghee, and clothes of great antiquity, recycled through the village umpteen times, for clothing is in short supply and the resultant outfits are bizarre. On old-fashioned bar-scales he weighed the salt and ghee which Gulfam ordered. He used no scoop but his hand, which he licked finger by finger between serving. He licked the ghee lasciviously before he plunged his hand into the sugar sack, licked the sugar before he served the tea. This was where the things ended up that did so much to make a cargo-jeep memorable. The bars of red soap, schoolbooks, a jar of bubble gum. The children's eyes fastened on the bubble gum and a clamour ensued, calmed only when each child had some, and Gulfam had paid the man with a few rupees tied into a corner of her dirty shawl.

Sometimes Gulfam would pass her hand over her eyes and stare wearily into the middle distance. She looked away through the green-framed window, over the stunted cabbage patch, the neighbour's roof, the walnut trees, beyond the village and out across the river to the road and the ochre rockwall beyond. I wonder what she would say if I told her I chose not to have children—at least, not yet. She dispenses hugs, kisses, scolds and food. This afternoon she was at her customary place at the stove, again preparing food. Perhaps it was on such an afternoon, when she was tired and dreaming, that she cut off her index finger. She explained how she'd done it: the knife, the chopping-board, the geyser of blood, the wide-eyed horror, the pain. But—she turned her hand about for my inspection—it's all right now. With that voice perfectly pitched to carry out into the lanes and fields, she called for her boy to go to the stream for more water.

The kitchen door duly darkened, but not with a boy dragging a jerry can. A ghost filled the frame. A scary ghost, a featureless spirit of awesome potency. It swayed a little, like a sapling in a cold breeze. Then it doubled over and its head fell off. Revealed Anwar Ali and his giggling friend. The two boys were piggyback, and upturned on Anwar's head was a conicular wicker basket used for transporting everything from dung to firewood to sleeping babies. Around that they'd wrapped an old chador, like a grave-cloth. We all laughed, but I wish I could have spoken to them. Several thousand miles separated our culture, but we both knew a ghost when we saw one. Are there ghosts in the village? Jinn with their feet on backwards? Old Tibetan tales; smothered babies and one-eyed spirits?

Then he was gone, and back a moment later with a wild grey kitten on a string, and then a years-old calendar with scenes of Switzerland. There were pictures with castles and cars. "This *garee*?" Anwar Ali said, pointing to a Volvo parked in a snowy Swiss street. A wagon, yes. This: a church; this: a mountain village, a far cry from your own. I took a great shine to young Anwar Ali. He was clever, polite, spirited. Through him I made most of my conversation, as we wandered in and out of village houses. Anwar oscillated between the formal demeanour of his father, in whose absence he assumed the position of man of the house, and of the schoolboy with his pockets full of buttons and string. "Bongo!" Gulfam called him. Son!

After the calendar Anwar Ali made ready with some new entertainment for me, and appeared with a leap and a jump at my side, not now as a ghost but as a bear. He danced a bear-dance, dressed in a real bearskin. The head and paws were removed and the skin was sewn up like a sack, and Anwar Ali was inside it, growling. There was my answer, perhaps, to the fence of briar and thorns which protected Olam's home. Within that fence we played a sort of cricket-cum-volleyball with a burst ball. The children ran about, mock-fighting, climbing trees which rained apricots down to the dust. I would have eaten them, having long since given up fears about the water and fruit. But windfalls are *ganda*—dirty. Only fruit plucked fresh from the tree is fit to eat. The little children ran about in ragged tops and no underclothes, fell into ditches and rolled around in hay-fields. Evening is playtime; they charge around the village with tin cans on strings. You never see a child on a British street now. Too much fear and traffic. Too much "safety."

A lanky unpleasant youth appeared to whom I took an instant dislike. He wore not the shalwar-kameez but a pair of blue track-suit bottoms and a thin top with Japanese writing on. The clothes brought out the Tibetan in his features, though he was gaunt of face and sly. He was as thin as a bean, and he lounged against the wall watching me out of the corner of his eye. Anwar Ali pulled my shoulder and whispered a word. "He is Pugee!" It meant nothing. I shook my head.

"In English?"

"You are name?" said the bean. "You are country-name? How many days you are in Pakistan?"

"Pugee!" whispered Anwar.

"I don't know what it means."

"Spy!" said the bean.

"Yes, he is spy!" whispered Anwar.

"You are a spy?"

"Yes." He slapped his chest. "I am SPY."

It was harvest time. The short summer was already drawing to a close. Olam had made his way back again from Khapalu and laboured up the lane from the fields to his house beneath a mound of hay larger than himself. There are no carts in the villages; the wheelbarrow the boys were playing in was the only wheel I'd ever seen there. Both men and women laboured hard under heavy weights of sticks and straw, dung and children, like little figures in a Brueghel painting. A man could look old and wizened at forty-five; goitres wobbled at older women's throats, their eyes turned weak and milky. Carrying seemed to be people's life's work, as it was in prehistoric times.

It was evening, in the kitchen. "Garee," said Anwar, and we all strained our ears. A wagon was indeed coming this way. The children pressed to the window and looked out into the darkness. Its headlamps lit a line of light on the other side of the river. The sound of its engine, trapped in the tall sides of the valley, reached us faintly. It stopped for a few minutes, as the passengers unloaded their bags and sacks and prepared to descend the steep bank to the river-bridge, and come home to the village. The hen roosting on its box woke and chucked, and abruptly ran across the floor amongst us. The baby lay asleep on Olam's lap, and a woman from next door came in to ask him to read a letter to her, from the army where her husband served, she being uneducated and Olam having the power of literacy. Gulfam was teaching me Balti words: *mindoc*, flower; *shi-sha*, lamp. Proudly she called out the sounds: Balti! *chuli*, Englis? *apricot*.

Anwar translated my words of English and Urdu into Balti for his mother. I wondered how many generations it will take before the programme of roads is complete, the schools are built, the Urdu-speaking doctors arrive to tend the new much-needed clinics, and the freshly painted schools resound to the chants of Urdu and English. Will the Balti words she calls so proudly go the same way as other languages—Gaelic in my own country? I felt again the sad excitement with which Ken and Jungly John had both infected me. And Jungly John—the day we'd arranged to meet was fast approaching. I wanted to go on and meet him and learn what he could tell me of the old culture, so that I too could read the signs which doubtless surrounded me. Often nowadays I felt as though I were at the brink of some knowledge or understanding. Tomorrow I would go on up the valley.

I excused myself for bed. Anwar Ali was master of the lamps—it was his job to fill them with kerosene, and light them. He took a lamp to show me the way, first outside in the yard where he lit my path to the evil-smelling long-drop by the gate. There he set down the lamp to make eerie flickers on the low mud wall around the latrine. He slipped away. The stars were out, the mountains dark black against the starlit sky. Around me, the huddle of houses settled for the night. There was an occasional cough or child's cry. As I washed in the stream, I could hear a radio faintly down in the village. It was playing "The Sting."

I was sad to leave. I'd fallen for Gulfam and her family, and didn't like to think I wouldn't see them again. I certainly didn't want to outstay my welcome either. There were great farewells. Anwar Ali walked me to the edge of the village in the morning light. The village ended suddenly. On this side of a stone wall was a field of peas. On that, nothing but dry dust and boulders. A beaten path led over a stile and down to the river, where a blue glacier stream joined the Hushe river, forming a blue slick in its grey race There, at the union of the rivers, Anwar shook my hand, and accepted my thanks with a gravity beyond his years. This was the border; farther he would not go. Before me lay a flat bridge of planks, lashed together with metal cable. There was nothing to hold on to. I stepped on to the bridge; it listed under my weight. I looked back for Anwar Ali, but he was gone.

Where the planks were missing, the river roared sickeningly down, sending up a cold draught. At the far side of the bridge the path lost itself in a steep bouldery bank. It was a scramble of 60 feet up to the road, where the wagon had stopped last night. Now, if I turned and looked back across the river to the village, I could see how beautiful it was, how the blue stream which watered it poured out of a deep cleft, where high snow-faced mountains hid behind a fanfare of lesser hills, barren and brown. Khane was an apron of green and yellow terraces, layered like feathers, and a huddle of flat roofs and graceful poplar trees. Downriver, bluff after bluff jutted out into the torrent, and a barrier of huge and distant mountains closed the valley off. The road was still in shadow. The rising sun was picking out the highest peaks in a golden light. People who have travelled tell me you see this golden light nowhere else. And the shade of blue of the sky is not sky-blue, but cobalt above tapering down to the merest eggshell in the distance. The river twisted in and out of the shade. A wagtail landed on the roadside, bob-bobbing its tail. Nothing else moved. I fastened on my sack and began to walk.

"Objectives," Jungly John had said, contemptuously. In this valley, the objective for Western mountaineering and trekking teams is Masherbrum. But I suppose we all have them, half-articulated. Alison: to save souls. Ken: to take notes on a changing culture. Gulfam—if it is an objective—to bear and raise her children well. The road rose, and from the vantage point I could see it carry on for ever, a flattened track of dust through a boulder-field. At its end, hours away, was my temporary objective, the village of Hushe. Olam had given me a bamboo staff with a leather thong for the wrist and I strode out with it, enjoying the walk like I'd enjoyed no other, quite alone.

The little hotel in Hushe village was empty. I rested in the room I was shown, because the walk was long. I like the simplicity of such rooms. They are restful. I like the angles. I like the angle formed by my walking stick leaning against the wall, the pleasing simplicity of the washed walls. The lower third of the wall was pale green, the upper portion white. I like the pattern made where the wash has fallen off, and the heavy wooden window-frames, and the logs that support the ceiling, although I know trees are hard to find. Everything is organic. Earth, wood, the hemp of the charpoy. There is sacking to cover the earthen floor. I like the rough little latch on the door. It's cool enough here to appreciate the colour and textures, and notice them. A similar room downside and you would just be sprawled sweating and enduring. It has a convalescent feel, like a room in a painting, an interior empty but inhabited. I would love such a room for my own. And that which I carry with me is being honed down to a satisfying minimum: a change of clothes; a shawl, a stick, a black notebook on a wicker table. My tin dish, comb, toothbrush, knife and torch.

There was cloud that afternoon, lifting and falling. I was too tired to do much except loaf about the hotel yard. I walked among the fields. The pea pods were ripe. The hotel's proprietor was Roza Ali, a high-altitude porter of renown. He showed me photographs of himself in Europe, himself in Italy at the home of Reinhold Messner, the two of them in front of a rose tree. Photos of this base camp, that, of people on glaciers, a woman in shorts laughing as she set up a tripod. Sometimes his hotel is so full, people sleep on the floor. He talked about famous mountaineers, such an expedition to such a peak, with encyclopaedic knowledge. Men's expeditions, and latterly women's. Swiss, Polish, British, French, their expedition postcards are plastered on the walls.

Hushe is spoken of as the most wonderful of all the villages. It's hidden behind a bluff so you don't see it until you are on top of it. Hushe, home of the most wonderful people, musicians and dancers, looked to me a filthy run-down collection of hovels full of children too used to streams of Westerners passing through their village. They shout "Ha-lo Ha-lo Ha-lo" like cuckoos and beg pens, sweets, "one rupee." I was not instantly enamoured of Hushe, but these things take time. There are two little shops, selling foodstuffs to expeditions. Tins of cheese and fish, bits of tape and karabiners. There was no sign of Jungly John, but that didn't surprise me; this is not a predictable kind of place.

The hotel had the sort of Mexican feel you get in movies. Ennui. A dirty boy sat on the concrete steps, mending a lamp. His friend lolled on a charpoy. Their clothes were very dirty. One had round his thick black hair a scarf that was once pink. The other wore a mismatching shalwar-kameez and an oily torn anorak. He looked like a garage hand in a place you'd never take your car. The sun went down and the air was chilly. It's high here. The garage hand began to sing as he fiddled with the lamp, and sang well. He warmed to it and stood. His voice attracted others, who peered in the gateway to the hotel's compound. They clapped on the off-beats. Still singing, he began to dance with the high steps of a man trying to get chewing gum off the sole of his shoe. And stopped.

"This harmony," he said to me.

"Do you play also?"

"Drum. Pipe."

For another hour we sat; he sang on occasion with a few words of desultory conversation in between. I sang a sad Scots song and he answered with one of his own.

"Childrens, you?"

"No. You?"

"One baby." He drew his finger across his throat and lolled his head. Dead. Quickly, he began to sing again.

"An old song?"

"New."

"Hushe song?"

"I am singing Hushe, Punjabi, Pathan, I every day singing. I pipe, I drum. Music, harmony is good."

Another voice reached us—it was the broken sob of the evening call to prayer. The singer cocked his head. "Muslim men pray."

"Not you?"

He smiled, but did not reply. That was left to an urchin who had his head laid adoringly on the singer's oily anorak. He said, " 'E is leettle bit Muslim. He is *ver'* sing, *ver'* drum."

I left Hushe in the morning, and on the way out of town met the singer with a sickle in his hand, going to the fields.
"Where go?"
I was going to forsake Jungly John and go back to Gulfam and Olam's place. "Khane!" I said to the singer. But it was more than just a change of village. I'd reached the farthermost point of my journey, and leaving Hushe was the first step on the long journey home.

He folded his arms and laid the sickle across his breast. Behind him, the sun was beginning to pick out the summits of mountains. Two women passed with huge wicker baskets strapped to their backs and a gummy-eyed baby in each. They asked for medicine for the babies' eyes. I suggested washing in warm water, but they looked askance at that.

"Yes," said the singer. "This Khane, ver' clean place. Khane peoples washing. Hushe peoples, no washing." He laughed merrily. "Hushe peoples, mens, children, *no washing.*"

"Why not?"

"No washing!" With a wave and a merry laugh he turned off into the fields, singing a few high notes.

The road curves down through a cultivated river-valley, and then a rocky outcrop seals it from the world outside. There is a suspension bridge across the boulder-strewn river. To cross the river by the bridge was to enter a cold place, still in dawn's shadow. From there the track rose steep and dusty until it emerged on to the flank of a hillside. It was no more than a scratch, miles of tyre tracks across a sandy boulder-field. The serrated ridges of mountains plunged down from left and right, with black faces of shadow on the east sides. It is a landscape of such scale and drama that the slightest human touch—a cairn, a village, a goat carved on a brindled rock—takes on a numinous glow. A crow glided across and landed on a rock nearby. I saw no other living creature.

On my left the land sloped and then fell down into the river gorge. On the opposite bank mountains rose to mirror those on this. Behind me, the valley writhed and was lost in a jagged wall of mountains. Hushe village was behind its bluff of rock, when the path swung to the west, the huge cone of Masherbrum swam into view, coated in a soft veil of mist. Ahead of me, the road raced the river down to its confluence with the Shyok, where the raft would be making its first crossing. There too a jagged wall of pale and distant mountains met my gaze. I was imprisoned in a huge place. Around and ahead: mountains, and the sky above no more than a fissure of bright blue. Long shadows were forming from the rocks as the sun crept into the valley. To my right, great motionless chutes of scree poured from the cracks between mountains. And the tenacious villages shone green and golden in the morning light. Is it any wonder they sang for the changing seasons? The too-brief summer of colour and growth and movement would soon be over, and they had to prepare. The villagers would be gone to the fields with their sickles and baskets, or on to the high grazing with the goats. The stream of village boys would be making their mischievous progress to the schoolhouses, where the summer sun would stream through the windows and distract them from their lessons. And in other places, the doctors would be attending the first of the day's patients, the princess would pluck her plums for breakfast, Gulfam would carefully tear chapatis in half and share them among her children. Jamila would be applying a little make-up, before wrapping herself in a burqa and making for school. And I was alone on a dusty track, under a strengthening blue sky. It was a beautiful day, a beautiful high summer's morning. It would be a shortish walk, four hours and downhill into stronger air. I wanted nothing to interrupt it. I wanted to walk, look and think.

We surprise ourselves sometimes, with what we are capable of. I didn't think I was a person capable of walking down a Himalayan track on a summer's morning, all alone. But I am, I was. A simple enough thing, to walk between two villages with a bamboo stick in one hand. But everything presents itself to our Western minds as choice. To Gulfam, and to Rashida and Jamila, who felt for me a slight pity as they wrapped themselves in their black robes, or displayed to me the awesome majesty of their much-used bodies, I wanted to explain notions of choice and risk, and how we embraced both. Gulfam had affected me with the delight she showed in her children; Rashida with her humble acceptance of her Gilgiti life and the way she said, "We have no worries."

I walked a few miles, then rested the weight of my rucksack against a boulder and looked at the villages downstream. There was a cairn, with a stone set upright on top. A wayside marker, a shrine perhaps? Orange lichen grew on the rocks. I picked up a stone and tried to throw it down the hillside to the river. I could have children, and maybe no worries. But I was a person walking down a track in Baltistan all alone on a Wednesday morning. I was capable; and sometimes, a glimpse of what we could be opens in our minds like the fearsome blue crevasses I'd seen on glaciers. I could be a person who lives here. Somehow, like Jungly John, a wandering monkish figure gone native. Tie a few things on to a donkey and walk the Himalayas. No matter how ridiculous the discovery, the hint of a possibility, it poses a choice; either you act upon it, or annul it. In my rucksack was James Baldwin's novel, and I recalled a passage which had so arrested me:

Many years were to pass before he could begin to accept what he, that day, with the stream whispering in his ear, discovered, and yet that day was the beginning of his life as a man—still struggling to find the grace that would allow him to bear that revelation.

This was no stream whispering in my ear, but the violent roar of glacial melt carving a channel through barren banks of rock. Grace, revelation, this was strong beer. And hard to admit to. I sat on a boulder and for a long time looked at the awesome land around me.

It was 8 a.m. Rashida would have finished her half-hour of exercises by now, and maybe would catch a half-hour at her dictionaries before the day's work. Already she might have swept out her demesne, the little room and the yard. But I could travel, and wander about on dusty roads, learning things. "Why?" she would say. It was time to begin learning. To speak the language and work with these people—that was the next stage, and it was possible. Odd, but possible, a possibility like the dry track under my feet. But it would mean forgoing the children, and the shadowy figure that filled the vacuum when they asked, "Where is your husband?" My body would remain immature and sticklike. I could only guess what Gulfam felt when she buried her face laughing in her children's smelly folds, and there was Alison, whom I envied in a way—the certainty of what she was, what she was doing and why. I envied her her faith, and understood why Muslims so often pity us our lack. A pair of pied wagtails swooped low and landed bobbing on the roadside. It would get hot today. The sky was turning bright blue. I ate a biscuit and walked on. If you aren't well under way by 8 a.m, don't bother.

As well as the sweets I'd bought from the trekkers' shop in Hushe, which were immediately shared, I gave Anwar Ali my head-torch, and showed him how to broaden and narrow the beam, where to find the spare bulbs secreted behind the lens unit, and how to replace the battery, when necessary, with the couple of spares I found for him. He thanked me gravely, then grinned from ear to ear. I went to bed, but first looked out to see what was causing the giggling and shouts outside. The entire family were prowling around the darkened lanes of Khane, looking at things by torchlight.

Hushe valley was a holiday from Pakistan. A different atmosphere prevailed there. I cherished the images I had: of the rounded haystack by the roadside, protected by a charm twirling in the breeze; of Gulfam's smoke-blackened kitchen, their hospitality. At Maculu I got a lift on a jeep; it was the most ancient jeep in the world. It was better to walk. An old man with hairy ears travelled in the cab next to me. I made him feel uncomfortable; he might never have sat next to a strange woman, all his life long. I blamed on him the occasional puffs of foul smell until I realised they coincided not with him lifting his woollen cap to scratch his stubbly head, but with the wrenching gear changes. On the back we carried a load of oil-drums and bales of hay, with the boy who owned the bales sitting on top like a cherry on a cake. With slow and odorous progress we left the Hushe valley and followed the Shyok through villages where old-fashioned houses leaned out over the track. It was a pre-jeep track, too narrow for the vehicle. Certainly, no carpet.

At the village of Chibo the driver, the smelly old man and I were joined by a long-haired soul with a resemblance to Descartes. The father of Western Rationalism reincarnated as an Islamic peasant? He was taking cow-skins to market. The bales were removed and the choice aroma of gearbox, old man, and oil-drums, as if deemed a cocktail not quite foul enough, was enhanced by the brittle hides of Descartes. We followed the river for hours. The smelly old man dug me in the ribs and offered a pineapple sweet. The sun rose to its zenith and, with none of the cooling breezes of high Hushe to comfort us now, the smell grew worse, and evil plumes of black smoke rose from the engine.

With typical perversity the jeep chuntered on until the hottest part of the day, then stopped for good. It was on the most arid stretch of road. No water, no habitation. Two inches of shadow clung to a dry-stone wall and there we sat, watching the driver groping in the open bonnet of his jeep, sucking and spitting petrol from the fuel line. I thought he would retch. We pushed, it started, failed. *Yah-Allah*! The driver got back in, leaned his head on the steering wheel. He looked sideways and shrugged. The jeep was his livelihood. The jeep was *khatam. All-ah*!

No living soul appeared on the long straight road. Not a drop of water trickled down a single irrigation ditch. Not a vehicle churned up an iota of dust. The sun beat down. Through the haze, just at the edge of vision far up the road, five men could be seen on a flat roof. They were making the obsequies of prayer. Then they came out on to the road, shouldered tools and set off in the opposite direction. The metal of their spades glinted in the sun.

Epilogue: Return to Gilgit

There was no sun, but a steady falling rain, which was turning the ground to mud. We'd stopped the jeep in the bazaar, by a grocer's stall. Under a damp awning were tidy heaps of oranges and cauliflowers. Men thronged around us, men and boys, every one wrapped in a thin blanket. They pushed handcarts or carried water, bought or sold. A boy, a newspaper vendor, was staring in through the jeep window. Behind him the grocer called his wares, and as he called, he whetted a long knife on the edge of an oil-drum.

Mohammed Ali Changezi leaned over from the back of the jeep. "Your shawl," he said. "I think it's better like this"—and he waved his hand around his face.

"Over my head, you mean?"

"Yes. In these places it's better."

"Should I go in the back?"

"No need. But the shawl is good. In the Northern Areas it's okay, but down here, these people, a lot went from here to fight for the Taliban, and a lot were killed . . ."

As the paperboy stared, Mohammed Ali sent the driver, Ibrahim, to do the buying, and now bulging polythene bags of peas, peppers, oranges and bananas were being manhandled through the window.

"You can get these in Skardu, but not so fresh. I think we won't have lunch here. Later, okay?"

Later, the rain turned to snow. We were still ten hours south of Gilgit and it was snowing. Ten hours more altitude to gain. On the hill in front of us, two little Suzuki wagons and a mini-bus revved and slithered helplessly.

"Do you think this is madness? To come in winter?"

Mohammed Ali laughed. "There's no snow in Gilgit. Only here. Gilgit never has snowfall. Skardu does. It's −13° in Skardu at night."

We watched as six men climbed onto the back bumper of the mini-bus, and began to bounce in unison, trying to shift the vehicle across the road onto a place with better purchase. On either side of the road stood silent pines, taking a slow dusting of snow.

"Scotland's like this," I said. Actually, it's not. Beyond the bouncing mini-bus and the hapless Suzuki wagons, and the people who milled about on the road, a convoy of painted lorries waited.

"Anyway, I put four new tyres on the jeep, for you."

"Thank you."

"And Ibrahim is now a driver, after five years' apprenticeship."

"A five-year apprenticeship, before you're fit to drive the

Karakoram Highway?" Ibrahim inclined his thin head shyly, never taking his eyes from the road. When he saw his moment, he put the jeep into four-wheel drive, and skirted round the skating mini-buses.

Mohammed Ali Changezi is a man I'd known for many years. Since 1984, as he will remind me, because he has a memory for dates and events. He's the owner and manager of a tour guide business from Skardu. In the summer, he takes groups of Japanese and European adventure-tourists, trekkers and mountaineers into the Karakoram mountains. As a young man, he was always thoughtful, but age has hardened his thoughtfulness into gravitas. His thick hair and beard, which were once coal-black, are greying now. In the back of the jeep, surrounded by luggage and vegetables, he turned his prayer-beads as we drove.

We travelled on, Ibrahim's thin hand pulling the gear lever. It was the first of February. Through the snow and on, among the terraced villages of Kohistan. We were now following the Indus, and were on the Karakoram Highway proper.

"You can drive; you can drive the Highway yourself!" Mohammed Ali had joked, when we'd spoken on the phone, me in Fife, and him in Rawalpindi. I was asking how things stood, was it too risky, too wintry to make a trip to the Northern Areas? How would he feel about accompanying me? I had decided that I should not go alone, not this time.

Not in winter, not with the USA bombing Afghanistan and troops massed on the Kashmir border . . .

Below us, far below, down slopes of mud or scree or cliff, the Indus coiled. This was a different river from the one I remembered. None of the grey broiling broth of summer, it was a deep, opaque turquoise. We followed the river-gorge around bluffs and along high ledges, under overhangs of rock, and through rutted places where waterfalls had gouged the road. Somewhere around here had been the landslide I remembered so well, which I'd had to cross by moonlight. I remembered the thin voice from the roof of the bus: "Sleepee here! Five hundred rupees you love me?" But the road was clear. All in all, I'd leave the driving to Ibrahim. I contented myself with offering him the occasional sweet, or a banana. He spoke little, concentrated on avoiding goats, and people bearing loads of firewood. Once, on a whitewashed wall by the roadside, I read the English words "Proud to be Islamic Fundamentalist." Then the trees petered out and we were journeying between walls of reddish rock. Now and again, a suspension bridge, or just a box on a pulley-wire, swung out across the river to the villages on the other side. Like the river, the villages were in their winter colours. There were no bright greens, no yellowing crops, but muted battened-down shades of earth and brown.

We stopped the night in a cold hotel, and ate, the three of us, wrapped in quilts: potatoes with chapatis. We were two hours short of Gilgit.

Gilgit! Market town of my dreams. The bazaar, the mountains, the walnut trees, Shia girls and politics. In my mind, Gilgit had taken on near-mythic status, these last ten years. I'd folded it away. Since that morning years ago when, walking down out of Hushe, I'd decided it was time to go home, I'd folded away the maps. I'd never even looked at the photographs, they were too potent. The great adventure of my life, my youthful excess, my travel-book, the green shalwar-kameez I was wearing even now, albeit with thermal long-johns, all had been folded away. The letter Rashida sent me, with her proposal of a life which would pass in peace, with no worries, all these things I'd folded away. I'd had my melodramatic moments, I admit, when, up to my elbows in nappies, I promised myself that I'd see the Himalayas again before I died.

Then had come the phone call from the publisher, and I was

offered what Rashida had called a "golden opportunity"—a reason to return and the money to do it with. And Phil said, Yes, go. It's time you went back. But go with Changezi. You'll be all right with him.

The morning dawned bright and cold. We loaded up the jeep and were ready, but before we set off, Mohammed Ali offered prayers. He did this every time we set off in the jeep. He prayed over his upturned hands, drew his hands down his face, then handed the driver a ten-rupee note. Ibrahim would take the money and wipe the steering wheel with it, and then tuck it into the glove compartment. If this little ritual amused me, it was because I didn't know about the accident two years before, when the jeep, not this one, had dived off the road near Askole, and rolled 120 feet down toward the Braldo river. The driver, who was not Ibrahim, had jumped clear, Mohammed Ali spent two months in hospital, and the passenger, a lone foreign woman— she had been killed on the spot.

As we pulled out onto the road, a bus blared past. It was a Masherbrum Tours bus heading down to Rawalpindi. Inside I glimpsed its passengers, a leg here, an arm, and as the dust settled behind it, I stared after it in something like disbelief. Among the passengers was, so to speak, my younger self. I had ridden in these buses. Ten, twelve years ago, I'd ridden unaccompanied in these buses, sweating and edgy, through summer nights. I'd been unmolested and unharmed. But it seemed so unlikely now, like a weird dream.

We stopped twice that morning. Once, to see some ancient Buddhist rock-carvings. The Buddha sat in all serenity, but the carvings were flecked where local people had thrown stones at them. And we stopped at the place where the the two mountain ranges, the Himalaya and the Karakoram, collide. With a kind of holy dread I looked up at the summit of Nanga Parbat, aloof, remote, so other-worldly, so snow-driven, so unutterably high. The nappy days were done.

And then we were bouncing into Gilgit, past the military bases and the bus station, a Montessori nursery, past a swanky new statue of ibex, along a new broad street of shops.

"Now we are in Northern Areas," said Mohammed Ali, almost in relief. "Look—women!"

A man brought an oil-heater into the hotel room and lit it, but its fumes soon filled the cold air and, convinced it would kill me, I turned it off again. The room had a huge overhead fan, and an air-conditioning unit. When I turned the fan on by accident, mistaking its switch for the light's, it stirred the cold air to an icy blast. Then both light and fan cut out, another power failure. We were the only guests. From the window, I could see the flat roofs of Gilgit bazaar, the snowy, jagged mountains rising on all sides. The sunlight was bright and cold. It was no good; I had to go out.

I went next door and pressed my ear to the door. It was a little after mid-day. Mohammed Ali might be praying, his prayer-mat and stone orientated toward Mecca, his hands open in front of him. But I could hear the sounds of a telephone conversation, knocked and went in. Mohammed Ali was sitting up, fully clothed, in bed. He hung up the phone.

"In Gilgit," he began, "take the jeep, won't you? Or walk, but Ibrahim or I will walk with you."

I gave him a long look.

"There are many intelligence agencies . . ."

"I remember." *Centre of Intrigue . . .*

"Now more than ever. They will be watching you . . . You are the only foreigner in the Northern Areas."

"You're joking!"

He nodded toward the phone. "I checked."

I sat on the chair and pulled my coat about me.

"It happened before. A boy in a stripy jumper. He was about nineteen."

"He was being paid by the real intelligence. A boy can go anywhere. They'd pay him some money and say 'keep an eye on her . . .' You are doing nothing wrong, and once they are satisfied you are doing nothing wrong, you will not be troubled. They will be anxious for your safety . . ."

Mohammed Ali looked at me over his glasses.

"Look. I'll tell you. If you go out, someone will be walking with you. Either I tell you, or I don't, but I will have people walking behind you. I have friends in this town and I will have them follow you. For your protection. Some people are very angry about American policy—they can't tell whether you are American, German, British . . ." he trailed off.

We looked at each other a moment. I was out of touch, out of season, and disinclined to argue.

"Okay," I said.

The muezzin's call rose into the air. Mohammed Ali smiled.

"Now, it's time for me to pray."

I could stand at the hotel gates, couldn't I? The railings where the hotel opened onto the bazaar. The street was bright and jostling, and my time in Gilgit was too short to spend it in cold hotel rooms.

So, while Mohammed Ali prayed, I stood outside at the gates and tried to orientate myself. The bazaar seemed bigger, longer, cleaner than I recalled. Or maybe it was just cool, none of the summer foetor. But still there were men pulling handcarts of oranges or fertiliser, and shops hung with jumpers, stacked with apricots and "Chinese Varieties." The light hurt my eyes. Cows shambled among the traffic, jeeps and Suzuki horns blared. I'd done it. I was back in Gilgit.

Outside the hotel was a rickety wooden bench and three men were sitting there.

One rose and, in English, offered me his place but I declined. Then of course, nothing would do but he had to go to a nearby shop and fetch a proper chair, dust it, and insist that I sit.

I thanked him, and because I couldn't resist, I said, "I haven't been in Gilgit for ten years. It looks bigger . . ."

"It's the business with China. How do you say, boomtown?"

"And cleaner."

"It's this General Musharraf. His policy. He has made wide streets and banned religious organisations. You know, before, Sunnis could broadcast through loudspeakers against Shias, and so on, this is banned."

One thing I like about Pakistanis—they don't do small talk.

"So. You think he's a Good Thing?"

"Ninety-five percent of people are behind Musharraf. He's ridding Pakistan of corruption, and extremists."

"Not democracy, though, is it?"

The man just laughed. "Give him another five years, let him finish what he's doing."

I had no long indolent summer stretching ahead of me. Rather, I had to squeeze my return to Gilgit into barely two days. So, in the early afternoon Mohammed Ali walked with me through town, toward the Golden Peak.

There was a bench there too, and a couple of men sitting in the cool sunshine, and there I had to leave Mohammed Ali. Whatever his anxieties, he was a man and a stranger, and could accompany me no farther.

There was a small yard, and a screened verandah. When I entered it, and lifted the curtain that covered the doorway, my heart was in my mouth.

Before me was a small, windowless room, I could make out two women. One was tying a nappy onto a baby.

"Kathleen?" she said. Then she was on her feet, softer, plumper than before, hugging me, kissing first one cheek, then the other.

"I cannot believe my eyes!"

And there was Salma, rising to greet me as Rashida ushered me into the room and sat me down on the floor-cushions. For a moment we looked at one another, then Rashida pulled her striped shawl from her head and pointed.

"Look!" she said. "Grey hair!"

Ten years.

"But who is this?" I asked, pointing to the baby. He lay on his back, swaddled in many layers of clothes, with black kohl smudged round his eyes.

"My kid! One month, only. One month today."

"Congratulations! Number . . . ?"

"Four. You?"

"Two."

"I cannot believe my eyes!"

We crowded the small, dark room, the three adults and several children. An oil heater burned in its centre. Then a handsome young woman of sixteen or so arrived and shook my hand, kissed me and greeted me in good English. I glanced at Rashida for help.

"You don't recognise her?" said Rashida "It's little Hina!"

The girl I'd last seen dancing along, holding her mother's Salma's hand. Or I assume it was Salma, because the woman had been all swathed in black.

We were laughing. "And now," Rashida looked at me sternly, straight in the face, "you must tell me the changes you observe in me. You must speak frankly!"

"A little more . . . plump, perhaps?"

"Yah-allah," said Salma, wearily.

"But you must tell us, how did you find us?"

They hadn't gone far, was the truth of it. This may even have been the same room where Rashida had shown me her wedding gifts, the twenty-five pairs of shoes. Even Jamila, who lived "in another area" took a mere twenty minutes to arrive. She had the same feisty look about her, she kissed me on either cheek, and I was thrilled. "You're older!"

Rashida's daughter brought in a dish of oranges, and as we ate, I told them how I'd found them.

I could have walked here, to the Golden Peak, and easily found my way from there to the green gates of their father's house, But Mohammed Ali had given me an old-fashioned look, and reached for the phone.

"This major," he said, "what was his name again?"

He had picked up the phone and spoken to I don't know whom, some oracular version of Directory Enquiries. I'd long lost the business card the Major had given me. "No matter, it's a small town," he said. God knows who he was speaking to but he was talking about minerals and offices. He hung up and began re-dialing.

"I have the number of the Major . . ."

"Bet you it's the wrong major. There's loads of them."

I heard my own name, a date, a description of the water-giving incident at Muharram. I sat back in the chair, beginning to enjoy myself.

"It's the wrong major!" Mohammed Ali laughed, his hand cupped over the mouthpiece, "But he knows the right one. As I said, it's a small town. And here is the address . . ."

Then we were back in the lane with the public library. A sandy lane with a half-frozen stream. There were children, boys with cricket bats. It was the cricket season. The TV in Rashida's room was on with the sound muted. It was showing a test match.

We passed the door to the library, and then, by some blue metal gates, Mohammed Ali had asked, "Did you come here?"

"To a room with a stuffed ibex—but I don't remember the gates . . ."

He rattled the gates and at length a small man appeared and stepped through them. It certainly wasn't the Major. Occasion-ally Mohammed Ali directed a question to me. Rashida's name. Her husband's name. The small man's face cleared. Ah, my cousins!

"So," Mohammed Ali said, when the man stepped back inside, and the gates closed.

"The Major is not here. He's in Islamabad."

"What a pity. I rather hoped we might DISCUSS!"

"He's in Islamabad because he is a political leader."

I laughed aloud. "The Major's a political leader? Of course he is. Of course he is! Good for him! He'll be thumping a few desks downside. Sorting the constitution single-handed. I hope he took his typewriter! Do you know the expression 'in his element?' Min-erals to elements. Ha!"

The last time I'd seen him the Major he had been in uniform. Then the Gulf was the trouble-zone, and of course, Kashmir. Now, ten years on, it was Afghanistan and, again, Kashmir. I don't know what kind of political leader he'd become, and I was sorry that I wouldn't see him, but I wished him wisdom, and restraint.

I really was beginning to enjoy myself. The sun was shining and again I was in Gilgit, and Gilgit was pretty much the same. At the gate to the library I peeked inside. There was the long low building, like a croft, where I had first met the Major, where all this adventure had begun. It was surely bigger, too.

"Yes, it has expanded. More books."

"And so," I said to Rashida, and Jamila and Salma, "we had your address, and just outside the Golden Peak Hotel, there was a bench and we asked for directions. But this is a small town. A small town on a Sunday afternoon. The man we chanced to ask was your brother-in-law, Rashida. We'd only asked him directions to his own house!"

So, I'd been handed over, from Mohammed Ali to this brother-in-law, who had led me through a narrow lane, where a thin grey sewer ran, a lane which led past many metal gates, always bolted from within. I could hear children's voices and women's.

"And then, we were in this walled yard, and the brother-in-law was opening the screen-door, and there you were. Still here!"

Jamila laughed. "Still here!"

"Still here," said Rashida.

"Yah-allah," said Salma.

We were older. Positively matronly. The ones I'd recalled as little children suddenly were students of psychology, of IT, shyly admitting to ambitions to become university lecturers. The babies whose births we'd half-dreaded—"creation of babies . . . is difficult"—were girls in Islamic shawls and boys playing cricket in the yard; and now we'd had our families, the question was—how best to stop?

We sat around the oil-heater, with a kettle on top, and told about our lives, the lives of women with families. We had young children and frail, elderly relatives, and jobs. That's what ten years had done; turned us from Shia girls and Western girls into grown women— mothers and daughters, wives and teachers. Despite what Rashida's letter had offered me, our lives were not one long summer of protection and ease, but spent managing responsibilities and anxieties.

I told Rashida my mother had suffered a disabling stroke and her first, swift question—who is looking after her?

Contraception. The price of dresses. Maternity leave. Housework, babies, our students, and their lax attitudes. Our suddenly elderly parents. What happened to the peace, and no worries? I could have been at home, except I was cross-legged on the floor, and all my friends were wrapped in shawls, and I was on the other side of the world.

"Yah-allah," sighed Salma, again and Rashida laughed.

"Always she is remembering God. Over and over."

•••

I went back the following day, Monday, and saw Rashida alone. The others were at their own homes, or even at work, because Jamila still held her teaching post. Rashida teaches too, but she was on maternity leave. I'd liked to have met Hussain Ali, but he was posted away from home, which didn't help. Rashida was tired.

"Did you bring your photos?" she said. "I am anxious to see them!" The room was quiet and dark. The baby slept, the children were at school, Rashida's mother-in-law was elsewhere. In a rare moment of calm she looked at pictures of my home and my children, far away in Scotland. I'd brought a couple of framed prints, as a gift, just in case, and I gave them to Rashida. One showed a Fife fishing village, and the other, Loch Lomond. Pitched roofs and low hills, boats and rowan trees—the Scottish landscape in its summer purples and greens, its blue, blue water, its low light. On the Loch Lomond scene, Rashida noticed at once the trees' reflection in the water. She ran her fingers over the picture.

"Like fairy-land," she said.

I suppose that, here, there is no water still enough to hold a reflection. The water is always falling, always on the run. I showed a picture of the view from my garden, with the wide Firth of Tay in the background. Slow, flat, plentiful water. Here were my children Duncan and Freya on a beach.

"Have you ever been to a beach, the sea?"

She had not. She commended me on my family, then handed the photos back.

"I couldn't live without my children," she said.

"You could. Believe me, for a week or two . . . You'd feel much less tired."

She shrugged. "But I must . . ."

"Must what?"

"Look after. I must look after them all."

I looked around the room. Her black burqa was hanging on a peg on the door. I had to ask the question which had long troubled me.

"Were you angry with me? About this book?"

She looked up from under her shawl and scowled. "Yes! For a short time. But it's an old matter now."

I knew they'd read it. I'd sent a copy to the Major and received a gracious reply. As for Rashida and Jamila, there had been a few letters, years ago, then no more. Had I offended them? These, after all, were women who observe purdah, who draw black shawls over their heads, then across the nose, nothing may show! I'd learned more since then about the privacy of Muslim family life, and Rashida had often used the word "shame." Could I turn up in Gilgit and merely knock on the green gates, in the hope that they would welcome me? Could I turn up in Gilgit and fail to knock on the gates?

And yet, and yet. We all have duties and tasks, and mine, as travel-writer, is to our common humanity. Travel-writing is less about place than people, it describes people's lives. How can we acknowledge our common humanity without showing something of that humanity? How can we show that families are pretty much like families, without revealing something of each other, of ourselves? Who draws the line, when we write about decent, ordinary people? The writer does, that's the truth of it. I wished for myself what I'd wished for the Major: a bit of wisdom and restraint.

The baby cried and Rashida moved away to rock his cradle. When her back was turned I asked: "Do you want me to leave?"

"Yes." she replied, sharply. Then she looked at me. I could have hugged her, because she was smiling and I knew I was being teased. "But only after tea."

We talked over tea about development, about life's hardships, and as she stacked away the cups and folded the cloth from the floor, I asked Rashida what she would like to see happen, in Gilgit, in the next few years.

She tucked her shawl behind her ears, and thought for a moment. "A proper sewerage system," she replied.

From Rashida's small, uncluttered room, I walked back up the earthen lane onto the street, with its running sewer, and then walked the length of the bazaar, back to the hotel. At the gate to the Golden Peak, I glanced in—they'd taken it down a storey. I walked on, past the main mosque and the side alley where the butcher-meat hangs. The beggar-woman who used to crouch by the Post Office, in her full burqa, like a shot crow, she was gone. The chowk, where I'd stood on a low wall and watched the men of Gilgit flagellate themselves, was wider now and occupied by a row of handcarts selling acrylic jumpers and combs and bangles and water-pistols, the cheaper end of the "Chinese Varieties." A man passed me, tugging a goat on a string.

I had to wait to cross the road, as jeeps and carts and Suzuki wagons passed, something I've no recollection of having to do before. I passed sellers of apricots, of toilets, of garden plants. I passed an Internet café, but its door was shut up and locked. Take away the heat, and Gilgit seems almost normal. It's the heat that drives us half-mad, and over-wrought.

No one approached me. No one said, Hello, yes! Where are you going? and I began to wonder if I'd imagined it. In all the discussion about danger and risk, my gender was never mentioned. If there was danger, it was political, and an incident could destabilise the whole town. People said:

"Gilgit is a mix of people, Shia, Sunni, many Pathans . . . in balance, you know?"

"Many people are very angry with American policy, very angry with UK and Pakistan governments for supporting them . . ."

"This Taliban . . . they killed 40,000 Shias in their time. We are not sorry to see these bastards go."

"I watched the towers come down on TV, in a hotel in Skardu.

My mind was spinning, my mind was saying this is not true, this is some sort of joke . . . *this is not the Islamic way!*"

Mohammed Ali was propped up in bed, fully clothed, even with his coat and woollen cap, and his half-moon glasses at the end of his nose as he read. His book, he told me, was called *The Habits of God*. He seemed more relaxed.

"I spoke to the District Commissioner, and he said, "Of course she may walk in the bazaar! There are no terrorists in Gilgit.'"

But what does one believe? Jamila had told me, emphatically, that Prince William had got married that very morning. "It's true," she said. "It was on TV."

We had been invited to dinner, and drove that evening to a newly built grand hotel, a place of upholstered chairs and white sweeping stairways. It was appointed to perfection, down to the monograph on the crockery, an R for Rupal Hotel. Our host was the hotel's owner, Mr Nasir. "He is king!" they said. "King of Astore!" He seemed an unlikely king, a portly, unshaven man, but then, he had his cares.

We were six for dinner and I the only woman. Liveried waiters showed us to our table, where a brazier burned at either end. I was mindful, as the waiter drew back the chair and dusted the seat, of my shawl dangling over the naked flame at my side. Our table was on a gallery which overlooked a lower dining-room. Down there two dozen young women, teachers on a convention, chatted over their meal.

Mr Nasir, the Raja of Astore, had built this, the biggest hotel in Gilgit. It had opened, and then . . . but we were a jolly party. "When this Kashmir crisis passes, when the war in Afghanistan is over, when the Pakistan tourist development people actually get out of their Islamabad offices and set foot in the Northern Areas, then the tourists will come, then the hotel will turn a profit and all again will be well."

"Look at us now," we said, "this is how it will be! Around this table we have Christian, Shia, Sunni, men, women, Eastern, Western. There will be serenity and peace . . ."

The king smiled glumly as the dishes were set before him. Mohammed Ali said grace, and after, one of the guests laughed and turned to me.

"This king, he is old religion."

"Old religion?"

"I pray only to fill my stomach," growled the king.

We were going to Baltistan, to Skardu, Mohammed Ali's home town. It meant another six hours' drive up the Indus Gorge. Ibrahim was hunkered beside the jeep, checking the tyres, and the oil. I stood on the pavement outside the hotel, and watched a convoy of brightly painted, tinkling trucks turn from the main bazaar into a side street. I say watched, but I could hardly bear to. The trucks, all painted with tigers and roses and fighter-jets, all decked with mirrors and bells, squeezed into the side street. Each was laden with timber, and balancing on top of each load was a man with a long wooden pole. His job was to lift the electricity wires that swagged over the road, so the truck could pass safely beneath them.

I couldn't watch. I couldn't even lean against the metal railings of the hotel yard, in case we all fried. Only when the last truck had turned, with awful slowness, into the side street, its rider hoisting the wires with his pole, did I notice yet another man with a longer wooden pole. He was on the pavement beside me, and was using the pole to throw a lever high on a street pylon. I dared to breathe again.

•••

One thing I had quite failed to understand, in my few days there, when I'd jolted into town on the back of a jeep, was the size and importance of Skardu. What I'd taken for a dusty bazaar, a geo-political cul-de-sac, was a town of 50,000 people, spread wide over the alluvium plains. From the hill which bounds the town to the north, I could see miles of houses and poplar-trees, and the dry gouge of a summer river. When two military helicopters flanked a mountain, heading for the border, I realised I had the scale all wrong. Against the mountain the helicopters were the size of crows.

Because all the hotels were closed for the winter, I was staying in Mohammed Ali's Skardu offices. By "office" he meant a walled yard, a compound, with low buildings along two sides. It was quite a community. There was the storesman and a cook, and two students who took board and lodging there in return for a little work. They'd made up a room for me, with a bed and stove. The days were a succession of visitors, linked through dense webs of kinship and friendship and business. In the evenings, we sat around watching telly, or reading, or, in the case of the two students, bent over their books. When the lights cut out, as they often did, one of the students brought in a hurricane lamp. They fed the stove with sticks, and the stove fizzed, and the smoke smelled sweet.

The electricity here is sporadic, if not because of lorries, because it's hydro-power, and in winter in this frozen world, there is little running water to drive the turbines. We ate sitting on the floor. At evening prayer-time, the devout Mohammed Ali would wash and spread his prayer-mat and turn in the direction of Mecca, while the rest of us watched dramas on TV, or the news. The news was domi-nated by Kashmir, by Israel, Presidents Bush and Musharraf. The dramas were interrupted by adverts showing beautiful smiling people gliding round houses with tables and chairs. They sold Tip-tons tea and Pond's face-cream and Ariel washing-powder.

This Ariel washing-powder. It's Ariel Sharon, isn't it? His company.

Ariel Sharon?
Israel!
Yes, I know, but it's not owned by Ariel Sharon.
I think it is.
I don't think so—Ariel's a character in Shakespeare, a sort of spirit of
the air. And this thing on the roof, for the TV, what you call an
antennae, we call that an aerial.
In Shakespeare?
Yes.
Not Ariel Sharon?
Shouldn't think so.
Well, who owns this washing-powder company, then?
Don't ask me. Lever Brothers, or somebody.
Lever Brothers. Yes. Jewish, aren't they?

Wednesday was a day of appointments. I'd asked Mohammed Ali
if I might meet people, and he took me at my word. He took me
up a rutted, dusty residential street to meet Mr Yusuf Husanabadi.
Mr Husanabadi was in his study when we called, kneeling at a low
table, writing by hand into a large ledger. Though a wood stove
took the chill off the room, Mr Husanabadi worked in his leather
jacket, and he had a pink quilt pulled over his knees. He was a pale
erudite man, working quietly among his books. Books! More than
the stove and quilt they warmed the plain room, like a low
murmur of conversation, across the centuries. On shelves to the
left and behind him, on the floor around his desk, lay bound
books and manuscripts and reference works.

He set down the pen and greeted us gravely, then came to kneel
by the stove.

I nodded toward the low desk, the precise handwriting.

"Please tell me what you're working on?"

He bowed his head slightly, and folded his hands in his lap.
"The history of Baltistan. It has never been written before. I am

compiling the complete history, in a single volume, from the Tibetan nomadic settlers in the fifth century BC, through the middle ages, the arrival of Islam in the fourteenth century, to the present day. I am working from old documents—a medieval manuscript here, a travel narrative there. I have been working for two years."

"Mr Husanabadi," said Mohammed Ali, "translated the Qu'ran into Balti."

Again the grave nod of the head. Here was a composed, concentrated intellectual who knew what he was doing.

Over tea and biscuits we talked of the border, the potential of Skardu to again take on the status it had before. Mr Husanabadi's little granddaughter came in and whispered in his ear, she was whispering in Balti. Did I realise this Balti language was spoken way beyond Baltistan, over the border into India, and across a 1200-mile stretch through Ladakh, Sikkim? That before Partition, Skardu had been the winter capital of this mountain region, with Leh as summer capital? That the two linked cities now sat in different countries? That a natural community, the Tibetan-descended, Balti-speaking peoples of the Indus catchment, were divided from each other by political borders and wars? Everyone had family over the border, whom they never saw. Skardu faces east, so to speak. Prior to the building of the road, there was no communication between Skardu and Gilgit. Gilgit was fourteen days' forced march away, if you were minded to go there at all. All this Mr Husanabadi told me in his calm and measured way.

"So. I am compiling this history. And perhaps you would help me?"

"If I could."

He told me he was seeking two sixteenth-century manuscripts, which had been written by two ambassadors of the Mogul court, narrating their travels in Baltistan.

"I don't know where these documents are," said Mr Husanabadi, regretfully. "Whether they are in India, or perhaps in Europe."

He looked up, a neat man, with a white beard.

"I need these documents, for my history."

It was a line which resonated with me long after we had left. "I need these documents, for my history." I tried to imagine being part of a community with no written history. There were 50, 000 people in this town alone, with no volume they could read to confirm who they were and where they had come from, they or their ancestors, or why things are as they are. As the people moved into mass literacy, the stories and oral histories might be forgotten. The time was acute.

"They will be grateful. Your granddaughter, here. Her generation will be grateful to you."

Mr Husanabadi inclined his head. He knew full well the task he'd set himself.

We left Mr Husanabadi's house, blinking in the cold bright light, and walked toward the bazaar. It was my turn to talk, and I was full of it.

"If the borders were permeable, like Mr Husanabadi was saying—if they opened the borders, and you could travel up river, why, you could travel from Skardu to Mount Kailash, to Tibet! Just think—from Rawalpindi, Karachi even, right up the Karakoram Highway, into the mountains, K2, Gasherbrum, over into Ladakh, Himascal Pradesh, right up to holy Mount Kailash, Lhasa for heaven's sake. Pilgrims, tourists, Muslims, Buddhists, prosperity, peace and serenity. Why, Skardu would be like Kathmandu . . . Skardu would be the tourist capital of the world."

Mohammed Ali looked at me as if I was stupid, like it had only just dawned on me, which it had.

"Yes," he said.

"Skardu, the new Kathmandu! Can you imagine?"

"Not really. We have no bars, or nightclubs. But—we do have a good bakery now, good cakes."

On a side street, a car was drawn up outside a shoe shop, and in the back of the car, a shawled woman was trying on shoes. The shopkeeper carried pair after pair of shoes out to the car, and handed them through the window. Then a hand would appear, giving them back.

"Okay, a Muslim Kathmandu. You've been to Kathmandu, haven't you?"

Mohammed Ali sighed. "Too many tourists. Too much pollution."

"But what if it happened, if the borders opened? And all you Balti peoples could travel and meet again. Your culture would regenerate—and think of your business—all those tourists! What would you do?"

"I'm having a house built, in a quiet valley beside the river. Another year and it'll be finished, inshallah. That is where I would go."

The poisoned chalice of tourism. That which destroys what it seeks. Our conversation had touched a nerve with Mohammed Ali too. Back at his office we had tea and over tea he said, "Kathleen, these people are so poor. In the villages. So poor. They need tourism. Tourism will help them, the widows, and the children . . . a little money. There are so many widows. They cannot work, buy medicine. Once, we took twenty-five boxes of clothes out to the refugees," he pressed his fingers to his temples, "but it was not enough. Do you understand? It is never enough. Even when the boxes were empty, they kept coming, the poor people. We came back here, into town, and you have seen these second-hand clothes shops in the bazaar? We bought everything . . ."

"Who's we, Mohammed Ali?"

"This charity. I founded a charity . . . Social Welfare Association, Baltistan."

"You didn't tell me."

"My mind, do you know? It upsets my mind. It is never enough. This is what the holy Qu'ran tells us. Almighty Allah is telling us. Help the people. Love the people."

But just then, the low blue door of the room opened, and admitted a cleric, whom Mohammed Ali rose respectfully to greet. A wizened man in a white turban and a floor-length woollen cloak. "Not Taliban!" said Mohammed Ali cheerfully, as the two men sat down to talk.

When did I start to feel uneasy, uncomfortable? It was dark, the snow gleamed in moonlight on the mountains, a few pin-pricks of light in the houses spread on the plains below.

The journalist lit a cigarette.

I said, If Bin Laden wasn't behind it, who was?

He was in it with them.

In it with whom?

The USA!

They murdered their own? Flew their own planes into their own buildings? Will you tell me why, exactly?

There were no Jews in the Twin Towers, you know that? Wasn't that strange?

Oh, PLEASE!

I glared out of the window. He took a drag on his cigarette. There was a long pause.

Then Mohammed Ali said, Only one person knows the truth of this thing.

Yes! said the journalist. President Bush!

No! Allah. Almighty Allah. In time He will be judge of this deed.

I woke to a clatter of pots, and the splintering crack of an axe falling into wood. It was seven-thirty on an overcast morning. Outside, the air smelled of woodsmoke.

Because it's so cold at night, they drain all the water out of the jeep's engine, and now Ibrahim was standing on its front bumper, filling its radiator with a kettle. Beside the jeep stood a cone of frozen snow. "It's our K2!" I crossed the yard to the water butt, to fetch water to wash, but the barrel was sealed by a shining disc of ice.

Mohammed Ali came from the room, where all the lads sleep. He selected his shoes from a heap at the door, pulled a blanket round his head, and looked at the sky. "It'll be snowing in the villages. Snow's good. The people need it for water, and when it's snowing, it's not so cold."

There's always some jollity about going to the villages, a sense of adventure or holiday. Into the jeep we loaded warm clothes, sleeping bags, and, oddly, a bag of dirty laundry. We were four, Mohammed Ali, and myself, the driver, and a man called Shabir, a cheerful, badly shaven man with a lop-sided smile who told me he was my own age, thirty-nine, though I'd never have guessed. Shabir was an employee of Mohammed Ali's, cook, I think. Since a near-death experience at K2 base camp one winter they had been bound like brothers. They'd been taking a party of Japanese on a reconnaisance trip. They laughed about it now, how there had been more snow than anyone could remember, waist-deep, head-deep, and how they'd been down to flour and water, before they made it out again.

He wore, we all wore, shalwar-kameez, and as warm a jacket as we could find. Mohammed Ali was, as ever, pristine. His hair and beard were combed, his shoes polished, his well-cut clothes were spotless. He'd bought a new woollen cap, and wore a smart green Western jacket. My coat and shoes were thick with Skardu dust, My dress smelled of smoke and kerosene. In the jeep, Mohammed Ali offered prayers, Ibrahim hanselled the steering wheel with the ten-rupee note, and we were off through the bazaar and out of town. A pretty girl at the roadside bobbed to wave at Ibrahim, and he blushed, and the older men teased him, and I realised just how very dashing he must have looked, with his leather jacket, at the wheel of this shiny jeep.

The road led through villages of flat-roofed houses and spare, wintry trees. At a pir's shrine—a pir is a kind of Islamic saint—we stopped to make an offering, a little money popped into a letterbox. The shrine was a rectangular chamber, hanging with flags. And then we were out in a plateau of high-altitude desert, where the road was no more than tyre-tracks across a mountain-ringed expanse of heavy sand. A fox ran in front of us; other than that, and a red jeep tilting away in the distance, I saw no other movement.

I twisted round in my seat.

"Have you ever seen a snow-leopard, M'med Ali?"

"Many times."

"Just once would suit me."

We were heading for Shigar valley. Once we'd crossed this desert we'd descend to river level and travel upstream, through many villages, for a good six hours of driving. If we stayed on this track it would lead eventually to Askole. I'd liked to have gone there and seen what changes the road had brought, but in this season Askole was cut off by snow. We were heading instead for the village of Chu Tron.

Private transport. I could grow to like it. This jeep wasn't going to break down. Ibrahim wasn't going to lay his head on the steering wheel and declare the jeep *khatam*, finished. If I wanted to take a photograph, or go behind a rock to pee, a simple word was all that was required. There was a point, with the desert plateau behind us, when the road turned in switchbacks down to river level again, and I asked if we could stop there for the view, because the whole of the Shigar valley lay before us, bound by its mountainous walls.

I left the men in the jeep, and walked just a few yards across a boulder-field. A high, cool wind played about me. Three or four hundred feet below was the thin turquoise band of the river, weaving between snow-covered sand-banks. Upstream, on the shelves of fertile land between the mountainsides and the river, were villages. There are words we reach for out of habit, like desolate, bare, barren, colourless, but these are not true. There were colours, but subtle, just a breath of pale blues and snow-greys, a smudgy brown denoting a village at the riverside. Above the river and villages, mountains slammed upward, young, hasty, sharp-edged. Now and again the summit clouds parted and an impossibly high jagged fragment of rock and snow seemed to float all on its own. But for the wind, all was silent.

We stopped for lunch at a rest house, and ate a vegetable stew served with round unleavened bread. In the floor of the rest house was a trap-door, and a bamboo ladder that led down to the byre below. Goats were looking up at me, and a child, with his arms full of fodder. Then we drove on through more villages, between stone walls, past more goats and people burdened with firewood, some lads playing volleyball, a yak, and a gang of shawled women with their backs turned to us, washing pots at a stream.

It was late afternoon before we crossed the river by a suspension bridge and drove toward our destination. We were above the snowline now. Once across the river, the jeep-track rose again and clung to the mountainside. Twice Ibrahim inched us through avalanche debris. I glanced at the gulleys above, figuring if they'd avalanched recently, they were less likely to do it now.

"The wind must be getting up," I remarked to no one in particular, because a snowy dust was rising all around us. We drove past women with bundles of clothing, and entered the village. Then, to my astonishment, a naked child sprang from a doorway. Only then I realised the wind-driven dust was nothing of the sort—it was steam. Steam, issuing out of fissures in the earth.

"Good," grinned Mohammed Ali. "Tonight we can have a hot bath."

But first, we had a message to run, news to convey. The two college students who lodge in Mohammed Ali's Skardu offices come from the next village to this, and we were going there to take news of the boys to their families. Both the boys were shy, handsome, and bright. One was exceptionally bright.

"Anyway," said Mohammed Ali, "I want you to see this house."

We walked through uneven winding alleys. The villages were honed down, elemental. There were sounds of chopping wood, and a chirping pair of coal tits. We walked between walls of wattle and daub and basketry. Huge walnut trees rose above the flat roofs. What I remembered most about walking through Askole was the smell of goat's dung and smoke. But it was too cold for smells, now.

Beyond the village were snow-covered fields. Under a tree stood a patient dzo, a Himalayan beast, a cross between a yak and a cow. Toward us, making for the hot springs, came old women and girls, carrying laundry and tin plates. We exchanged a word with everyone. Their shawls were the only bright colours in the land-scape. On their feet, as they trudged through the snow, they wore plimsolls, or flip-flops.

We went in single file, Mohammed Ali, Shabir and me. I was asking Shabir about his family and he numbered his children, and spoke in admiration of his wife—an expert farmer. He raised his arms like a muscle-man. My wife is very strong! On every roof were creels and baskets woven of willow. To be a farmer you have to be strong.

We climbed a ladder onto an upper floor and were welcomed by a young woman, a girl really, of about fifteen.

"This is M's wife," said Mohammed Ali, naming one of the two students.

Then we took our shoes off, and stooped into a dark room. As my eyes adjusted, I made out a little hearth burning in the middle of the floor. Folded against one wall were a dozen quilts. On a shelf on one wall were some tin plates. There were no other objects, except a carpenter's plane.

As news of our arrival spread, the room filled with members of both the boys' families till we were a crowd of fifteen or so, sitting in a circle round the fire, cross-legged on a goats' wool rug. Mohammed Ali, Shabir and I seemed bigger than everyone else, or our clothes were brighter.

The old woman beside me plucked my sleeve and spoke.

Mohammed Ali whispered, "That's M's mother."

"*It can't be . . .*"

He translated from her Balti, a language which sounded like a gong. "She said, 'I can't speak your language, and you don't have a word of mine!'"

It was true, and because I couldn't take part in the cheerful conversation, I could look at the people's faces as they talked. Faces, under hats and shawls, half-lit by a little window cut in the earth-wall. The old woman to my right, M's mother—her face had collapsed in on itself, a button nose and watery eyes. The handsome teenage girl who'd greeted us stood leaning against a pillar that supported the blackened roof. A toddler, held on a man's lap, stuck her bare feet into the ash of the hearth. The man was all in browns, as though he'd risen from the earth of the floor.

I looked about the room, its rafters, earth floor, the robust hand-woven rug we were sitting on. The people were pleased for the news, animated, they laughed and gestured.

Then Mohammed Ali leaned over and whispered, "This girl, she is not normal."

But I hadn't noticed the girl he meant, because she was sitting outside the circle, with her legs drawn up to her chin, watching us closely, and as soon as I spotted her, another girl, her sister perhaps, moved protectively toward her, and cradled her head, and moved her legs as though she couldn't move them herself. Some words of Rashida's came back to me.

"I must," she had shrugged.

"Must what?"

"Look after them."

Someone began coughing, a thick deep intractable cough.

And then the curtain lifted and a bent old man shuffled in, greeting us in a rasp. "This is M—'s father."

"The student? It can't be . . ."

The beautiful boy, who shyly lit the stove and leapt to his feet the instant the power cut out, to fetch lamps. The boy of twenty who was taking straight A's in every subject he touched. It wasn't possible that these could be his parents. This shrunken crone at my right, the hunched man who was entering the room now. He was dressed all in dark browns, in a torn jacket and cap. He was stunted, the goitre at his throat spilled over his old jersey. His voice was damaged, he could only rasp. His mind . . . I don't know about his mind. He came shuffling in and took his place, anxious for news of his boy.

Iodine is one of the few things I carry with me. I carry it to purify water, and clean scratches or cuts. I had it even now, in my pocket, a little glass bottle with a dropper, and could close my hand round it like a talisman, as the bent old man shuffled into the room. It's wrong to see people only as ailments, but as they laughed and gestured, that's what I was thown back on. Faces, laughing, scolding, gesturing hands. It was like being in a painting, a Goya, perhaps. On every adult's lap, a toddler. The open, full-faced teenagers, the collapsed, half-blind crones. The cretinous—horrible word— father of the beautiful student. The "not normal" girl. I would never know their names, or their personalities, or talents. I'd never unravel the dense web of relationships that bound them to each other and to this room. They were each other's mothers and fathers, wives, sisters, sons. And there was cerebral palsy and iodine deficiency and that awful cough, and women worn out and done at fifty-five or sixty.

We stood to leave, showered with messages for the boys, and were escorted, hospitably to the edge of the village, where the houses stopped. By a walnut tree, the young man waved us off.

From there we walked back through the path between the snow-covered fields. We walked in silence. I was the first to speak.

"Mohammed Ali, who's putting the boys through college?" I asked, as if I didn't know.

We walked on a few yards more before he answered, his hands behind his back, his prayer-beads entwined in his fingers.

"God gave me the chance to help. The boys will get good jobs, inshallah, and then it will stop, do you understand? Then, it will *stop*."

It was Shabir who led me from my room, out into the darkness. Icicles hung from the eaves. What, I thought to myself, has been the strangest evening of my life? By the light of a hurricane lamp he led me down a dark lane. The women with their bundles of clothes had vanished, the children dressed and taken home to bed. Only I and Shabir with the lamp were abroad. By a rough wooden door set in a stone wall, he stopped. High in the walls were niches, through which steam escaped. He handed me the lamp.

"This is lady's private bath."

The door swung open. I lifted the lamp and by its gloomy light, saw wraiths of steam fleeing away from me, chased by the draught from the door. There was a splashing of water. Before me was a rectangular pool, surrounded by a narrow ledge. I entered, holding the lamp high, and the door swung closed behind me.

The floor of the bath, under the water, was grey earth and silt. I could see stones down there and unnervingly, a bone. The ledge I balanced on was so narrow and broken I hardly dared move. Above me, through the steam, was a skylight, and beyond it, the dark mountainous winter sky. I set the lamp down on the ledge, with great care. Please, I prayed, don't let it go out.

Off came the boots and coat and shawl, all smoke and kerosene, the shalwar-kameez, the thermal long-johns, the vest, socks and underwear, and then I lowered myself, first one foot, then the other, into the blissful, scalding bath. I wanted to think through the day, but the water was so warm, so soft and relaxing. It replenished itself all the time.

The people of Askole don't wash in their hot springs. The people of Chu Tron and all the villages around—you can't get them out of the water. In the morning light I saw where I'd been. There are two communal bathhouses, a men's and a women's. There are two private ones, too, which I'd been privileged to use. From both, especially the women's, came a constant peal of voices. From early in the morning children arrived with baskets of breakfast dishes. From far over the snow-dusted river plain, figures trudged, bringing laundry, bringing themselves.

We left Chu Tron after prayers and breakfast, relaxed and clean from the baths. Every thorn-bush was draped with green and red shawls and children's jerseys, and torn anoraks, and the women's thick tunics, a light snow dusting them. A fox in its winter greys bounded up, away from the village. On a high rock, it turned and looked down. Above it, the mountainside rose and kept on rising up into heavy cloud.

It was Friday, mosque day. We crossed the river back across the suspension bridge. Its wooden planks buckled under the weight of the jeep. At the village of Hyderabad we stopped for prayers. The men were going to the village mosque, and I was shown into a rest house, but I said I would rather go for a solitary walk.

I followed the jeep-track a while, it was frozen and rutted. Then I climbed onto a boulder. Behind me, the mountains rose and a whole flock of choughs, with red legs and red beaks, issued from the mountainside and wheeled across the valley. It's only 8000 feet or so, but the air is cold and already lighter, it has a sinuous quality.

A high movement caught my eye—bigger birds, eagles or lammergeiers, were turning in the air, coasting and settling on a high pinnacle of rock. I sat for a while, watching the birds and the movement of goats across the hillside, the river before me, the mountains' impossible rise. The sky was lifting a little, revealing a scrap of blue. The constant, intractable challenge of poverty. I'd taken a few photographs, quietly, of village houses. The old houses were being replaced by concrete, and already people were complaining that their new houses weren't as warm as the old earth-floored, wattle-and-daub affairs. I'd taken the photos to show an architect friend at home, an eco-architect who is advising the Scottish executive on the merits of traditional buildings, who travels to international conferences to speak with enthusiasm about clay floors and lime-wash and thatch.

What is worth keeping? Can't we keep our relationships and our willow baskets and our songs and looms, yet say goodbye to deficiencies and blight? There are charities working here, NGOs a-plenty. There are programmes to provide each household with iodised cooking salt, and electric light. There are schools and mobile clinics, annual "medicine camps." What happens, though, if all the clever ones leave? Ken McDonald in Askole had taught me how much intelligence it takes to run a village, and live so close to the land. Can't we draw up inventories of what is worth having, and keep them?

The world is sorrowful and beautiful, and it was lunch time. Because he is the kind of man who understands these things, I told Mohammed Ali I'd been to a mosque of my own making, a rock by the riverside, with a view of the mountains, and of eagles turning in the breeze, and I'd been thinking about poverty. He nodded. From the rest-house window, he pointed out a half-built house nearby, next to the river.

"That's mine. That's where I'll live when I'm old, inshallah, and you and your family will visit me there. And we will sit on the verandah, and talk about the world."

"We'll do that." I smiled. "I'll bring a cake."

I want to tell the story of Abeera and Shabir, as it was told to me.

Shabir, with his dusty blue mountaineering jacket and his lop-sided grin, who came with us to Chu Tron. Their names are not Abeera and Shabir. But that afternoon, instead of heading back to Skardu, we drove on up the valley a few miles, to a little house set back from the road. The mistress of the house greeted us warmly on her veranda. Her hens squawked from the roof, her three daughters gravely shook our hands. We kicked off our shoes at the door, and ducked into the warm living space.

This was a different kind of household to the poor one at Chu Tron. Though it still had the low raised platform for sleeping and eating on, and the quilts folded against the back wall, and the wood-stove, a double one next the hearth, and an array of tin plates and trays on the mantelpiece, everything was bigger, brighter. It had, you might say, a woman's touch, with decorations made from cut newspapers, the plates arranged just so. Abeera had parted her hair severely and held it at each temple with three shining kirby-grips, just visible below her red shawl. Just visible round her throat was an impressive lapiz necklace. She saw us all seated and then, hunkered at the stove, set about preparing boiled eggs and cinnamon tea.

There was something in the atmosphere of jollity, and when a man came in, a strong, tired-looking man dressed in a blue blouson jacket, the cry went up "Osama! O-sam-a!"—and "Osama" looked faintly embarrassed.

Mohammed Ali whispered to me in English, "He's the leader of a gang of miners—gem miners, in these hills. Last time we came they were making—you know, with bombs."

"Blasting?"

"And because he is the boss the men call him Osama. And this place they call Tora Bora, ha ha!"

The tea was served in Chinese bowls, with much polite fuss. A neighbour arrived—there is always a neighbour—a woman who was so hard of hearing she couldn't speak too well.

"This is Osama's wife, and their son. She is very nice."

I wondered idly which of these men was Abeera's husband. The old man folded in a corner I took to be her father-in-law, the rest I could account for. Mohammed Ali, Shabir, Ibrahim, the driver. Osama. No matter, maybe he was at work—men have a habit of wandering off for days or weeks on end, working or studying far from their village homes.

When we left later, Shabir shook my hand farewell, because he was staying on in these parts to do some work on nearby tree planataions. A Japanese NGO, the Himalayan Green Club, was responsible for these plantations, and there was work to be done, opening new sites, irrigation work, that kind of thing, before planting began again in March.

I waved to him as we set off in the jeep. I'd enjoyed his cheery company, his lop-sided grin.

"Shabir's staying there," said Mohammed Ali, mildly, as we drove off down an avenue of poplars.

"Yes, he said he had plantation work to do."

"Is that what he told you? Ha!"

We drove on. Mohammed Ali pointing to fields of trees planted by the NGO, in some response to the deforestation problems. Then he said, "You know, I couldn't believe the change in that woman. I did not recognise her."

"Abeera?"

"I'd only met her once before. And that time, I thought she was old. I thought she was an old woman. Her hair was all dirty and the children all round her knees. She was a widow."

"There's a story here, isn't there?"

"He's only gone and married her."

"Who?"

"Shabir! She's his second wife!"

"Well," I said, "he must have seen beneath the dirt. She's a pretty woman . . ."

Mohammed Ali relaxed into the story. Ibrahim smiled as he drove. He told me Shabir had come up here to do this tree work before, how he'd met Abeera, and "slowly, slowly" things developed, then Shabir had asked his friends to arrange their marriage.

"Did you notice when we arrived, how they shook hands, how she pulled his hands so?"

"I thought everyone was merry. But what did his first wife say?"

The first wife, the expert farmer, the very strong—she had gone nuts. Hearing the rumours, because Shabir didn't dare tell her, she'd sent her brothers up the valley to see if they were true. They returned with bad news.

"She was very, very angry. Then she sent another man up the valley, a highly respected person, to check again what the situation was, and he came back with bad news. She even came to my office, and shouted at me!"

"At you? Why?"

"Because I had asked Shabir to come up here and do this work. Work, not to . . . well, how was I to know he would find this Abeera? I was angry too. But then, she said okay . . ."

"Okay?"

"She said to Shabir, 'Okay, but . . . I want your land.'"

Now we were all laughing. Mohammed Ali, Ibrahim at the wheel, and me, laughing as we bounced along.

"It's true—she had a paper drawn up, putting into her name all the land she worked. Shabir signed. Well, he's got lots of land."

"Just shows—land is more important than men. Clever, though."

"She is a clever woman."

Later, when we were back in Skardu, Mohammed Ali asked: "You people don't do this, do you? Temporary marriage, second marriage . . ."

"No. Leastways, it's a big secret. Sometimes there are secret affairs. It happens. Is there anywhere in the world this doesn't happen?"

"But do you see, she was a widow. No income, and these three daughters . . . she was so poor, absolutely poor . . . and now. Well, I didn't recognise her."

"Shabir's providing for them?"

"Of course. That is the point."

"Are you trying to tell me that this system is to benefit widows? It is to help widows?"

"Yes. Yes. It is for widows. Nowadays people do it too much, marry here, marry there, but properly speaking. There are so many widows . . ."

Shabir and Abeera. Shabir and his two wives. Or two women who knew what they wanted and saw their chance of getting it? Men, women, money, and land. Did Abeera set her cap at him, so to speak? See him coming with his cheery lop-sided grin? That was one thumping great necklace. Did Shabir travel with us to Chu Tron, and bathe in the hot springs, always longing for the morrow? I keep looking for some moral high ground, but find none. Every time I think of them, at the end of the valley with the chickens and the trees, and the other woman, the very strong proprietor of her own land, I do what everyone else does: shake my head and smile.

Mohammed Ali caught my eye, and said, apropos of nothing, "When I came to visit the UK, there was only one thing I didn't like. That old people, old *parents* are sent away."

What do people want? A sewerage system. Peaceable, open borders, that accord with the land. A language, and a culture, rose bushes. A professional job—for every job advertised in Gilgit, 100 young women apply. Peace. *Where can one go for peace?* Some help around the house. A decent tourist season. *They asked me if they would lose their jobs, if the hotel closed, others have lost their jobs. That is fifteen families. I told them I would sooner sell my land.* Schoolbooks. A husband, and a necklace of lapiz to wear when he arrives. A farm of one's own. That pretty widow at the end of the valley. Free iodised salt. A cure for grey hair. A baby. To go home. *I pray to fill my stomach!* A house among the mountains, beside the river: *For the first two nights, I hear only the river, then it becomes inside me, like my heart . . .*

Even back in Gilgit, a week ago, news had been reaching us of a big funeral which had lately taken place somewhere in Baltistan. Whose, I didn't know. Mr Nasir, the hotel owner who prayed only to fill his stomach, had mentioned it. Only today, when we were half-way to Khapalu, did I make the connection.

The sky was lifting, as the forecast had promised, as Mohammed Ali had prayed it would. Clear skies meant aeroplanes, and we were booked on tomorrow's flight down to Islamabad. If the weather closed in again, then it was two days' jeep ride down the Karakoram Highway. Forty minutes' flight, or twenty hours' drive.

People were spreading dung into their fields; spring comes a little earlier here than Chu Tron. Soon, the fields and trees would soften and turn green. We had saved the best till last. Khapalu is the most beautiful valley. This was the valley I'd looked on from the roof of the palace and proclaimed wonderful. It was here the funeral had lately been held.

"Who has died?" I asked as we turned from the main road up into Khapalu town.

"The old Raja has died. Katcho Mehboob. He was in his nineties. But his daughter is here."

This was stirring something in my memory: a palace, three young lads, one in a checked jacket, who had said to me, "The king is on a visit. Only his daughter is here . . ."

"Yes! She is my friend."

The princess, as I'd called her, who had been sitting in her orchard, who had given me mulberries and permission to visit the palace, could it be the same woman? Could there be two?

"Her title is Rani. Rani Shah Jebeen. And we must visit her to pay our respects."

We climbed from the bazaar up through bare terraces. Had these been the hills I'd walked up, all cherries and lilac, where I'd chanced to meet the three young men? The water which had fallen in a sparkling sheen now lay in the channels in grey swirls of ice. No flowers bloomed.

We walked up a cobbled lane. Here was the little Venetian bridge, here the flower garden I'd stopped to enjoy for a moment, bone-hard and frozen. It was the same place, but so closed down and wintry that I struggled to recognise it. I was nervous. This was a serious and formal visit. Mohammed Ali, bless him, was briefing me.

The woman's father, the Raja, had died. The house was observing forty days of mourning. She was receiving visitors on this account, and we were making a visit to offer condolences. We would enter the reception room, she would greet us, we should say something appropriate. We'd be invited to sit. Prayers would be offered for the departed. We'd stay a decent interval, and that would be that.

I was casting around in my mind for the phrases we use on these occasions: the perfectly pitched Irish expression, "I'm sorry for your trouble." "May I offer my condolences?" I offered a prayer of my own, that, inshallah, I wouldn't make a fool of myself, or by extension, Mohammed Ali. I was reaching back a long way, to Scotland in the 1960s. A rough democratic Kirk of Scotland education that had prepared us to behave as well in peasants' huts as the reception rooms of Rajas. To my old primary school and Sunday school teachers, I was suddenly grateful. My clothes, well, my clothes couldn't be helped. My not-beautiful winter boots would, of course, be left at the door.

Mohammed Ali bowed me in first. We entered a large reception room, with an opulent red carpet, and flat cushions round the plain walls. A wood stove fizzed against one wall, and beside the stove, wrapped in a fine woollen shawl, was the woman who had given me mulberries. She lifted her hand, which I shook, briefly. I said my few words of condolence, then Mohammed Ali did the same, then Ibrahim, the driver.

Again the old-fashioned word "comely" came into my mind. The Rani sat now cross-legged, now with one knee drawn up. Her shalwar-kameez, of which I could see only a cuff, was lilac. Her socks, which peeked out from the shawl, were lime green. Mine were royal blue, my shalwar-kameez was emerald-green, my shawl a blue tie-dyed affair. I kept on my Goretex jacket.

I would liked to have said to Shah Jebeen that I had met her before, fleetingly, years ago. That she had been sitting in an orchard, her lips and fingers fruit-stained. That it was an afternoon I remember as one of the happiest of my life, a high summer day of flowers and clambering round in an old palace. It was day which she herself had bestowed on me with a regal wave of her hand, but which she would never recall. I would liked to have thanked her, but we were a sombre and funeral party, and it wasn't occasion to mention it.

We sat against the facing wall, and a polite conversation ensued between Mohammed Ali and Shah Jebeen. I noted the English words "blood pressure," "heart." Then Mohammed Ali spread his hands, palms up on his knees, and prayers were said for the old man who had died.

On the windowsill stood two vases of silk flowers, and beyond, out of the window, a wall of snowy mountainside rose.

Shah Jebeen was in complete social command of the situation, wrapped in her long shawl. When the conversation paused, and the room was hushed but for the fizzing of the stove, there was no sense of unease. And then, gently, she would lift her chin and another topic would be introduced. Ibrahim said nothing, I said nothing,

Mohammed Ali and Shah Jebeen sat opposite each other and spoke in voices just loud enough to carry. Then, of course, the door opened and plates of small cakes arrived, and a silver samovar of tea.

I felt like a child again, sitting in a formal room while the adults talked, looking about me at the pattern of the red carpet, and the cushions, the stove and samovar, the mountains soaring up past the windows. We ate cakes and drank tea, and then, at some ungiven signal, some subtle shift in the tenor of the conversation, we rose, and gravely took our leave.

From the roof of the palace—of course we went to the palace—we saw the wintry valley spill down to a slow distant river. From the balcony, the heavy ornate carved balcony, we could view the polo pitch, the naked, frozen palace gardens, the mountains, the people far below spreading dung on their fields. Water would thaw and run, and it would transform everything it touched into yellows and green, mulberry and plum.

A sign had been pasted on the palace's carved solid doors, saying that the princes Nazir Ali Khan Yabgo and Zakaria Khan had handed over the fort to the Baltistan Cultural Foundation, who would inshallah find the money to preserve this unique architecture, because these buildings, where the Tibetan met the Persian, were like nothing else in the world.

"I haven't seen her for twenty-five years," said Mohammed Ali. "She was beautiful then. I was beautiful, too, when I was young. But she was proud. And I was also proud . . ."

"Was she married?"

"Of course." He smiled. "And so was I."

I still have the letter Rashida wrote me, postmarked Gilgit, 1991. She describes her changed life as a married woman expecting her first child as "a new and strange experiment." It was for me too. To come back to Pakistan was to meet my younger self, childless and unhurried. One of the odder experiences of this short trip was also one of the more ordinary: making a phone call home. I made the call from the H.Q. of the Signals regiment. I was surrounded by Urdu-speaking soldiers with moustaches and epaulets, but one gets used to that sort of thing. The strange part was hearing two little children in a far-away land say, "Hello Mummy, when are you coming home?" and feeling my throat tighten.

I have another letter too, from the old days. Oddly, it's from the man who had shared the raft-crossing with me, the one with the shopping trolley on wheels, who had kindly given me tea and commandeered Olam to walk with me to Hushe. He hopes I am well and mirthy, and I hope he is too, because he is one of the many to whom I owe a debt of gratitude, a man I met for half an hour years ago. He lumbered Olam with me, but at Olam's house and the few days following, I had the time of my life. Next time, next time, we would all come, the kids as well. We've got an invitation to a house at the riverside in Shigar, for conversation and cake.

"Has anything changed?" I'm asked. Of course. Change is our resting state. Rashida, hunkered on the same floor of the same small room as I left her, is changed. On her falls the duty of care, for the children and the old ones and even her students. Her hair is greying. I was wakened during the night in Chu Tron by the soft thundering sound of an avalanche. Even the mountains, especially the mountains, are in change. People die, and we gather in formal reception rooms, people are born, and their new, blue eyes are rubbed with kohl. For many, their deaths come far too soon, too shockingly. This we know from the television, which nightly brings us pictures from Kashmir, from Palestine, from Afghanistan and the USA. There are small disasters too. Mohammed Ali knows this, and it mounted into a spiritual crisis for him. He knows it from his jeep accident, his charity work, from the destitute who come quietly to his gate.

•••

It was my last morning, and the sky over Skardu had cleared. For the first time in over a week, the plane would leave. It was full of over-excited children, whose parents couldn't face the thought of a twenty-hour bus ride. It took an age to clear the runway, then we were rising among mountains, then above them, and we could see hundreds of miles of snow-covered mountains, jagged and scrunched, ranks and ranks of mountains. Among them, to the north, was a huge one, head and shoulders above the rest: the perfect, terrifying cone of K2. I watched it as long as I could through the oval window, twisting back in my seat.

We were following the Indus. Then, as soon as that, we were descending into Islamabad. We were strapped in for landing, the nose of the plane was pointing steeply down, we'd heard the whine and thunk of the landing gear. Then suddenly, a child went pitching down the central aisle of the plane. At once, everyone lunged for him. The men, women with chadors drawn over their faces, everyone. A man down the front caught and held him, and the rest of us—we all looked at one another, and shook our heads.

Selected titles from Adventura Books

The Unsavvy Traveler: Women's Comic Tales of Catastrophe edited by Rosemary Caperton, Anne Mathews, and Lucie Ocenas. $15.95, 1-58005-058-1. Twenty-five gut-wrenchingly funny responses to the question: What happens when trips go wrong?

A Woman Alone edited by Faith Conlon, Ingrid Emerick and Christina Henry de Tessan. $15.95, 1-58005-059-X. A collection of rousing stories by women who travel solo.

Dream of a Thousand Lives: A Sojourn in Thailand by Karen Connelly. $14.95, 1-58005-062-X. The award-winning account of a young woman immersed in the heart of Thailand.

Journey Across Tibet: A Young Woman's Trek Across the Rooftop of the World by Sorrel Wilby. Foreword by the Dalai Lama. $16.95, 1-58005-053-0. An inspiring story that captures the sensibility of a remote land and its people.

East Toward Dawn: A Woman's Solo Journey Around the World by Nan Watkins. $14.95, 1-58005-064-6. After the loss of her son and the end of a marriage, the author sets out in search of joy and renewal in travel.

Expat: Women's True Tales of Life Abroad edited by Christina Henry de Tessan. $16.95, 1-58005-070-0. A collection that answers the question travelers so often ask: What would it be like to live here?

The Curve of Time: The Classic Memoir of a Woman and her Children Who Explored the Coastal Waters of the Pacific Northwest, second edition by M. Wylie Blanchet, foreword by Timothy Egan. $15.95, 1-58005-072-7. The timeless memoir of a pioneering, courageous woman who acted as both mother and captain of the twenty-five foot boat that became her family's home during the long Northwest summers.

Seal Press publishes many outdoor and travel books
by women writers.
Please visit our Web site at **www.sealpress.com.**